THE MORAL LIVES OF ISRAELIS

THE

MORAL LIVES

OF

ISRAELIS

REINVENTING THE DREAM STATE

DAVID BERLIN

RANDOM HOUSE CANADA

PUBLISHED BY RANDOM HOUSE CANADA

Copyright © 2011 David Berlin

Published in 2011 by Random House Canada, a division of
Random House of Canada Limited, Toronto. Distributed in Canada
by Random House of Canada Limited.

www.randomhouse.ca

Library and Archives Canada Cataloguing in Publication

Berlin, David
The moral lives of Israelis : reinventing the dream state / David Berlin.

Issued also in an electronic format.

ISBN 978-0-307-35629-1

1. Israel—History—21st century. 2. Israel—Politics and government—
21st century. 3. Israel—Foreign relations. 4. Berlin, David. I. Title.

DS128.2.B47 2011   956.9405'4   C2010-904241-7

Cover and text design by CS Richardson

Printed and bound in the United States of America

10 9 8 7 6 5 4 3 2 1

To Deborah

Intro: Omit par. I. all parents make mistakes + have to apologize later as the new culture evolves. Then, as they age, they are out-of-step and unable to catch up with their "alien" "children". must believe it too + know no better. all parents whatever the surrounding circumstances.

Introduction

T his book is about many things, both personal and political, most of which took place in Israel over the past decade. It is a book about the death of my Israeli-born parents, the trust I put in them, the betrayal of that trust and my attempts to contain the damage of that betrayal while they were alive. What my parents—and indeed what the entire first generation of "Sabras" whose lives straddled British-controlled Palestine and the independent State of Israel—said to their children was *"smokh aleinu"*: rely on us, leave it to us. They said they knew what they were doing. We, their sons and daughters, believed them and wanted to believe them. But the fact is they had no clue what they were doing and even less of a clue about who they were. And now things in Israel and among their children are a mess.

It has not always been this bad. My parents left Israel in 1953 when I was almost two years old. By the time I decided to return on my own, sixteen years later, I was tall, dark and some said rather handsome, but also passionate and maybe crazy. Israel, for its part, was both in its heyday and at its last gasp. The

1

Mayflower generation, my grandparents' generation of immigrants to Palestine, were fading into the background. My parents' generation, which did not include my own parents anymore, because they'd left to raise their family in Canada, were very much in charge. My generation, the first to be born to the independent state, was attempting to come into its own. The grave consequences of Israel's euphoric victory in the 1967 war with Egypt, Jordan and Syria had not yet hit home.

I came back to Israel in my late teens not as a Jewish refugee, nor because I wanted to make sure that Israel would remain an insurance policy against future anti-Semitism. I wasn't particularly interested in Jewish self-determination or in a more intensely Jewish experience than I was getting in North America. In point of fact, I had just about had it with Judaism. Like so many children of the 1960s, I was all about a future in which the world would be defined by love and peace. Remember that?

I came to Israel because I thought the new state was all about getting it right: Zionist thinkers and political leaders were brimming with cosmic ambition. They seemed intent on showing the world what it means to create a country that is at once a secure state and a refuge, a welcoming new home for strangers. To my adolescent eyes it seemed clear that such an experiment would necessarily entail establishing the best modes of social, political and economic organization. Secular Jews in Israel would insist on such things, driven by the prevailing idea that Jewish morality itself needed to find secular expression. The concept that drew me in, along with hundreds of thousands of Jews and non-Jews alike, was the possibility that we could show the world what it means to found a country upon this morality, which Judaism had long ago introduced to the world.

This was the intense, and I'd argue virtuous, spirit that permeated Israel at the time. Which is not to suggest that when I arrived in Tel Aviv in the late summer of 1969 everything was perfect. It was, in fact, far removed from the rather blurry image that I had packed into my duffle bag when I left my parents' home in Toronto. But it was also a good approximation, a believable beginning. There was, to my chagrin, not a single decent snooker table, not a single croissant or movie theatre in all the land. And yet this experiment in creating a state spilled forth sufficient promise to keep us all there, noses to the grindstone, or in my case for the next three years, eyes to the sights of a rifle, as I did my stint in an elite unit of the Israeli Defence Forces (IDF).

Every scholar and artist, every social activist and politician, seemed bent on looking in on Israel's grand experiment, seeing for himself what exactly was happening there, trying and failing to define precisely where it was that this country thought it was headed. For the next few years—until October of 1973 and the Yom Kippur War—this idealistic spirit of experimentation was everywhere. It was present in the twinkling eye of our grandparents, in the cold, witty pragmatism of my parents' generation, and in the innocence of my own generation, who had not experienced and were not privy to the real story of the great conflict between "our" version of the war of independence and the "Naqba," or Catastrophe, which was how the Palestinians remembered things.

In those years, the spirit was present (if sometimes hard to detect) even in the smallest-minded and most infuriating public *siakh* (discourse). The spirit was undeniably there, if even less detectable, in the Soviet-style institutions by which Israel was then governed. To be sure, the nascent attempts to replace religion as an organizing principle with modern, secular institutions seemed backward compared with the unifying force of 1960s youth culture, or even the peace, order and good government I knew from my years in Canada.

Employees in the Histadrut, the big Israeli labour union, for example, were most animated during coffee breaks in which they drank tea or horrible Nescafé, whose magical qualities they extolled in a German-inflected Hebrew. Service, even the most straightforward of tasks, dragged on like a Siberian winter. One called to order a phone in September and got the confirmation that it might be installed the same month—but three years later. Those of us who had experienced more efficient systems expended a great deal of energy rationalizing: our country was still young, experimental and poorly financed. "Things will get better" was both our mantra and a method of self-hypnosis. What I did not quite get was that time and circumstance were already working against us.

In the early years, as Zionists of the second and third *aliyah* (immigration) were trickling into Palestine, there were no very clear predictions about how, where and when this experiment would come into its own. My paternal grandfather, Gershon, once told me that the optimists among his peers thought that it would take maybe a century to figure things out. "Realists put their hard-earned kopecks on three hundred years," he said, "and even then we would remain in the red." The point was not to reproduce this or that revolutionary ideology in Israel; it was not to adapt some earlier vision or model. We were committed to starting from scratch.

Nothing that had been tried by others was necessarily right. Like other socialists, left-wing Israelis had been sold on Marxist ideas, but they were already getting the feeling that maybe Lenin—and certainly Stalin—was not all they had once thought him to be. Nor were these Jewish seculars willing to absolve the original blueprint drawn up by Marx and Engels of responsibility. To many, the old "system" suffered from the same basic flaws of which it was so critical. It was at once too beautiful and too ugly, too open-ended and too deterministic; it made one feel alternately euphoric and confused. In short, Israel's pioneers thought Marxism was another "opium of the people." Besides, there was also Bakhunin, and Kropotkin, and the less-than-orthodox doctrines of Antonio Labriola and Enrico Ferri, to which Vladimir Jabotinsky, the father of right-wing Zionism, was drawn. And there was French Syndicalism and British liberalism and American egalitarianism, and entire libraries filled with lesser dreams.

These motley immigrants had an unshakable faith that there is such a thing as getting it right and that if they put their minds together they could get it right. It was only by getting it right that the results would be good enough to serve on the *magash hakesef*—the silver platter—which is how the great Israeli poet Natan Alterman thought Israel's future needed to be served.

By the late 1960s, it seemed to most Israelis of any generation that we'd gotten two main concepts settled. The first had to do with the state. The decision was made to go forward as a nation-state fashioned on the Western European model. This decision back-burnered two other options that had been very much alive in the earlier years and dated back to well before the founding of the State of Israel. One of these options, associated with the visionary founder of political Zionism, Theodor Herzl, was that Israel, wherever it might be geographically, would be a "Gemeinschaft"—a social compact founded for the common good, and thus a loosely governed polity with no central, fixed authority. It would not institute democratic values such as fixed elections but would be run by voluntary associations. To many of the first pioneers, including my paternal grandfather, this model had huge advantages, not the least of which was the possibility that as a non-European system of government it might hold more appeal for the Arabs in the region.

The other idea, which was in the process of being jettisoned by the time I arrived, was Asher Ginzberg's vision of the country as a cultural centre that would focus on secular institution-building, guided but in no way governed by ancient Jewish morality. Ginzberg (also known as Ahad Ha'am) thought that Jews should resist wholesale and therefore indiscriminate immigration. They should opt for a selective return, in which only the best and the brightest among us would be invited to make the aliyah.

For many reasons—including the Arab Revolt of the mid-thirties, the rise of the revolutionary Sabra movement called the Canaanites, Hitler's ascent to power in 1933 and the Nuremberg race laws of 1935, but mostly the growing impatience of the young Sabras—the earlier sense that the movement had all the time in the world, which my grandfather had described so well, was lost. Suddenly many of of the Jewish leaders in the "Yishuv" believed that the ongoing conversations about the nature of the country needed to be on the fast track. The new urgency began whittling away at the idea of an "open society" and at the open-ended conversations for which the younger Sabras had never developed much tolerance. By the time Hitler declared the intent of his Third Reich, the earlier goal of an entirely organic consensus had been left in the dust.

⁂

Over the decade I spent in Israel, from my late teens to my late twenties, the nature of the country (whether Gemeinschaft or cultural centre) and its purpose (as cultural centre, as homeland, as refuge) hardened and became fixed. Very soon, no one except maybe the "Matzpenistim" (radical communist types) was prepared to discuss any option except the centrally governed state. The notion of selective immigration was also off the table. By 1978, as I was preparing to leave for graduate school, the status of Israel had acquired the inevitability of self-evident or maybe even God-given fact. The early legislation of a "state of emergency"—or constant war footing for the country—was never repealed and indeed remains in place. It means today what it meant when it was first introduced—that we are embattled and will do whatever it takes to survive.

This hardening reached into every interstice of Israeli society. One lesser-known example, in my view the most insidious, was the new definition of " Jew" that was enshrined in the Law of Return in 1973 on the watch of the Baltimore-born prime minister Golda Meir. Meir proposed, and the legislature passed, Addendums 4A and 4B, which redefined Judaism. No longer would it be sufficient for any prospective immigrant to self-declare and to assert he did not belong to another tradition. In the new definition, a Jew was more or less what the Nuremberg laws had said a Jew was—the product of Jewish parents and grandparents. From that point on to be a "Jew" in Israel was a matter of race and biology. And so it was that the original spirit and in large measure the experiment as a whole became unrecognizable, and for me entirely distorted.

On October 4, 1999, my parents moved back to Israel. Their departure and my desire to stay in touch triggered a second return for me, which extended well beyond the time of their respective deaths. Over the course of my intermittent visits to Israel, a distinct pattern emerged in my mind. The "dream state" that I and others of my generation once carried and perhaps still carry about in our heads, and the "facts on the ground"—the State of Israel as it exists today—have gone their separate ways. The approximate match I felt back in the late sixties is now no approximation at all, but two entirely different pictures, with no overlap. It perhaps goes without saying that I, a native son who had invested so much time and energy, and sacrificed so many good friends and family members to that dream state, viewed the yawning abyss with increasing pain and alarm and terrible, aching melancholy.

ONE

Family Matters

My parents called me Zafrir, which in Hebrew means zephyr, a cool morning breeze like the one that blew me into Assuta Hospital on May 14, 1951. The morning I was born, that gentle current of air soon broke into the flattening, scorching wind that the Arabs call *hamsin* and Israelis call *sharav*; even the insulated walls of Israel's first private hospital could not hold back the disabling sirocco that attacked Tel Aviv from the south. "I sweated you out," my bittersweet mother never failed to remind me. "My own father was swept out of the hospital on the waves of his own perspiration. And your father? Well, he was called up to the reserves. I stuck with you," she said. "But your name? That was your father's doing. He loved the name as he loved the boy who first carried it, Zafrir Carmelli, who was your father's sunnier side. The two of them grew up together on the farm and then Zafrir was killed on the Castel, an old crusaders' fortress on the road to Jerusalem. The Arabs took it over from the British and a sniper's bullet went through his head. That was your father's blackest day and the pall hung about him until you were born. You brought him back to life."

But there is more to my name than the blood of a beautiful boy. Roll it on your tongue, breathe in its vowels, and let the rhythm of its consonants work itself out and you will hear the entire history and greatest hopes of the Sabra generation, Israelis whose lives straddled the desert of the colonial powers and the creation of the State of Israel, which gained its independence three years to the day before I was born.

Zafrir is a dawn wind that carries hope for the day that will follow. To allow one's hair to blow in it is to imagine that the restless heat that will soon be kicking at the door does not matter; what matters is only the crisp and silky touch of the early light; what matters is only the here and the now. It was Chaim Nachman Bialik, the great Hebrew poet, who taught the Sabras (or New Jews) how to put the old language to new uses. To him, Zafrir was not only a breeze, but one of those esoteric Kabbalistic spirits—a goblin, a sprite, a gnome. The morning wind, or *ruakh tsafririm*, was Bialik's April, which sprang lilacs from the dead earth. It was not cruel but mischievous; it was not a harbinger of false hope but a reminder that there is more to heaven and earth than either the old rabbi or the realist could dream.

Zafrir is a Sabra imprimatur, a signature of their times. It bears no resemblance to Motl or Tevye or Rayzel, names of the shtetl. When you say it out loud, it challenges you to be who you are, not as all men must be, but like Atzmon and Zohar and Noga and Miron, to become a foundation—to be the rock of the first generation born to freedom. The two *r*'s are throaty and uvular, as in the Arabic letter *ghain*, which is where the Sabras got the phonemes they used to create Dugri, the blunt, staccato patois they carved from the ancient Hebrew. To many Sabras, the opportunity to pay homage to the Arab, and to the Bedouin in particular, was almost an obsession. For them, the image of the nomad, clad in a kaffiyeh and wrapped in the enigmatic desert shroud, brought to mind the aboriginal, the preternatural, the *Ur* source for which these native sons and daughters yearned. Which is one of the reasons why my maternal grandfather, Yunkl, hated my name.

He was a shtetl bourgeois, a merchant who refused to buy into the religion mostly because he believed that all convictions came at a price and he preferred to pay for nothing. But then again, it was he who footed the bill for the private hospital where I was born. And it was he who doled out the keymoney for the apartment on Shlomo HaMelech Street to which my mother and legions of my parents' nearest and dearest soon accompanied the newborn, and where they immediately set him to one side while they drank and sang and exchanged *chizbatim* (tall stories).

"My father wants to call him David," my mother said to my father when he arrived from the base late in the day. "Asik, can we do that for the old coot? It'll just be a middle name—nobody will know, we'll never use it. Maybe it won't even appear in his documents." My father, whose name was Asher but who went by Asik, shrugged.

"It's for a good cause," my mother said without much conviction.

"What cause is that?" Asik asked.

"*Shlom bayit*—order in our household," my mother replied.

Asik shrugged and it came to pass that I was called Zafrir David after Yunkl's favorite dead brother, Doovidl.

What neither my father nor my mother had factored into their decision was just how bound to the actual physical reality of Israel were all the meanings of the name they had chosen for me. What they never imagined was how living away from Israel would loosen the bond, carry off a consonant here and a vowel there, and that before long there would be not a trace of Zafrir, but only David, at which point Yunkl, the old Jew from Poland, would declare a mighty victory.

———

One Monday morning, in the fall of 1953, my parents, Asher and Rachel Berlin, left Israel for Canada, where they pitched their tent for the better part of half a century. Why did they do that? Why did they leave their dream state and for what? The question is compelling when one recalls that both Rahela and Asik had given all they had—their best time and their best friends—so that Israel could rise and go forward. Why leave, and why so soon? Why abandon the family they loved and hated, the *hevre* (friends) they adored, the cafés that ran them a tab? How could my mother, who wandered by the shore and stared out at the sea when she was sad, who was an ocean child and who loved the Mediterranean, leave it behind? How could my father leave the farm whose scents were his life, betray it all, and for what?

Neither of my parents spoke a word of English when they arrived in Canada. They hated the cold and it took my father more than twenty years to learn how to make a buck. Nor was Canada in the early 1950s particularly Jew-friendly. In the immediate post-war period, Charles Blair, an official in Prime Minister MacKenzie King's government, compared Jewish survivors seeking asylum to hogs at feeding time. When he was asked how many of these hogs Canada was prepared to accept, he offered an unabashed "none is too many." Governor General Vincent Massey agreed.

Many Canadians, English and French, rallied behind these leaders. At the time, there were strict quotas and restrictions on Jewish students. Those who applied to the University of Toronto needed to score higher than others. The level of Jewish admissions to McGill was capped at 20 percent. In the early 1950s, a dozen men's clubs were restricted and Canadian hospitals were loath to accept Jewish doctors. Nor was immigration to Canada made any easier for the kind of Jews my parents were. These young Israelis did not think of themselves as Jews at all, maybe even as "un-Jews": brash, full of chutzpah, post-Jewish Jews who were not the least interested in Diaspora Jewish culture. Nor were they ready to adopt the parochial values of the secular Jewish community in Canada. In fact, the Jewish establishment in Toronto, where my parents and I ended up, was far more conservative than others in Canada and tended to think of the Sabras as Philistines whose noisy spirit needed to be broken and tamed to fit the assimilated British posture.

And yet my parents stayed in Toronto, where they suffered the cold, the cold shoulders and their poverty—though that abated once my father figured things out. They shovelled snow while their old friends in Israel dug graves for those killed in battles.

They did not participate in the joys and in the woes and they were not in Israel to bury their own parents. Except for an interval between 1970 and 1975, when my parents separated and my mother ran off to Israel to be with her mother, they never got the experience of living in the dream state to which their entire youth and much of their adult life was devoted—until the fall of 2000 when they returned home to Israel to die.

To write of the unhappy family circumstances that caused my parents to leave Israel is to write very close to the ground. From this level the pettiest annoyances and the largest tectonic movements often seem of the same order of magnitude. A mother's stubborn insistence on cooking with artificial flavouring can be as compelling a reason to leave a country as a profound moral disagreement about whether a war should be waged or not.

The characters in this particular drama, my family, are not different from the characters who play the lead in other families' dramas. My mother's father, Yunkl, was like any other self-centred, authoritarian patriarch. What made him interesting was not the unique shape of his spleen, but that his spleen had the same quality as the spleens of the small-minded, conservative element that made up one part of the Mayflower generation, that wave of immigrants who arrived in Palestine from Eastern Europe dreaming of their own country. Asher Ginzberg, the father of cultural Zionism, feared this kind of pioneer would overwhelm the Labor Zionist movement and he argued that immigration to Palestine should be reserved for only the best and the brightest.

When my mother said, and she said this more times than I care to remember, "Had we not had you, we would never have left the country," I thought she was guilt-tripping me, which she undoubtedly was. But then again, before I was born, the two sets of in-laws, my mother's parents, Yunkl (Yaacov) and Yudit Mass, and my father's parents, Gershon and Pessiah Berlin, had no reason to be in the same room together. I was of course too young to appreciate the cosmic posturing, the comedy, tragedy and human misery that mostly my paternal grandmother Pessiah and my maternal grandfather Yunkl heaped one upon another. Maybe I should be grateful for having been given a ringside seat, and thank my parents for entertaining me with the theatre that their parents played out upon each other and upon their children. But whether I should feel grateful or not, I was in the audience for many of these off-Broadway spectacles. I am quite sure I saw and heard almost all there was to see and hear, even living thousands of miles away in Canada. Not one day went by when my parents did not re-enact the old matches, vividly and with such attention to detail, including the smell of armpits and the most obscene gestures, that everything else about my childhood is a blur.

Apparently, Pessiah threatened never to see her new grandson (me) should her son's wife give birth in that "bourgeois pigsty called Assuta Hospital," which Yunkl had paid for. "He can stuff all his gold bullion right up his capitalist arse," she declared. Then there is my mother screaming at my father, "How come you didn't come to my rescue? You knew I couldn't even think about having Zafi in that filthy hospital your mother recommended. You knew how terrified of the dirt I was. And you knew that I wanted my mother by my side. I mean, I was nineteen, for Christ's sake. I didn't even want to have a baby."

Gershon, my father's father, thought his wife might have a point and tried to persuade his son and new daughter-in-law to check into the publicly funded hospital. "Remember, even your more-gracious-than-Grace-itself father took sides against me," my mother yelled. "That's true," my father said. "But your father is an egocentric son of a bitch, the incarnation of vanity, and my father is not. And don't forget, Gershon did tell Pessiah she was being a fart."

Pessiah finally did get off her high horse. But then at the maternity ward she evidently quoted Gogol or Turgenev to Yunkl— something about not blaming the mirror for your face. Ready to smack her, Yunkl realized she was far too short. "If I gave you my head," he said to Pessiah, "it would not fit on your shoulders and I would then remain as headless as you were born."

"Class warfare" is how my father summed it up. Pouring another stiff drink, he said, "Your mother, Yudit, is hardly a *tallit shekula tehelot* (lily white). Every time we handed her the baby, she made a face like he smells of shit. Her Polish nose picked up the scent, which undoubtedly lingered from her man."

When I thought back upon all the Sturm and Drang which was my upbringing, it often struck me that the real family tensions were not between Yunkl and Pessiah, who were the ones who noisily contended, but between the two grandfathers and the two grandmothers. Yunkl was the diametric opposite of Gershon. Yunkl was a living version of Ayn Rand's philosophy; in his every aspect he demonstrated nothing more or less than the virtues of selfishness. Gershon demonstrated the opposite, the selfishness of the virtuous man.

Yunkl was a *khupper*—a grabber. He took, he did not wait to be offered. He was the first at the food on the serving platter and when it came to women, he took them when and how he wanted them. He lived as if with an unquenchable thirst. In place of conversation, Yunkl had sayings. He was a walking book of proverbs, which is to say that he was never at a loss when it came to finding the same words he'd found the day before. The proverbs protected him. They were his shell and his bubble. Except for the day my mother came home with my father for the first time—that day, Yunkl was actually speechless. "Your father walked in with his hair all greased up and with a pistol tucked into his belt and my father stood there, immobilized," my mother told me. Asher, whom Yunkl viewed as some cowboy from the country, was not what he had in mind for his oldest daughter.

According to my father, Yunkl did finally come up with some line about a Jewish *sheygitzeh* whore who fell in love with a Cossack and broke her father's heart, but my mother has no recollection of it. "I wanted to whack him," my father said.

"Maybe you should have," my mother replied. "That would have saved us both the trouble of getting married."

———

Yudit, my maternal grandmother, was born in Warsaw. When she was in her teens her mother, who had run the family hat business in Warsaw, was killed on a stroll down Jerozolimskie Street near what is now Warsaw's culture ministry. A brick fell from one of the buildings, cracked her skull, and she died instantaneously.

With her grandmother, Yudit made a pilgrimage to Palestine, intending to mourn and ask for respite at the Wailing Wall. As far as I can gather, neither the young Yudit nor her grandmother had any plans to stay in Palestine, which struck them both as a wasteland. In Jerusalem, my grandmother told me, they never found the wall. My great-great-grandmother died and Yudit decided not to return to Warsaw, which was "haunted by my mother's ghost." At sixteen, she moved in with an Orthodox relative who lived in Zefat. Soon she met Yunkl, who did not court her, but paid her guardian to arrange a marriage. In one of her very few intemperate moments, Yudit described the first time she met Yunkl: "He had the most un-kosher face of any man I had ever seen."

Yunkl never really was prepared to be faithful to a wife. He wanted a cook and a womb and maybe someone who would put up with him when he cheated, which was always and with everyone, including Yudit's sister, known as crazy Bela. The only thing sacred to Yunkl was money. It gave him the power and respect he demanded. Money trumped everything. He used it against his children and on visits to him we, his grandchildren, were forced to sit and review the same old stamp and coin collections with him over and over. "I know why you visit me," he would say. "It is because you are trying to protect your inheritance."

⸺⸺⸺

When my mother turned fifteen, her family moved from Haifa to Tel Aviv, mostly to avoid the consequences of Yunkl's dalliances but also to live near his only friend, Levital.

"I changed when we moved. One day I was a Polish princess, the apple of my father's eye, and the next I was a rebel. The first time I stayed out all night my mother called me a whore and hit me with a broom for a solid week."

Rachel was athletic and learned to walk a tightrope. She became one of the better swimmers on the beach at the bottom of Keren Kayemet Street. Her hair was thick and black, twined in a waist-long braid. She refused to pluck her eyebrows, which grew together, making her look like a Frida Kahlo self-portrait.

Her new Tel Aviv friends called her "la spirito mundi" because she claimed to have no past and was committed to making up the rules as she went along.

She and her chic Sabra gang treated all the old ideological quarrels that blew through town as so much hot air. From their perspective the questions the old Zionists were squabbling over were mostly moot, if only because the answer was clear—it was *them*, they were the answer. She and her friends and her counsellors in the scouts and the young people she counselled and the young poets and artists who mingled and drank in the Café Kassit on Dizengoff Street—they were the answer. She and her friends realized that the train was skidding out of the station and that the old guard was still hung up on where the food car should be hitched. "What we got," my mother told me, "was that everything depended on us."

My mother's hoity-toity girlfriends all rolled their eyes when farm boys like my father rolled into town on their motorcycles. The girls all knew better than to flirt with them. "But I thought they were pretty damned cool," my mother said, "and I thought that your father was the most handsome man I had ever seen. Maybe because I was from Haifa, which was less uptight than Tel Aviv back then, maybe because my father cared about money and couldn't stand the idea that I loved a guy with not a penny to his name and no profession and no future. But I did love him and I loved his wild side and I dared to go where most of my girlfriends would not."

Wherever it was that she was ready to go at seventeen, she was not quite ready to get married. She always said it was my father's idea to wed and he went about asking in a most peculiar way. In fact, he did not ask at all but got his good friend

Atzilla from the farm to spread the rumour that Rahela had become pregnant.

She came home one day to find her mother fuming. "Have you been sleeping with that farm boy?" she demanded.

"None of your business," my mother said.

"Are you pregnant?"

"No! I am not pregnant."

"But have you been sleeping with him? Don't lie to me!"

"Okay, dammit, so I have been sleeping with Asik, so what?"

"So what? So it is only a question of time."

And within the week Yudit was arranging the wedding.

⸺⸙⸺

My grandfather Gershon was dark and leathery, and had eyes as black and bottomless as a desert night. His wife, Pessiah, was short and stubborn and kept her hair, which may have always been grey, and was as steely as steel wool, in a tight babushka bun. Gershon and Pessiah were socialists, except that Pessiah secretly coveted the expensive things at which she would turn up her nose. Both were highbrows, but Gershon's wisdom was derived from the heart, not gained from books. "Everything that is white is sweet," Gershon would say, parodying his wife's taste for generalities. "Take for example, sugar . . ." To my paternal grandfather, only individuals mattered.

Pessiah was born in Uman in the Cherkasy Oblast province of Central Ukraine. Her family was poorer than the branch of the Berlins in Kiev, but she was sure her people were of better stock. "After all, the great Nachman of Breslov, the founder of Breslov Hasidism, was not buried in Breslov but in Uman,"

Pessiah would say. "And a man does not choose his place of birth but only where he will be gathered." Also, her older brother, Avraham Koralnik, was a world-class intellectual. "How could I have married such an aimless man," she would complain, "a man with no ambition and no desire to rise above a goatherd?" But Pessiah would sometimes admit that "Beroosh," as she called her husband, was a sweet man. Then she would add her usual acid: "Not everything that is sweet is sugar—for example, gold potassium cyanide."

Gershon was born in Minsk, Belarus. He was the eighteenth child of a wealthy and secular family whose aspiration may have been to singlehandedly give birth to a nation. Gershon's father, Aharon, was something of an activist in a town whose population at the turn of the century was more than 50 percent Yiddish speakers. *As der Messiah vet kumen*—when the Messiah comes—was like an anthem in that community. What it really meant was that whatever needs to be done will never be done.

My paternal great-grandfather was a doer. He designed bridges for the czar and he read the *Communist Manifesto*, which Karl Marx and Friedrich Engels had published fifty years earlier. "My father was particularly taken by its energy," Gershon once told me. "For him, it wasn't so much about the workers, as it was about working, thinking for yourself instead of letting the rabbi do it for you, or maybe not thinking at all until the Messiah *vet kumen.*"

In 1897, the year Gershon was born, a cadre of Minsker students struck out for a worldwide revolution of the sort Marx and Engels had envisioned. That same year they convened what has become known as the first-ever Bolshevik meeting, which apparently took place at one of the warehouses

Aharon owned. The Russian czar, Nikolas II, did not much appreciate the new anarchist spirit and ordered that many of the Minsker Jews be called up to serve in the Great Russian Army.

Aaron's wife, my great-grandmother Gitte, would have none of this. "God will eat the czar's kishkes before my sons become his Cossacks, " she said. So the family packed up and six months after the czar's decree they were unpacking in New York City.

Years later, Gershon remembered Manhattan as if it were Honolulu. His most vivid memories were of eating pineapple and playing a ukulele, which was the only thing he brought with him when he eventually emigrated to Palestine.

I could never quite make out what kind of business the family ran in Manhattan. Sometimes it sounded as though it may have been a pharmacy. Other times it seemed that my great-grandmother bought and sold vestments wholesale to Orthodox Jews. But whatever it was, by 1913 it was not—either because the store was burned down or because Aharon had gone bankrupt or both. My great-grandparents and several of their married children and families left New York for Warsaw; all of them perished in the Nazi camps. Others moved to Brazil and to Argentina. Three middle brothers remained in New York, ingratiated themselves with Tammany Hall, and came out owning a chain of gasoline stations. Gershon and his youngest brother, "Todik" (who was named after Theodore Herzl), made their way to Palestine. Gershon took up residence on the shores of Lake Galilee, where he helped found Israel's first kibbutz, Degania.

Gershon was a cosmopolitan and a free spirit. In Palestine he learned to speak Arabic and to work the soil. He spoke other languages, of course—Russian, English, German and French. Though he never made more than a living and mostly made less, he was, in his heyday, considered one of Israel's most gifted creators of new fruit. Family lore has him pegged as the graftsman behind the giant citrus, the pomella, which is the happy union between an orange and a grapefruit. He etched in copper and sang for the children of the kibbutz on holidays.

But Pessiah was a professional woman, a pharmacist who would not stoop to women's work on the kibbutz. Until 1929, when the Arabs massacred the Jews in Hebron, she had been the town's druggist and doctor, and now wanted more comfort than a kibbutz could offer. Besides, from her point of view, kibbutznikim were not only snobs but meddling busybodies. "Mostly that's what kibbutznikim made," she would say, "they made *heshbonot*, lists of who did and who didn't do what they were supposed to be doing."

To appease his wife, Gershon reluctantly moved from one kibbutz to another until he and Pessiah finally ended up in Tel Mond, a privately owned farming settlement, or *moshav*, where he built a matchbox of a house and painted it as white as the flag of surrender. For many years Gershon worked as a project manager in the Gaza Strip. He never dreamed of occupying this land but spoke always of a New Middle East in which Arabs, Jews, Christians and whoever else wished to join in would work co-operatively and govern themselves in the same way.

Sometimes Gershon's sense of "co-operative" went overboard. I learned this when my father's youngest sister, Lela, came to visit. We were flipping through an old photo album when a picture of my father as a child slipped out of a yellowed pocket. In the photograph, he is standing near Muli-Baba, the Arab-owned store on the main drag of Tel Mond. "It was the only trading post for fifty kilometres in every direction," Lela told me. He is dressed in baggy shorts and a sleeveless undershirt. His face is smeared with dirt, his hair thick and crew-cut. There is nothing naive and quizzical about his look. He does not have that mischievous "Dennis the Menace" air that the Israeli historian, Amos Elon, has claimed was the signature mark of Israelis of his generation. In the photo, my father looks defiant and fierce. He is holding the reins of a donkey and they seem intimate. "The donkey was the only thing more stubborn than your father," Lela said. "I think they understood one another."

When I asked her why my father looked so neglected, she became wistful: neglect was a way of life in the moshavim. "Kids were forced to harden quickly. We became a *bar'ed* generation, cold, icy, hard. Some, like your father, may have become rather savage, like the cactus that learns to take root in any soil. We were left to fend for ourselves in a world in which there was very little time to be young."

"But why is my father so filthy?" I asked.

"Well, I think this was just about the time when your grandfather gave away the family bathtub. He was like that. Someone came by and asked for the bathtub and he gave it to him. It was all your grandmother needed to make her lose her mind." Which according to Lela, Pessiah did, quite early and quite often.

When he was fifteen my father and a few of the more macho *hevre* from the moshava volunteered for the British army. The boys wanted to fight Hitler's big general, Rommel, whom they all knew as the Desert Fox. The boys were all underage and could not possibly have got past the sentry except by lying about it. They did not have to lie about their experience handling a Sten 9mm British automatic machine gun with a side-mounted magazine. Many of the boys had done some killing around the farm. I once overheard my father boast that by 1941 he had killed at least two, maybe three, Bedouin boys he'd discovered in the chicken coop.

Most of the boys who volunteered spoke some Arabic. Many had Arab friends, though fewer of them after the 1936 Arab Revolt in which British soldiers randomly executed some seven thousand young Palestinians. What is for sure is that by fifteen my father was more than capable of killing a man. I would say he was a natural; he lived within that circle of time and space in which everything that goes around comes around. For him, killing of the sort one did in order to defend the few chickens in the coop was neither moral nor immoral. It was just part of life.

Before the day was out, the parents of all the boys except my father had dragged them home by the ear. "Once we were there, we all prayed that our mothers would come get us," my father told me years later. "But Pessiah did not come. Two days later I was trucked off to El Alamein."

When I asked my father how he felt about all of this, he said, "What do you think? I felt betrayed."

A few years before my father was whisked off to North Africa, there was a raging debate in the Yishuv, the pre-statehood Jewish community in Palestine, between those who thought Israelis should join the Allies to fight the Nazis—Ben-Gurion and his group—and those who felt it was necessary to keep fighting the British—the Irgunists and the Stern Gang. The latter group wanted to take advantage of British weakness and distraction in order to end the mandate in Palestine. Gershon wanted to fight the Nazis and he wanted the British to remain in Palestine as long as possible "to give us and the Arabs more time to figure out how to live together."

My father told me that when Gershon told him this, it was the only time he ever wanted to hit his own father. He didn't.

—∞—

So the fifteen-year-old farm boy Asher Berlin was shipped off to El Alamein in North Africa where he learned to use a Tommy gun, drive a half track, and run messages behind enemy lines. My father's friend Motke Dror once told me that very soon after my father arrived in Africa he found himself at the mercy of some British officer who thought he might put the boy to his own uses. Motke's smile widened sardonically as he spoke.

"Apparently your father could not have agreed less and I am afraid to say that he has never had much respect for good form or for the old stiff upper lip. In any case, by the time Asik was done with him, this British officer had lost a lifetime of sexual ambition. Your father barely managed to get himself discharged from the army before he was charged in a British military court."

When I asked my father about his time in Africa, he claimed that the fog of war had muddled up his brain. He called this condition "having a plonter," which is a Yiddishism meaning "tangled," as may happen when an excess of toilet paper prevents the toilet from flushing. "Plonters" were regular occurrences with my father. Each time I asked him to spell out a truth that was inconvenient he would declare himself out of service.

In fact, most of what I have cobbled together about my father's life has been hard won and came my way from others.

Apparently he was recruited to the Palmach, the strike force of the Haganah (the underground Jewish defence organization, precursor of the IDF), for a time. The Palmach was an elite unit that initially consisted of no more than a hundred young men, many of whom had been trained by the British to fight against the Vichy regime in Lebanon. According to my father's sisters, he served in the *plugah meyuhedet* (the special forces) of the Palmach, but for how long they could not say. They knew nothing about why he was finally discharged except that maybe he did something sufficiently alarming that the chief of staff of the Palmach, Moshe Dayan, locked him up for three months.

—◆◆◆—

Consider a story my father never told me. I heard this after he died from my cousin, Ariel, a philosophy professor in Haifa who became something of a priest to him — my father felt comfortable enough with Ariel to confess an event that must have burdened him his whole life. That he talked with Ariel and not me was hurtful, but I recognized that he was less at risk of being judged by Ariel than he was by his own son.

"Several months before the War of Independence broke out in 1947," Ariel told me, "there was some shooting in one of Haifa's Arab neighbourhoods — the one just up from the harbour. Our soldiers imposed a curfew and one of their Arab speakers travelled up and down the streets, announcing on a megaphone that every male over a certain age was to come out into the streets with their hands up. The special forces were called in to comb the buildings to make sure that everyone had in fact complied with the order.

"Your father was assigned a floor of a building and when he entered one particular apartment he discovered, crouched in the corner, an old Arab man with burning black eyes. Dressed in a long white jellabiya, a red-checked kaffiyeh wrapped around his head, the old fellow was squatting in typical Arab fashion. Your dad described him as defiant, adding only that his forehead was not only creased but seemed to contain riverbeds and a canyon or two. The whites of his eyes were not white but black as coal so that they ran fluidly to the iris and pupils. Somehow I got the sense that the fellow was exalted, maybe head of one of the big *hamulot*, the Arab families who lived in Shfaram or maybe in Haifa itself. Your dad locked the man in his gaze, which, as you can imagine, could not have been an easy task. And then he said that something funny happened."

"What?" I asked.

"Well, I am not quite sure. Your dad maybe did not mean that something actually happened."

"So what didn't happen?"

"Let me put it this way. Your father said, 'The old Arab reminded me of my father.' Our grandfather, Gershon."

"He what?"

"He said he reminded him of his own father—that is what he said. Apparently your father was confounded by that thought and for a few moments he could not quite figure out what to do. And then he ordered the old man to get up and get out, join the lineup outside. 'Y'allah, *rukh meen hon*,' Asik had said, waving his hand in the direction of the door. He repeated the order once and then again. But the old bugger did not budge."

"Maybe he was deaf or blind or both," I offered.

"That's exactly what I asked. But your dad just went on with the story. He said that he felt strangely nauseous and then felt something burning into his forehead, like a tattoo or the mark of Cain. But to be perfectly honest, I think he was making this part up, or maybe this was just something added in the dream version of the event which your dad said has haunted him ever since. But then again, maybe he was just buying time so that he might reconsider whether he should finish the story or not. But he did.

"He said he took out a magazine from his belt and fitted it into the Sten machine gun, pointed it straight at the old man's head and fired a first round. And then he loaded and fired a second round and then loaded a third magazine and emptied it. By the time he was done, there was very little left of the guy, very little that was not splattered over the walls. And then Asik stopped talking, as though there was nothing more to be said and nothing that called out to be understood."

"What do you make of it?" I asked.

"I don't know, I guess your dad was a bit crazy."

Consider this story, which my father did tell me. It was meant to be a bedtime story and he repeated it many times over the course of my childhood, each time with a slightly different coloration. But it always summoned for me the smell of the zoo that had been just down the block from Philon Street, where my maternal grandparents lived.

The story my father told was about him and his old buddies from the farm. There was Moishe Va-Hetzi, or Moishe and a Half, who was 50 percent taller than everyone else. And there was Shimaleh HaMelech, who planned to be king when he grew up, and a lively fellow named Haim Ben Haim. There was also Zafrir Carmelli, my namesake, who was killed near the Castel.

"On muggy afternoons when we weren't out milking cows or picking oranges or in the army," my father recalled, "we'd gel our hair with animal fat, wax the old mustachios, get into Shimaleh's jeep, and head up to Jerusalem. We'd park near the Orthodox Jewish neighbourhood, Meah She'arim."

In my father's account, the ultra-Orthodox Jews hated everything the Sabra stood for. They refused to believe that the Zionist movement had replaced the Messiah. "They didn't hate the Arabs, they hated us," he told me. "When I was young the *haredim* (Orthodox) seemed far more dangerous than the Arabs. The Arabs just wanted things, but these guys wanted to destroy the very ideas we were building on, the centre of our beings. So we would drive to Jerusalem, put the jeep into crouch and just sit, really quiet, not moving a muscle, scanning the neighbourhood like lions. When we'd spot one, our prey, we'd pounce, tie his feet and hands, and drag him back to the jeep. We'd always pick really ugly, smelly ones. We could never understand or get over their outfits—the black overcoat and the fur-rimmed hat in the heat of Jerusalem. And of course, all of them had *payis*, the sidelocks that blew in the wind when they walked. Usually the guy we picked was an adult—we didn't prey on young kids— but every one of them walked with such a sense of purpose that it made us crazy. We knew they had nowhere to go, but they walked the streets as if commanded by some supreme, mightier-than-thou authority.

"We would take our prey into the jeep and snip off his sidelocks, at which point he would cry out for help from the Messiah: "Avinu Malkeinu," he would squeal. We would explain to him that the Messiah had already come and had sent us to save him from himself.

"We didn't really hurt him. Just scared him. Sometimes we would offer kosher food, but most of them refused because they could not be sure of its purity. Even water was refused, which we all found ridiculous. We would finally let him go with the advisory that he should go back home and tell his family that he wanted to join the real Jewish people and serve in the army for the glory of our people, not pray for the destruction of the State. That's all we did. It was our mission."

Today, hyper-Orthodox Jewish Israelis still refuse to recognize the State of Israel. They have engaged in treasonable offences, including passing secret information to the late Palestinian leader, Yasir Arafat, who paid them handsomely for it. Orthodox Jews have even voluntarily attended conferences organized by anti-Israeli Holocaust deniers such as the Iranian president, Mahmoud Ahmadinejad.

That Israel's first prime minister, David Ben-Gurion, did not act against them was a mystery to my father and his friends. But the Orthodox rabbis in Palestine blackmailed the Yishuv leadership by threatening to persuade the UN commission, which was sent to investigate the status of the Jews in Palestine, that there was no real consensus for an independent state. My father was following his nature: what goes around comes around.

To understand the relationship between Gershon and his son, my father; to unravel the complex love–hate relation between these two men and, by extension, between the Mayflower generation and the Sabras; to understand what part this drama of betrayal, illusion and reality played in my parents' decision to leave Israel so soon after the state was established; all this has taken me the better part of forty years. Looking back, all I can say with relative certainty is that my grandfather was an idealist, a utopian thinker, a dreamer who was quite content with the little he had—and what little he had did not include a real understanding of his dream.

My father, on the other hand, acted on the dream and his own self-interest in a Jewish state, under a flag and in the army, with the unshakable determination that something like the Holocaust would never happen again.

But the two generations did not talk to each other. Neither the Sabra youth nor their elders—the Mayflower generation as a whole—took the time to flesh out the dream. Had they done so, I believe they would have established not a Jewish state but a secular commonwealth, which would have worked well in the region and which would have kept the Orthodox religious community from overwhelming the state and undermining the entire Zionist project.

Had either the pioneers or their sons and daughters understood themselves not as secular Jews but as Jewish seculars, not as types of Jews but as types of seculars, the entire history of the past sixty years would have been very different.

The undeniable generosity of spirit, the humility and the modesty that are part of the ethos of the founding culture—my grandfather giving away his bathtub because some else needed it—brings to mind the archetypal citizen of Socrates: unselfish, virtuous, but without a sense of the greater good. My grandfather gave away one tub; my father thought, why not have a thousand bathtubs instead of just one? Build a world where everyone has what they need.

My father's generation was made of pragmatists and doers, not dreamers. On the day he was old enough to mix mortar, my father built a mixer powered by his donkey in order to make bricks. Two weeks later he built a primitive mould that increased the production of his bricks fourfold. A week after that he was selling bricks to his father's friends. The old guard was in awe of his industry but they worried about the crazy-making sense of urgency that my father and his entire generation introduced into what was their pastoral life.

For them there was endless time for thinking and dreaming, and for building, but their children did not subscribe to that schedule, nor were they sure that thinking or dreaming was so necessary.

"I think my son believed and maybe still believes that he betrayed me," my grandfather Gershon once told me. It was in the early seventies, just after I was recruited into the IDF. He was suffering from advanced prostate cancer and would soon be diagnosed with terminal lung cancer. His frame, once muscular, had diminished, raisin-like. The doctor had forbidden him to smoke, but sometimes, and this was one of those times, it seemed to me as though cigarettes were far more important to him than living.

"Ask your grandmother whether it might be all right for us to go walking in the garden," Gershon whispered in my ear. When I did, she frowned and cocked her Ancient Mariner's eye, but by then Gershon had linked his arm in mine and we were off to the far side of the great pecan tree, which he had planted on the day my father was born.

"Don't smoke, Beroosh. Zafi, don't give him a cigarette," Pessiah called after us.

Once upon a time Gershon's hands were as steady as a surgeon's, his motor skills so fine that he could have sewn the wings back on a fly. But now his hands trembled as he fumbled into his overalls for the filterless cigarette he had folded in three and tucked deep into his pocket. Quickly I offered him a smoke from my box of Sweet Times but he wouldn't hear of it. "Don't waste them on my old lungs," he said, "I prefer my own fags." Then he straightened out his own Dubek 10—also the cigarette of choice in Israeli military prisons. He put it to his lips, touched a match flame to its end and drew long and hard. Then he coughed and turned slightly green. When he tried to extricate the fag from his always weathered lips, a stubborn string of tobacco refused to come along; it stuck and the cigarette unravelled. By the time his arm completed the arc, there was nothing between his fingers but a hollow tube of no-ply cigarette paper.

"Never mind," he said. "Tell me all about your life—how are things going in our astounding army?"

I hesitated, but then told him how the other night our unit had unexpectedly been catapulted into the Jabaliya refugee camp in Gaza and that we had been entrusted to comb the fields for wanton fedayeen. Somewhere along the way, one of my best new friends, Gal Avinoam, was shot dead. It was a horrible shock and I was still in a daze. I couldn't believe that it really happened. That people just die like that. And I could not figure out what exactly we were doing in that refugee camp in the first place. Terrorist activity in Gaza had increased after we arrived.

My grandfather suddenly became very grey. I stuttered and apologized for disturbing him with such grimness. But he slipped his arm around me and we walked down a path he had created. On both sides were trees bearing green grapefruits and lemons.

"You know that for many years I worked in Gaza as a project manager," he said. "Many Jews of my generation were uncomfortable with the Arabs. But I have always been more uncomfortable with Jews, especially the eager ones who think that we are all about the state here. For sure we need something of our own. But we don't need it without the Palestinians. And we don't need all the crap that comes with having a state. I was in Tel Hai with Joseph Trumpeldor when the Shii gang from Lebanon attacked. People believe that as Trumpeldor lay dying he said, 'Tov lumoot be'ud artseinu' — that it is noble and good to die for our country. But Trumpeldor said nothing of the sort. He was scared to death of dying. And anyways, he didn't think it was good to die for anything. The point is to live for something. To die is good for nothing. I know because I am dying."

I asked him whether he thought my father left Israel so that his children would not have to serve in the army.

"Maybe," my grandfather said. "But you know your father and I never really spoke candidly. Not really. I love him more than anything. But he was always impatient, sure of himself and of his friends. They all wanted to get on with things. They wanted a flag and an anthem and our very own army. They were our children but sometimes I thought maybe I wasn't his father. I don't mean that literally, but it was as though they came from nowhere: they were kind of mythic creatures — beautiful and powerful, more like gods than men who wanted to make their home here."

My father claimed that his generation was the "desert generation" which, in the biblical odyssey, was permitted to see the
country from afar but never to enter it. In his view the Bible got
it right. "Those of us who stayed in Israel and who went into
politics made a mess of it. I am quite sure that had your mother
and I stayed we would not have done any better."

But of course they did not stay and so there is no real way of
knowing whether they would have done harm or good. Given
that neither of my parents had the skills or the desire to enter
public life, had they stayed in Israel it would have probably
made little difference one way or the other. But what I found
fascinating about this perspective is the picture of Israel's history
upon which it relied. As my father saw things, the continued
Israeli occupation of the West Bank and Gaza had very little to
do with the relationship between Israel and the Palestinians. It
was all about sibling rivalry, especially the rivalry between two
big-time Sabras: Chief of Staff Moshe Dayan and General
Ariel Sharon.

I remember a long conversation I had with my father about
this rivalry. It was on a summer Sunday afternoon in the mid-
1990s. We met at the Prince Hotel in Scarborough near his
house, had brunch, and then went for a stroll in the hotel
grounds. Out of the blue my father began talking about Moshe
Dayan, a man I knew he'd never liked but who he now claimed
was a far more rational man than Sharon. "Dayan was *bar'ed*,
icy rational," he said, "a little like your mother can sometimes
be. Do you remember what his daughter Yael wrote about him?
That he was afraid of being afraid—that the fear of fear was what
mastered him—that all other emotions, human, normal, healthy
ones, were pushed aside and stopped existing.

"Sharon was more like me. You know that he was born in Kfar Malal, which is really a stone's throw from Tel Mond where I grew up. Anyhow, what you need to understand about Sharon, and I know you had some contact with him in the army, is that he is all about the chip on the shoulder, which all of us farm boys had. All our lives in Israel we felt outdone by the clean-cut kibbutz types. Sharon wanted to be loved and admired, especially by Ben-Gurion, who preferred Dayan and Rabin and Peres and Yigal Allon. But Sharon kept after Ben-Gurion and he was tickled when he sometimes, not often, asked him to sit by his side at a meeting. Sharon felt like Ishmael might have felt had Abraham asked him to sit with him. He was flattered beyond belief.

"Anyhow, more than anything else, Sharon wanted to be chief of staff. He wanted to be a hero. But Dayan couldn't stand him. In the early 1970s, when you were in the army, Dayan was minister of defence and Sharon was given charge of the Southern command, which included the Gaza Strip. There was lots of terrorist activity in Gaza but Dayan didn't think it was our business. But Sharon saw an opportunity to become a hero. Clean Gaza up and you will become chief of staff—that is what Sharon thought. But Dayan is stubborn and he's in charge. So then Sharon gets this big idea. Let some Jewish tourists in and let them get killed and the Israeli public will force Dayan's hand. Do you remember the Arroyos?"

I said I remembered them, although I was not quite sure that I did.

"They were a British family, tourists," he said. "Sharon lets them through the checkpoint into Gaza and sure enough some terrorist lobs a grenade and kills their kids. The next thing you know you and your friends are in Gaza, too."

I interrupted. "I can't believe you mean that Sharon orchestrated the whole thing. How do you know that?"

"Zafi, you really are too naive," my father said, rather disarmingly. "Of course Sharon orchestrated it. How else did these tourists get through the checkpoint? Wasn't Sharon in charge of security in and out of Gaza? Anyhow, Sharon is thrilled. Dayan is fuming. And you know the rest of the story. Sharon moves his troops into Gaza, does what he does. And then, a couple of years later, Dayan announces on public television that Gaza is clean and that Israel owes General Sharon a vote of thanks.

"Sharon hears the announcement and realizes it's over for him. He will never become chief of staff because Dayan has just written him off, with thanks. Now he is fuming. He goes home, feeds his pigs for a while and dreams of revenge. And then comes the Yom Kippur War. Sharon goes into Sinai and basically does the Kurtz thing, all 'heart of darkness.' He takes over, gets a couple of hundred young Israeli kids killed for nothing in the Battle of the Chinese Farm in the Sinai across the Canal, becomes a hero and then he's ready for revenge. How does he do it? By planning to take down the Labor Party to which Dayan belonged, but to which Ben-Gurion and my father also belonged. I really can't forgive him for that one.

"I read in the Israeli papers that Sharon claimed that he and Menachem Begin created the Likud Party because they thought that Israeli democracy needed a strong opposition. But the truth is that neither Begin nor Sharon could even spell the word democracy. What they both wanted was revenge. Sharon for his reasons and Begin because Ben-Gurion always humiliated him, called him 'that guy over there,' even when Begin was in the Knesset. Then Sharon goes even further. He starts to usher in all those crazy settlers: Levinger and Porat. He actually sends his troops to help them settle the West Bank. Believe me, had it not been for Sharon they never would have settled there. And believe me also: Sharon couldn't stand those religious Jews any more than I can. But for the sake of revenge he would do anything.

"And you know what? If I were in his shoes I would probably have done the same. Maybe I wouldn't have killed the entire country for my ambition but I sure as hell would have found a way to revenge myself on Dayan."

I found my father's story shocking not only because of what he said about Sharon but because I had never really understood the sense of ownership over the country that his generation of Sabras felt—as though Israel was nothing but their plaything. They were gods who had established the place and now it was their sandbox. Was this the force behind the great unravelling of the Histadrut (the national labour union) and the kibbutz movement, which another Sharon lackey named Haim Ramon oversaw? And what about Israel's eighteen-year occupation of Lebanon, a campaign Sharon initiated? Sharon had promised Menachem Begin that Israel would be in and out of Lebanon in a matter of weeks. And Begin, who did not get that Sharon was a consummate liar, was duped. When Begin finally realized that he had been taken for a ride, he resigned, fell into a morbid depression, locked himself inside his apartment, and was never seen in public again.

And what happened to the Dayan types? The kibbutznikim, who once numbered only 3 percent of the population but over 40 percent of the nation's top echelons of officers, were no longer in the limelight. After the first few disaster-filled days of the Yom Kippur War in October of 1973, Dayan himself lost his cool and declared with no reservation that the project he called "the Third Temple"—the State of Israel—was now in ruins.

Young Israelis of my generation found Dayan's statement repulsive. We rallied around the defiant Sharon, but then our seamless, uninterrupted faith in our elders finally broke.

—∞—

Although it was difficult for me to rethink the history of the conflict as the history of a rivalry, I realized that this was how my father thought about things, and that allowed me to better understand his reasons for leaving Israel. And it also illuminated for me why he felt he was within his rights to go. He and his peers had done all that they promised to do: now there was a state. My father was always girded and prepared to return to defend it should the need arise. But he and the rest of his generation could not defend it from themselves. He knew that had he stuck around in the bubble he had helped to create, he would not have acted very differently than anyone else. Over time I have come to think that all the Sabras realized this. I believe that in the back of their minds or deep in the recesses of their hearts they must have understood not only that they had fulfilled their part of the bargain and had the right to leave but also that to stay was an error. How else to explain the extraordinarily ugly lengths to which many of them went in order to persuade themselves to stay?

Before the War of Independence, remaining in Israel had been a matter of honour and privilege and love. After the war it became a matter of duty. One stayed because one would feel too guilty for leaving. Sabras called friends who left *yordim* ("downers") or *nefolet,* meaning chaff or waste. A *yored* is a person who betrays his friends and betrays the cause; *yordim* are pilgrims on the road to hell. My parents and I were about to become all of that.

Exile in Toronto

F or weeks before we boarded the plane for Canada my mother and I would make believe we *were* the plane. She would lie on her back and I would step on her feet, lean forward and then balance myself on her knees and on her shins. I'd stretch my arms over my head like Superboy and then I would make engine noises. Soft rumbling noises at first, then climbing noises as she raised me to a cruising altitude. Merrily she sang *red eleinu aviron, kakh otunoo luh marom*—take us yonder, little plane, up, beyond the clouds and rain. She was the tarmac and the air that buoyed me up. I was the plane and the pilot—and dead serious about it. The more earnest I was, the more she laughed and the more annoyed I became.

When we got on the real plane at Lod Airport in Tel Aviv, no one laughed. My father claimed to have flown during the war, but he was as pale as the rest of us. When we reached cruising altitude we all relaxed and I became giddy. My parents let me out of my seat and I ran up and down the aisles in exhilaration. Baruch Segal and his wife Ruth, an actress who would become one of Israel's grandest, thought the scene was charming enough for them to introduce themselves to my parents. My mother was clearly taken by Ruth, whom she had seen perform twice. The KLM flight had a stopover at the airport in Amsterdam. As we entered the lounge my parents struck up a lively conversation with Baruch and Ruth. As they spoke about Israeli politics, I became fascinated with the size of the place, with the lights and the tulips that adorned the lounge. When the adults thought to look, I was gone. They began to search, and my parents were soon hysterical. Ruth found me an hour later flushing one of the new-fangled toilets in the women's washroom. For the first (but hardly the last) time in my life my mother slapped me.

Montreal, our original destination, was a write-off. "Anywhere that has more churches than the Via Dolorosa does not need another New Jew," my mother said, and besides, she was four months pregnant and Mont Royal had no escalators.

Two weeks later we moved to Toronto, where my father's friend Motke and his wife, Tamar, already had made serious inroads. Over the phone Motke promised my father a job driving a school bus. "What kind of school?" my mother asked my father when he got off the phone. "I think it's for Sabonim," he said, which in Hebrew means soap—the kind the Nazis made out of Jewish fat. "Perfect for you, my sweet anti-Semite," my mother said and laughed.

On January 8, 1954, my brother Daniel was born. The family moved northward, from a ratty apartment above a paint store on Queen Street in downtown Toronto to the ratty second floor of a house in Kensington Market. A year and a half later, in September of 1956, my mother noticed that Daniel had developed some lumps under his arms and in his groin. From his crib, which was next to my bed, I could sometimes hear him wheezing and coughing. One day shortly after that, my parents told me that my brother had acute childhood leukemia and from there on in was to be taken to the hospital frequently for radiation. "The good news," my mother said, more solemnly than is usual for good news, "is that you won't have to come to the hospital with us. We found a perfect nursery school very close to home. Next Monday you will begin school like a big kid."

Monday morning I woke up early and very excited. I got out of bed to check on Daniel, who was restlessly turning from side to side but still asleep. My mother had laid out a brand-new set of clothes on the little stool beside my bed. On the floor there was a pair of new running shoes, a new pair of white socks, and best of all, a shiny red lunchbox, which was already packed with a sandwich wrapped in cellophane and a Mr. Big chocolate bar. When my parents got up, my father lit a cigarette and put the kettle on. He asked me if I was excited about school, then told me that he would be here when I got home: he was not going to be working for a while so he could stay home to take care of Daniel. My mother got up and got dressed and she and I were just about to leave for school when Daniel started crying. My mother nursed him for a few minutes and then handed him, still crying, to my father, who walked him about to relieve the colic. Daniel did not stop, but we left anyhow. My mother assured my father that she would be back very soon.

"The name of your new school is Cedarvale," she said in the car, pronouncing it "Seder-Vale" as though it had something to do with Passover.

The school's foyer smelled of Lysol. A portrait of Queen Elizabeth II hung between two Red Ensigns on poles. We were late and my mother, flustered, looked around for the right room. Suddenly the anthem "God Save the Queen" came over the loudspeakers. I am not quite sure whether she recognized the tune but was too worried about the time to stop; more likely, she just did not much care for anthems. We kept on walking until a severe-looking man in a grey suit stepped out of an office and ordered us to stand at attention. My mother stopped, but shifted anxiously, clutching me by the hand. When the anthem ended, we heard children's voices.

"*Sof, sof, Heeganu*, we're here," my mother said in front of an open door. From behind her skirt, I peeked in to see children, cross-legged on the floor, calling out in perfect unison: "Good morning, Miss Carmichael."

"Good morning, children," the teacher responded.

"This is Zafrir," my mother said as we entered the room.

"Welcome to our school," Miss Carmichael said as she reached for my hand. I was not the least bit interested and clung to my mother.

"Zafi, I need to get back to your brother, so please . . ." She disentangled my fingers and Miss Carmichael led me over to the circle, where I listened to a story I barely understood. When it was over, I waved my arm to get her attention. I needed to go to the bathroom, I needed to get out of there. But Miss Carmichael ignored me. She walked over to her desk, picked up the class list and scrolled down to the name of the new boy. The manner in which the consonants in my first name played off the vowels may have exuded the scent of an immigrant, and made her uncertain of how to address me. But whatever it was that prevented her from responding, it took more time than I had.

"Yes, dear," she finally said, avoiding the name issue. But it was too late. "Dear" had warm piss dripping down my leg, forming a puddle on the floor, and the class was choking back their laugher. Miss Carmichael flashed them a look and they turned to stone. As Miss Carmichael took hold of my arm, I slumped away from her. "Not a peep," she said to the class.

We walked down the hall briskly, stopping in front of a door that turned out to be the principal's office—the man with the grey suit who had told my mother and me to stop walking. He looked down at me. "I see," he said. "Take a seat outside, young man."

Miss Carmichael went back to her classroom leaving me to sit for the longest while on the long wooden bench outside the principal's office, fighting back tears. Then my mother showed up. "*Meesken*," she said, "you poor child, I will be with you in a jiffy." I didn't hear much of what went on between my mother and the principal behind his closed door, but I did hear her saying my name, Zafrir, many times. And then I heard another name: David. When the door opened, the principal walked out, my mother behind him, fussing with something in her purse.

"David," he said, "your mother will now take you home and we shall see you tomorrow morning bright and early. David, will it be okay if we pretend that today never happened?"

I did not answer.

"Who is this David?" I asked my mother as we left the school.

"You are. It's your middle name. You remember Saba Yaacov? David was his brother. And your father and I named you after him."

"But it's not my name."

"Yes, Zafi, it is. To us you will always be Zafi, but David is your second name and it is a perfectly good name. The principal said that the children in your class will find it easier to pronounce. Zafrir is a beautiful name but Canadians can't pronounce it. Don't you think that's a good thing?"

"No, I don't. And I don't want to stay in this stupid school or in this stupid country! I want to go home."

"*Ani lo Maskeem*," my father said, pressing his lips together the way his mother did when she needed to dig in. "I won't allow it. My son cannot go around with a ridiculous name that reminds me of your father—who is the last person on earth I want to remember."

My mother cried, but insisted, "It is not about you."

Daniel cried, too, and then my father left. I thought, "If they agree to this, then it can only be that they aren't my parents— they are fakes—and I will not call two fakes my parents. I will call them nothing."

The next two years at Cedarvale Public School were mostly miserable. Sometimes my father, who now drove a huge silver gasoline truck, took me on a tour of Toronto gas stations. My mother spent most of her time in the hospital with Daniel, who was slowly recovering. And then one day my mother said that I would be leaving Cedarvale to attend a private parochial Hebrew school called Talmud Torah.

And our family moved farther north, to a second-floor apartment on Hotspur Road. Off the living room there was a small balcony that overlooked a field and a yellow brick building. "That is your new school," my mother said. "It's half Hebrew and half secular studies. I think you'll love it and you can walk to school by yourself."

What my mother did not tell me was that she had persuaded the school to exempt us from the exorbitant tuition and as a result she expected me to be on my best behaviour. Nor did she tell me that she would be a substitute teacher at Talmud Torah and that I would often bump into her when I was kicked out of class. But most important of all the things she didn't tell me was this: neither she nor my father mentioned God, whom I had never heard of until my first class with Rabbi Shokhet at the new school.

Secular studies at the Talmud Torah were already over my head. We studied Latin with Mrs. Colyps, who spoke it as fluently as Claudius and expected us to do as the Romans did. Mrs. Vowels taught French language, which she told us we had to learn if we wanted to be officially Canadian. Geography was the provenance of Mr. Bowley, an old Brit with many letters after his name, who could draw perfect maps on the blackboard without ever turning away from the class. Mrs. Sternberg, whom I liked best, taught English. She could shut us up in an instant by threatening not to read the next adventure of Peter and his friends in *The Ship That Flew*. Mr. Petlock, who, thinking back, I now realize was halfway out of the closet, taught the boys arithmetic and science.

The real trauma, however, came from the rabbis who taught us the Hebrew Bible and the Aramaic interpretations of Rashi and the Targum Onkelos. When we got things wrong they hit us on the knuckles with half a dozen rulers. They sent us to buy cheese buns at the Open Window Bakery across Bathurst Street from the school. Most of the children had never crossed the road by themselves and at least one of us got a job at the bakery and transferred to the local public school.

Rabbi Shokhet, who loved cheese buns even more than the others, often borrowed money from the children. He ate while we copied out lines from Hebrew texts. He nicknamed Perry Simon, who was cursed with an overactive bladder, "Mabool" — which in Hebrew means a flood of the sort that persuaded Noah to build an ark. It was fine with the rabbi if all of us called Perry Mabool.

Classes were ordered alphabetically: 2A was accelerated, 2B and 2C were for the slower, and 2D was for all the kids called retards. In each classroom, rows of desks were ordered from left to right. Geniuses (the *illuyim*) like Jeannette Pik sat in the smartest row along with others who were perhaps not as brilliant but were as well behaved. The rows by the window were often empty; the children who occupied those seats were either down at Mrs. Snyder's office getting the strap or hiding from the principal in the school basement.

Still, my classmates, no matter their classification, had at least heard of God before they began school. Phil Ladovsky and Tova Goldenberg and Martin Lockshin, for example, had been going to synagogue before they were born. In all his life, my father had never been in a synagogue. When I began to understand that the God I had just been introduced to was not particularly forgiving, I got worried and tried to persuade my father to come and pray. I told him that he should at least show up for Yom Kippur and that when he did he should wear only socks in the main auditorium. But on the Day of Atonement my father wore leather boots and he went to work as usual.

God was not happy and he took over my dreams. Baruch Segal, whom my parents had met on the plane from Israel, led the junior congregation and told the children that they could not hide from God. Because he was an Israeli like me, I believed him.

When I was twelve, I decided to go the entire eight days of Passover unleavened. It was an extraordinary bit of discipline and I reasoned that it gave me some experience of what it might feel like to be God, who did such things on an everyday basis. To pass by Hal's Smoke Shop with a dime in one's pocket and not buy a Mr. Big was to be the man I wanted to be. I took on a righteous swagger and then, at the end of the eighth day, my father walked into the kitchen, congratulated me on my feat and unwrapped a piping hot corned beef sandwich cut on the fatty side from Moe Pancer's on Bathurst Street near York Downs. Eating that sandwich together was the most Jewish thing I ever did with my father, whom I had not called by any name since the day I became David.

—◈—

One day my father announced: "At the end of the month—on the thirtieth of May to be exact—I am planning to kill the head of the Canadian Nazi Party. I have been assigned a mission by

N5, a Jewish organization named after Isaac Newton's fifth law, which says that for every bad action there is an equal and opposite reaction. They've asked me to drive a truck into Allen Gardens and break up a Nazi rally. I am supposed to lose control of the truck, which will then ram the podium and kill John Beattie, who is the head of the party. Do you want to tag along, Zafi?"

"For sure," I said.

But then my mother got involved. She didn't think it was a good idea for her husband and eldest son to spend the rest of their days in the Kingston Penitentiary. That would not work for her or for Danny. "Besides, I don't understand what business it is of yours," she asked my dad. "Haven't we done enough to save the Jewish people?"

The good memories worth mentioning from my mostly ridiculous childhood are those that have to do with the Labor Zionist youth movement. It was only during the regular Friday evening meeting and the irregular Sunday morning bull sessions, in the seminars that were held three times annually and in the two months of summer camp every year that I found a way of bringing together Zafrir and David, the two mostly incompatible sides of my identity. And it was only in the youth movement that I could bring my selves together without feeling that God was watching.

In the early 1960s, a Vancouver physician named Max Langer led a North American movement aimed at re-orienting Zionism as a whole. His idea was that Habonim (the Labor Zionist movement) should stop building bridges to Israel and take up selected topics that mattered to the Diaspora Jewish community. Langer's pitch was unsuccessful, but most analysts claim that he lost mostly because the old Israeli guard, which included ambassadors (*shleekheem*) dispatched from the kibbutzim, opposed the re-orientation. But because of Langer's efforts, the Zionist movement did begin to broaden its reach. For the Zionists in the Diaspora the ultimate goal was still immigration to Israel, but soon a hundred and one social and political ideas began competing for attention with that ideal. Members of the movement became far more interested in the Port Huron Statement, the founding document of the American New Left, than in the 1917 Balfour Declaration supporting the idea of a Jewish state.

In my experience of it, sixty or seventy young people would get together on Friday nights through the school year for a perfectly secular shabbat that always began with a communal singalong that traversed a full spectrum of songs, from the Russian folk songs that the Israeli pioneers had translated into Hebrew to the folk ballads and protest songs popular in the 1960s. We argued vehemently about civil rights strategies and protested American aggression in South America, Vietnam and Cambodia. We smoked cigarettes and pot and took overnight buses to the United States to go to demonstrations where we discussed matters ranging from conspicuous consumption and polymorphous perversity to existential irrelevance. SNCC, Nixon, Mao and nuclear non-proliferation were never far from our minds.

The movement's transition from Israel-centric to 1960s-centric came at a point when many of the old collectivist institutions were beginning to lose their hold on the Israeli imagination. I did not realize it at the time, but I do not think it is much of an exaggeration to suggest that the spirit of secular Zionism, which was in large measure about the possibility of embedding the old Jewish morality in secular institutions, moved at that time from Israel to the youth movement.

THREE

The Right to Return

spent the summer of 1969 making love to Robin Fenster from West Orange, New Jersey, and losing money to a card shark named Mike Green from Chicago. Joel Minkoff, whose father distributed beer in Madison, Wisconsin, provided the booze and Paul Blanc from Frisco introduced us to the music of Jacques Brel. All of this happened against a blurry Labor Zionist background in a leadership training camp held in Hunter, New York.

My grade twelve report card, which my mother sent on to me at the camp by mail, did not add up to much. Nor, as far as my eighteen-year-old self was concerned, did the Yorkville hippie scene back in Toronto. Everywhere in the streets young people were retreating into themselves, fighting hepatitis, fighting addictions, fighting each other. My parents had separated (my mother would leave for Israel in 1970) and for several months before I'd left for camp, I had been a vagabond, bedding down here and there, and often at Rochdale on Bloor Street, a social experiment now awash in bad acid and the acrid scent of a good thing going stale. A decade that had blown in on the promise of peace and love was quickly becoming reduced to "your issues" and "their issues" and mostly "not my problem."

News of the My Lai massacre hit the headlines in November 1969. It had a profound effect on those of us who hung on to the idea that the 1960s might still amount to more than the drug culture into which it had devolved. For weeks after the journalist Seymour Hersh's revelations about the war crimes committed at My Lai by American soldiers, we in the Labor Zionist movement reeled. Somewhere along the way I recall going numb and feeling an urgent need to get off the planet without having any idea of what that meant.

I decided, in early January of 1970, that getting off the planet meant a flight to Tel Aviv. Why this was the case is not clear, except that Israel seemed to exist in another world—which, as it turned out, it did.

My mother's younger brother, Moti, picked me up at the airport. As we walked to his car I could feel him sizing me up. To him, the shoulder-length hair and Gandhi collar meant that I was soft, that I had no concept of the real world. By the time we arrived in Tel Aviv, he was calling me "shmocky," which I did not much appreciate.

Moti's obsession at the time was a militant Zionist youth group to which he belonged, called Maccabee HaTza'ir. He had risen up in the ranks and had become a mini-Führer of sorts. In the evenings he loved nothing better than to review a guard of fourteen-year-olds and march them around this or that schoolyard. At thirty-something, my uncle was still very much a man being trampled by his father, my grandfather Yunkl. The fact that he had not broken free from his old man left Moti nauseated. "Life is a *nakhs*—a rotting stink that is best

when it is cut short," he said to me more often than I needed
to hear.

While I was living with my uncle's family a friend from
home came to visit me, bringing a lump of Lebanon's finest in
his bag. Moti, or maybe it was my aunt, discovered the hashish
and called the police. That was the end of a not-so-beautiful
relationship with my uncle.

———

Tel Aviv in the late sixties was more sand than culture. I knew
hardly anyone my age and for the next few months hung mostly
with Vicki Free, whose father managed a rock band called "The
Who." Vicki introduced me to "Barnyard," who was from Los
Angeles, and to Mick Jagger's younger brother Chris—we called
him Chick—and who was in Israel to sing the lead role in *Hair*.

In March of 1970, I enrolled in a high school aimed at
young Israelis who could not study full time. For the next four
months I took classes in Israeli literature, civics, math, science
and English—all in Hebrew. Mostly I did not study at all, but
I did begin to become Israeli, something I had not been since
the principal of Cedarvale first called me David.

I cannot really say how or when or even why I submitted to
this metamorphosis. Nor would I be very honest if I suggested
that I had any idea of what was actually happening inside me.
What I can say is that I was overwhelmingly compelled to have
not the "Israel experience" but the "experience of being Israeli."

And it was clear to me that I could not remain an eighteen-
year-old hippie from Toronto and get the experience I was
after. To become an Israeli I would have to forget the drug

scene, lose interest in Kurt Vonnegut and Tom Paxton, re-baptize myself in the Jordan river, gain an insatiable appetite for sunflower seeds and suffer no shame in spitting out the shells in public places. As I saw things, I wouldn't achieve my aim by picking oranges on a kibbutz or attending long discussions about socialist values. Nor was the experience of being an Israeli about the sense so many secular Jewish young people had at the time—that they could be among the first Jews to truly forget that they were Jews if only because everyone was Jewish. The most profound thing about being Israeli back then had to do with identity.

Living in Canada, I'd lost most of what it meant to be a Sabra and had become more or less like every other secular Jew. To be sure, I retained some of the signature chutzpah and I spoke Hebrew fluently, though not quite at the clip of a native son. For me, figuring out my Israeli identity was a slow process that began in those first six months in Israel, continued over the course of my army career, and for the rest of the time I was there, as I internalized "the experience of being Israeli."

Only four decades later have I begun to understand what that process was about. It was about standing my identity on its head. It was about changing from a secular Jew to a Jewish secular. It may be that I am the only Israeli who would argue that this revolution of identity *is* the experience of being Israeli.

What does this re-orientation mean to me? It means that I am committed to a concept I still understand only in outline. This concept is secularism—but not secularism as a negative category or as "humanism." Secularism is beyond the mono-theistic traditions (Judaism, Christianity, and Islam), puts them in creative tension, and has a positive idea all its own. The secular assumption is that the spirit that was once called God arose from life and not the other way around. The secular idea is that life itself arose from nowhere but exists in the eternity of creation. As a Jewish secular or a Christian secular or a Muslim secular, one treats the religion and tradition into which one is born as a culture and not as an absolute.

⊷⊷

There is no sign at the main entrance to the Israel Defence Forces' recruitment centre, which was once a British outpost. Arriving at the base to serve my three years of mandatory conscription, I was struck by just how makeshift the entire operation seemed to be. To be sure, most everyone was in uniform, but there was nothing uniform about them. Some soldiers were in full dress. Others wore fatigues and sandals, and still others were in T-shirts or an army shirt and shorts. No one saluted anyone; no one presented arms or marched in lockstep or did any of those soldierly things that soldiers do in Fort Hood or West Point.

For a moment I wondered what would happen if I just left. But then I joined the huddle that had formed around a pretty NCO wearing a nametag that read "Batya." She held a clipboard and with a smile took down the names of the more unruly young men around her. A few minutes later, two officers from the military police arrived and carted them off. Evidently the first stage of "selection" had begun.

A sergeant-major soon rounded up the rest of us, herding us to a wicket where we were each handed a dog tag with a number on it. "That will be your name for the next three years," the clerk behind the window said. Someone in the lineup said that the tag had more hope of surviving than we did. Others laughed. I did not find the joke funny. We were shuffled off next to a mile-high pile of kitbags and were told to pick one. "Each bag contains the same things," the sergeant said.

When we each had a bag, the sergeant told us to remove the army blanket from the bag and spread it out as though for a picnic. And then he instructed us to empty the bag item by item as he checked them off his list: two army blankets; three pairs of fatigues, three pairs of socks, underwear, one khaki-coloured army belt, four pouches, a water bottle, a wash kit, a mess kit, and a green beret, which in the IDF means you have no rank.

"Repack," the sergeant said, and so we did.

At the next station we were handed a helmet that would have made a fine Chinese wok. With it we received a slice of rubber tire and some mesh netting to create camouflage. At a fourth station we were thrown a pair of black boots and laces. After which we were told to change into uniform and head to the barbershop where an elderly reservist with a set of clippers soon made it impossible to pick oneself out from a lineup. Once the retrofit was complete, we were ushered into a tent and told what it all meant.

"For the next three years you should consider yourself army property," the sergeant said.

"Does that mean that we have just been nationalized?" a handsome fellow sitting next to me asked. The sergeant ordered him to do fifty pushups, which he pulled off without much ado. I immediately liked him and when he sat down again, asked his name. "Miron Yakuel," he replied.

Miron suggested that we volunteer for a reconnaissance troop called Shak'ed, which means "almond" in Hebrew. He said his cousin Naomi was the unit commander's personal secretary and that she'd help get us over the hurdles. I told him that I had a scuba diving licence and thought I'd like to become a frogman. Miron said that to qualify for the Commando Yami, the IDF frogman unit, you had to sign up for an extra year of service. "So much for that," I thought and tagged along with Miron to the Shak'ed cabin.

An officer, wearing a black beret and red boots and sporting paratrooper wings as well as the reconnaissance unit's insignia, asked if we wished to be fighters. "Definitely," Miron said, and we were escorted over to another huddle of young men who were busy lacing their boots and removing their shirts. Miron followed suit but I could not quite figure out what was going on and so just stood there. And then the huddle set off jogging.

That day I ran as fast as I could with loose laces; I ran as though everything depended on whether I would be accepted into this elite commando unit. I ran for the opportunity to become an Israeli, though I did not understand what that meant. I ran hard because I am not a natural athlete and because I smoked. I ran because my friends from Talmud Torah back in Toronto, Chaim Shainhouse and Seymour Cohen and Howie Goldberg, who *were* natural athletes, were not running and because this was my chance to separate from them. I ran because six million Jews did not run when they should have. I ran because I thought that my father, who maybe did not want me to run, would still be proud of me if he saw me in red boots and a black beret, with paratrooper wings. I ran harder when I thought I would collapse and I did not collapse. And then we stopped running and I bent down to tie my laces.

Miron passed me his water bottle and we were ushered back

to the shack, where I met his gorgeous cousin Naomi and a couple of other officers. I told Naomi that Miron and I were very close friends. A colonel figured out that I had not been raised in Israel, and asked where I was from. I said that I was born in Tel Aviv and that both my parents were Israelis but that only my mother was living in Israel. My father was still in Canada.

The colonel muttered something about the security risk entailed in having a parent living abroad and then asked me if I understood that I was volunteering for the single best infantry unit in the entire country.

I said that if they accepted me, the unit would be better.

Apparently the colonel liked my response, because he laughed, slapped me on the back and said, "You're in. Throw your bag and your body on the back of that truck."

Miron was not accepted right away, though, and was only hoisted onto the truck as it was pulling out of the recruitment camp. I later learned that his oldest brother had been killed in the Six Day War and that the army was reluctant to allow sons from stricken families to enlist in fighting units. His cousin Naomi had pulled some strings.

―⋙⋘―

Sha'ked was an elite commando unit with a long and glorious history. It was the cream of the Southern Command, which I soon discovered was led by General Ariel Sharon, who had acquired his fame as the founder of Paratrooper Unit 101, the only paratroops in the IDF to have ever parachuted during battle. That was during the Sinai Campaign of 1956. It had been Sharon's idea to parachute behind enemy lines at the

Mitla Pass. The fact that it was a largely bungled operation, and that many young soldiers were killed for no reason except to advance Sharon's career, was only known to those few Israelis who made it their business to know such things.

In 1970, the year I joined, the IDF recruited in four waves: November was for the kibbutznikim; February and May were for the graduates from the professional schools; and August was for the urban elite, all of whom would have matriculated. Many of the young men in the back of the truck with me that day came from highly accomplished Israeli families. One was the son of a former chief of staff, another of a sitting cabinet minister, a third hailed from one of Israel's top banking families. What became clear to me even at this early point was that the young men with whom I would serve were being groomed to run the country.

"Off the truck, *Augusteem*," Corporal Amiad barked, sounding stern despite a noticeable lisp. "Form three rows and come to attention. From this motley group of city slickers I intend to forge Israel's best fighting unit. Training begins at 5:00 a.m. Dismissed."

At 3:00 a.m. we were awakened and run into formation. Red-headed Sergeant Yair Assinheim paced before us, hands clasped behind his back. "Someone has helped himself to a bag of chocolate milk from the supply," he snapped. "That will not do. But if the culprit steps forward, we could all get back to whatever it is we were doing." No one stepped forward.

Assinheim smiled and looked down at his wristwatch. "Okay. If that is the way you want it, then you have precisely fifty seconds to circle the toilets over there and return to formation. Move."

Seventy pairs of boots moved, circled the john, and returned to formation. Sergeant Assinheim asked a soldier in the front row whether he believed the company had done as he had asked.

"I don't know, sir."

"Guess, soldier."

"I guess we didn't."

"Quite. Let's try it again. Move."

The same set of boots circled the toilets once more and then they circled them again, and again. Sergeant Assinheim asked whether anybody's memory had been jogged while jogging. "Who remembers helping themselves to the chocolate milk?"

For a second I considered stepping forward, figuring what could the sergeant do to me that he was not doing to us all. I flashed on Eli Wiesel's description of the death march to Auschwitz. Had one or two Jews stepped forward and attacked the Nazi guards, the rest might have gotten away with their lives. Was not the whole idea of Israel just such a stepping forward?

Then from behind me I heard a soldier mumble, "I just remembered drinking the chocolate milk." Then another soldier confessed too. Every soldier had been preparing himself to confess, just as I had. If the sergeant's purpose was to forge a single coherent unit out of seventy individuals, his strategy was working.

To this day, it remains a question in my mind whether forging such a bond was really what the sergeant intended. My best guess is that the kind of well-oiled machine that other armies pursue by various military exercises—marching in lockstep, saluting rank officers—was not what the IDF was back then. The idea here was not to transform individuals into killing machines, or even to create bonds between men so they would then be prepared to die for each other. The glue here was the figure of the Hebrew soldier, *khayyal Ivri*, whose pride derives in part from his difference from the old passive Jew but also from an understanding that he, as opposed to the secular Jew and the religious Jew, is the future. But all that was still questionable when I joined up. What soon became unquestionable was that the chocolate milk was an excuse for the collective harassment. It turned out that no chocolate milk had been delivered to the base that day and the red-headed sergeant's wristwatch had no second hand.

———

It did not take too long in training before my mind and body went their separate ways under the assault of constant and impossibly excruciating physical pain, the relentless harangues, the filth and the always lingering smell of the machine oil we used to clean our rifles, along with the shooting and stretcher-bearing marathons and, worst of all, the frequent order to pack up our belongings, including the pup tents we slept in, move them to the top of a nearby hill and set up camp again. Within a month, my body had become something that was just hanging in or that I was hanging on to for dear life. I became an observer, a witness to its travail. I was doing nothing but surviving, and bearing witness to the body that was the hapless host of all this pain.

I am not attempting to be disrespectful here, but was this not the experience that Holocaust survivors described in the camps? Was their raison d'être—their reason for enduring, which so many of them described as the "need to bear witness"—as much a description of the tenuous relation between themselves and their body as it was a desire to tell the story of the camps?

During the first few weeks of basic training, I made friends not with recruits with whom I shared common interests but with soldiers who could help look after me, or more precisely, look after the body that dangled from my soul like clothes on a line. By the fourth week of basic training I could hardly touch the food that the army cooks ladled out into our filthy mess kits despite my constant hunger. I was suffering from extreme diarrhea, dehydration, and an acute case of boils. And so it was that I found myself following around a burly young recruit named Danny Fite, to whom I had absolutely nothing to say. Danny had been born and raised on a moshav, an agricultural co-operative made up of individually owned farms; I wanted so much to be with him that I pretty much forced him to take me home on our first furlough. He was taken aback by my request, but perhaps because he assumed I had no relatives in Israel and needed the comforts of home, he obliged. When I got there, I could not for the life of me figure out why I had not gone to Tel Aviv instead. It took many months for me to figure out why I had imprinted on Danny, and in the end it all had to do with his hands. Danny the moshavnik had my father's hands.

Training ended with a 220-kilometre marathon from Beer Sheba to the port city of Eilat on the northernmost tip of the Aqaba Gulf. Half an hour before we set out, I was given the new pair of boots I had been requesting for months. I put them on and joined the troop. Inside an hour, the new boots were cutting into my feet and soon even my soles were raw and bleeding. But some crazy will kicked in and I decided that I would rather die than stop walking. With full gear on and in the extreme heat of the Negev, we walked for the next two and a half days. When the company was given a break, I didn't sit for fear of never being able to get up again. I slept while walking and I dreamed of an ice-cold Coke with lemon. I walked on even as the skin on my feet began to scab around the leather of the boot. Then we arrived.

Four friends had to carry me to the bus back to Tel Aviv, and when we got to my grandfather Yunkl's place on Philon Street, they carried me up the four flights of stairs to the apartment. A surgeon came and carefully cut the boots away and I could not get out of bed for an entire week.

———

After training, the unit was divided and deployed to various military camps within the Southern Command. I was dispatched to an expropriated Palestinian villa near the Jabaliya refugee camp. Upon the inhabitants of the camp, the IDF imposed nightly curfews that were strictly enforced. Our routine consisted of early morning patrols in the fields surrounding the camp. Any Palestinian found in the fields was considered a terrorist and was either arrested or killed.

One beautiful summer morning, the six soldiers of our squadron returned from a patrol and, as always, headed directly for the company kitchen. Normally we would shake awake the snoozing cook, who would groggily and reluctantly make our breakfast. But on this particular morning what we discovered in the kitchen was not the dozing cook but a very wide awake and very wide General Ariel Sharon, hovering over the eight burners of the stove, which was dwarfed by his unusual circumference.

Needless to say, we who treated Sharon as a legend were awed almost to the point of losing our appetites.

"I gave the cook the morning off," Sharon said, flashing his infamous toad grin. "What are you boys having?"

"*Lo kloom*. Nothing, sir. Really. We are not hungry, we have absolutely no interest in food, we just ate. But thanks so much for asking."

Sharon would not hear of it.

"Two eggs sunny side up for you, Private. And you? One omelette with onions, three scrambled eggs . . . Cheese, anyone?"

Sharon proved to be as good a commander-in-chef as he was in-chief. He could flip half a dozen eggs at the same time and never break a yolk. He heaved a pile of steaming pita bread to the centre of the table and at the same time managed to serve coffee to every soldier in the room. He worked just as easily with his left hand as with his right. And all the while he told bawdy jokes and described the sort of exploits for which he had become famous. None of us knew whether to believe him or whether it made any difference if we did.

After he'd finished serving breakfast, Sharon took a seat and gobbled down as many eggs as he had prepared for the entire squad. Except for an occasional "pass the pita," he did not speak while he ate. Apparently he considered eating a sacred act, deserving of his full attention.

Finally, he pushed his empty plate to one side, and asked, "Did any of you encounter anything suspicious on your patrol?" Had we checked for fires? Did we know that a fire that was not only doused but concealed almost certainly meant that terrorists had been there? Were we aware that Fatah members were digging bunkers near the cactus hedges at the edge of the cultivated fields? Did we understand that the recent spate of renovations in the camp meant that fake rooms were being constructed in which terrorists could hide?

And then, in midsentence, Sharon changed the subject. "What do you boys think about that *hashishnik*, Giora Neumann?" Neumann was Israel's first post-1967 conscientious objector. He and two female soldiers had refused to serve in the occupied territories. It was all over the papers. From his tone and from the pitch of his voice it became abundantly clear that Sharon was worried.

"Who does that *shtinker* (rat) think he is? What is going on in that dope-filled head of his? Does he think we should all be putting our lives on the line so that he and his buddies can hang in Café Ta'amon, smoke hashish and talk about peace?"

Sharon looked at each of us squarely. "What do you think, Private?" he asked.

"I think you are right, Commander. Neumann is an asshole."

"And what about you, Sergeant?"

Everyone agreed, a fact I found interesting because I knew that many of my peers had serious doubts about Israel's continued occupation of the Gaza Strip. Indeed, one did not have to be a military expert to realize that our aggressive searches and impossible curfews were creating more rather than less terrorism.

Sharon took the time to ask us a few more questions. He wanted to be sure of a consensus among us and to test whether the Neumann case had damaged our morale. As he left, he said, "Get to bed, soldiers."

But we did not.

One of us admitted after Sharon left that he knew Neumann personally and that he was a thoughtful and patriotic Israeli.

"Did he have a right to object?" someone else asked.

Even without Sharon's bullying, the consensus in the room was against Neumann. The argument went like this: If the country were bigger, then we might have the luxury, like the Americans, to debate the moral conundrum that conscientious objection raises. But as Israelis, we can't afford to indulge in armchair philosophizing.

Thinking about the situation forty years later, the moral morass that the country and the army were thrown into by the Neumann case could have been avoided by more thoughtful policies. Why had there been no option for Giora Neumann to choose to teach refugees wishing to find work in Israel, for example? Moshe Dayan, for one, had proposed a whole series of community-service-style, integrative initiatives, not just compulsory military service.

In his autobiography, Sharon writes: "His (Dayan's) priorities were to give the Arab population the ability to live normal lives, give them the benefit of many Israeli public services, allow them to travel freely and open up the Israeli marketplace and workplace to them. He did not expect the residents to welcome Israeli control, but he believed that even prior to a political solution, Arabs in the territories could live alongside Israelis in peaceful and relatively cooperative terms. These were precisely the goals that the terrorists sought to frustrate."

Sharon, concerned solely with the security risks, rejected Dayan's priorities.

In the fall of 1972, ten months before I was discharged, I was recommended to an American agency that seconded IDF soldiers to serve a two-month stint as a counsellor in a Jewish summer camp abroad. Needless to say, the prospects of a two-month leave from military life struck me as heaven.

I sailed through the first round of interviews and arrived in Tel Aviv for the final one on a dank December day. A pleasant older gentleman in a rumpled suit, with unusually bright grey-green eyes, greeted me in an office on Ibn Gvirol Street. He was holding a black binder and shook my hand heartily.

"You seem the perfect candidate," he said. "Your English is perfect and you are serving in one of the most renowned units in the IDF."

We talked for a long while about the summer camp.

"Imagine that it is parents' day and a father tells you that he is a big supporter of Israel but that he would not consider emigration. Nor would he support or encourage his children to leave the United States. How would you handle the fellow?"

I recognized immediately that this was the six-million-dollar question and I knew the answer he was after. "Just say it and you're in," I said to myself. "Give him a version of different strokes for different folks." But I couldn't.

"I don't like the idea of being someone else's insurance policy," I said.

I could feel the ice start to form. This was definitely not the right answer. It was a response that was too Israeli and not Jewish enough.

"Would you prefer that American Jews not invest in Israel?"

"If American Jews think they can buy their way out of

defending the country," I said rather quickly, "then Israelis have the obligation to put them right."

He looked genuinely puzzled. "Don't you think you are being a little harsh? After all, Israel is not for everybody any more than America is for everybody."

I didn't say anything. A thick silence settled in.

Finally the gentleman said, "I am afraid we will not be able to hire you. Thanks very much for taking the time to come." Visibly saddened and perplexed, he pointed me to the door.

I walked into the street mentally kicking myself. I simply could not believe that I had blown this remarkable opportunity. I really had become "too Israeli," even more of a purist in my investment in Zionism than most Israelis ever become. I suddenly felt an urgent desire to get out of the country.

———

From Tel Aviv I did not return to Gaza but to army headquarters. "I can no longer function as a combat soldier," I told the personnel officer, who sent me off instead to become a medic. Several months later I was attached to a troop stationed at one of the thirty-odd bunkers that constituted the Bar Lev Line, which snaked down the Mediterranean shore along the road that ran parallel to the Suez Canal. The consensus was that this line was impregnable, but it was not. Almost every week some group of terrorists or other managed to cross the canal and make their way into the Sinai desert.

Our unit's responsibility was to patrol a section of the Bar Lev Line and we did it with the help of night vision binoculars and a Zelda sonic radar device. Identification of moving targets was imprecise and on one occasion we destroyed a caravan of Bedouin hashish smugglers we mistook for terrorists. For a week or so the cache of drugs left behind got us all dreaming of villas in faraway places. But then the military police arrived and the villas faded like a desert oasis.

I was discharged on August 15, 1973. Six weeks later the Yom Kippur War broke out. Eight friends, all still sporting army issue haircuts, had gathered for a marathon poker game when my new girlfriend, Yael, called from the military base where she was serving. "Every truck and truck driver has been ordered to report to the base," she said excitedly.

"What's happening?" I asked. "Will they let you come over tonight?"

"Not a chance," she said. "There are unconfirmed reports that the Syrians are moving troops into the Golan and that the Egyptians have crossed the Suez Canal."

Dirges broadcast over the radio wrapped Israel in the pall of atonement. Suddenly there were interruptions; a piercing, mechanical voice spat out codes calling up reserves. "*Mavreg keess, mavreg keess*," it screeched, the words for pocket screwdriver. From the neighbouring apartments we heard phones ringing, which they never do on the Day of Atonement. At 2 a.m., Ami, a middle-aged officer who lived upstairs, clambered down with his kit-bag. I caught him in the hallway. "*Ma koreh?* What's happening?" "No clue," he said. "But things don't look good."

Another phone call from Yael. "I'm quite sure we are at war," she exclaimed and even as she did, the solemn radio music suddenly went upbeat. Saccharine songs packed with patriotism replaced the funeral marches. Codes came at regular intervals as the dawn's early light began pouring in through the blinds. And then came the news: Egyptian troops had crossed the Suez Canal, Syrian tanks were making their way into the Quneitra region in the Golan Heights.

The phone rang. "It's a fucking war," Yael screamed. "It's a goddamn fucking war."

⎯⎯⎯⎯

Months later, Israelis would claim that the Yom Kippur Miracle was that the war broke out on Yom Kippur—this is the only day of the year in which Israeli roads are not jammed. But it was also the day when most soldiers were off base and that was the anti-miracle. My friend Miron and I reported to the recruitment centre where we had met three years earlier. The base was unrecognizable. Bunkers ostensibly storing weapons and ammunition were locked and no one could locate the keys. Many turned out to be empty. Thousands of soldiers wandered about anxiously, their ears glued to the radio.

A cattle call came for medics and I was ushered into a helicopter destined for Sinai. As I boarded I was handed a bag filled with morphine syringes, another filled with saline solution, and an Uzi submachine gun. Miron, who had completed officers' school, managed to inveigle himself onto the Sikorsky that carried us to the base at Balooza in North Central Sinai.

The mess hall had just been hit and as I disembarked I caught a glimpse of a circle of soldiers standing about as stiff as candles on a cake. In the centre of the circle, a soldier lay bleeding into the sand and screaming into the desert air. I knelt down, checked his vitals, set up a saline solution and yelled for a stretcher. No one moved. They had been frozen in place by the shock and this had cost the wounded soldier his life.

—⊶∞∞⊷—

War feeds the rumour mill, and people believe greedily and indiscriminately. Soldiers thirst for some order where there is none. Lists of dead friends began to circulate almost immediately. I was on one of them. Someone said that the minister of defence, Moshe Dayan, had declared the destruction of the Third Temple. We all knew what that meant—the first and second temples had been destroyed, and Israel was the third—but no one knew what to do about it. Someone else claimed that Moshe Dayan wanted only to avoid blame for our state of unpreparedness. Apparently King Hussein of Jordan had warned Prime Minister Golda Meir that war was in the offing. But Dayan had assured Meir that the Bar Lev Line was impregnable and that the Egyptian Air Force, which had been destroyed only five years earlier, was in no condition to strike. But then I got a message from my brother who was stationed at the IAF base in Be'er Gafgafa, which Israelis called Refidim. The airstrips and helicopter launch pads had been bombed heavily.

Miron met a buddy who had served with us in Sha'ked. "Ariel Sharon is planning to cross the Suez Canal despite orders to the contrary. Sharon expects all his old fighters to join him." So Miron and I appropriated a command car and set out to join Sharon to the south, but by the time we arrived, the general was gone. Thankfully my brother Daniel was intact and in decent spirits. A light infantry division under the command of General Adan had broken through the Egyptian lines, he told us. Our troops had made their way to Bitter Lake.

Sharon was ordered to support the troops from our side of the canal but he refused the order. Instead, he took a considerable force in the direction of the Egyptian Third Army, cut it off from its supply chain and sent a reconnaissance unit off to the "Chinese Farm" on the Egyptian side of the Suez Canal. Some claimed that Sharon had turned the tide in our favour. Others said that he had sacrificed many more lives than would have been lost had he adhered to orders. Still others claimed that Ariel Sharon had a post-war political career in mind and that he was determined to carve out from the vestiges of this war the figure of a hero.

Miron and I made our way along the road to Suez, which was lined with the still simmering signs of destruction. By the time we arrived at the canal, Sharon had secured the beach-head and we crossed on a makeshift bridge. Cheery female soldiers handed us bottled water and loot bags filled with sweets and fresh underwear. From the branches of the few trees near the canal, bloated Egyptian bodies hung like party balloons.

On October 22, 1973, the first ceasefire of the war was declared and several foreign correspondents made their way to the front lines. But just as suddenly as it had begun, the cease-fire was violated. Once again the chalkboard black sky was streaked with scribbles of light that traced the random paths of missiles. Looking up at the sky I thought how much more appropriate this war would have been had it been waged nearer the city lights, which had long ago robbed the night of its darkness. The noise of the barrage was unbearable and when my eardrums stopped vibrating, the whole war went on mute.

"You're American, aren't you?" a colonel was yelling at me from up close. "I suppose I am," I responded.

"Take the Dodge Dart and drive those reporters over there back to their hotels in Tel Aviv. And then bring me back the keys!" he said, smiling.

I could not have been happier to oblige, but became melancholy when we finally reached Tel Aviv. The city streets were eerily empty and all the street lamps and the headlights had been painted blue to dim the prospects of an air raid. I dropped the journalists at the Hilton on Yarkon Street and headed to my mother's apartment in Ramat HaSharon on the city's outskirts.

En route I stopped at a supermarket whose front windows had been smashed. A half dozen glassy-eyed women loitered about, picking at the remains of the merchandise as though at a smouldering heap of debris. I took a bag of sorry-looking fruit and some yogurt and made my way to the cash register. But the cashier was nowhere to be found. An older man standing behind me said, "They shattered the front window a couple of hours after the war was declared."

"Who did?" I asked. "Hooligans?"

"Not at all," he said. "It was those women over there. I believe they are Holocaust survivors—not bad people, just traumatized. When they heard there was a war they lost their minds. They needed to hoard food."

On the other hand, my mother did not seem traumatized at all. Perhaps because she had been through a very different kind of war than had those Jews who had lived through the Nazi period. She seemed steady, perhaps even calm. When I asked her how she felt about having two sons on the front lines, she quoted the popular cliché attributed to the early Zionist hero

Joseph Trumpeldor—*tov lumoot bu'ud artzeinu,* "it feels good to die for our country." I never knew whether she was kidding or being serious.

Danny Fite was killed during the war. When it was over I visited his elderly parents on the moshav. They had just finished building a new home for Danny and the woman to whom he was betrothed. Danny's mother said that she wished that I, rather than her son, had been killed. I did not know what to say, and left.

In February of 1974 I enrolled at the University of Tel Aviv and rented an apartment on Pilikhovsky Street not two blocks away from the campus. For the next three years I became a tourist of the interdisciplinary sciences. I dabbled in political philosophy and in economics and in medicine and art and in law. My father, whom I had not seen since the late 1960s, arrived to take my mother back home. While he was there, he bought me my first car, a red Morris Mini Clubman, which I drove proudly to the military base in Jaffa where my girlfriend Yael still served. By then we were sharing an apartment and she asked whether she might drive the car home.

I agreed reluctantly. Not that she drove badly. It was just that she decided to turn right from the left lane and a bus that was travelling in the right lane hit us. Yael flew forward and her head hit the windshield, which put her into a coma. Somehow I was able to slip out of the car window, even though the entire chassis had collapsed. I pulled Yael out through the driver's window and, carrying her limp and bleeding body, managed to hitchhike to Ichilov hospital.

She woke from her coma, but she had suffered a major concussion that that made it impossible for her to sleep soundly. In the night she ground her teeth so hard it would wake us both. She became extraordinarily colour-sensitive and relentlessly interviewed all our friends, demanding to know why they had chosen to wear this or that particular shirt on this or that particular day. Most of our friends had loved the old Yael. She was Swedish-born and spoke Hebrew with an accent capable of charming the world. She was fair-skinned, freckled, athletic — a good-natured tomboy.

The concussion altered her character in profound ways. She became dark, often depressed, and lost much of her ability to tolerate people whom she had perhaps never much liked in the first place. At a dinner party one evening, she confronted the hostess in a manner that reminded me of the way Dostoevsky's Nikolai Stavrogin confronted Gaganov. Eight months after the accident, an IDF doctor declared that she was, once again, fit for service. But she was not, and because married women are exempt from military service in Israel, we married. But our love affair had ended amidst the shattered glass of the Morris Mini.

⸺◦⊗◦⸺

Israel in the aftermath of the Yom Kippur War was changing dramatically. Both the public and the government commission that investigated the war demanded that heads should roll. The Labor Party, which was held responsible for Israel's unpreparedness, began chasing its tail, losing its once formidable centre of gravity. One could figure this out from the government's crazy indecisiveness concerning the settlement project that Ariel Sharon was aiding. Or from watching the government spin from one scandal to another, even as the Likud Party, headed by Begin and Sharon, gained momentum.

Most of my friends were the sons and daughters of the Sabra generation. Like me, they were part of the first generation to be born after Israel had attained independence. I expected my friends to balk at the sudden and steep decline of the once powerful Labor Zionist ideology. But hardly any of them did. On the contrary, they seemed to want nothing from this country except to be left to themselves.

Most every Israeli I knew back in the mid-1970s was far more interested in high finance and in economics than in anything that might have a direct bearing on the political climate of the country. To be sure, the Israeli economy needed help and so it made some sense to study macroeconomic models. But if any of these people had interest in anything more than becoming independently wealthy, there wasn't much evidence of it.

In late 1977, even as I was in the last throes of an undergraduate degree, Begin and Sharon managed to corral the support of the disaffected Sephardic Jewish community. When added to Sharon's stature as a war hero and to his popularity as a leading figure in the growing settler movement, it helped win Likud the election, ousting, for the first time ever, the ruling Labor Party. This political upheaval, which has come to be known as the *mahapach*, or overturning, triggered the country's swing to the hard right.

For all these reasons, and also because I wanted to do graduate work abroad, and for one more reason besides, I suddenly found Israel claustrophobic. This "reason besides" had to do with what I earlier described as my need for the experience of being Israeli. To be sure, I was still decades from discovering the language and logic of this identity. But there was already something about the way that Israelis were arguing the old binary—Judaism as a religion versus Judaism as a culture, like an eternally spinning top—that made me feel incredibly nauseous. By September of 1978, I had every reason to leave.

FOUR

Two Eternal Returns

No Israeli can really leave Israel behind. The country is too new and too much in the news, and the dream is far too immediate to forget on the tarmac of Ben Gurion Airport. A culture as thick as Israel's and as layered as Judaism—a dream as ineluctable as the one Zionism introduced—leaves little space for the individual.

For me, the idea of being owned by a nation or a culture is a declaration of war; it is a life-and-death struggle that can end only in two possible ways: either the country retains its hold or the individual comes into his own. I've never had much choice but to slog on, fight a little, die a little, regroup a little, then mount another attack—or maybe once again try to resolve it all with some sweet talk whose purpose is to end the fighting and allow me to just live.

Half a century after they emigrated, my parents decided to move back to Israel. That was in the spring of 1999, about six months after my brother Daniel, who had lost his young wife to cancer, took his two boys and moved to Tel Aviv. My mother wished to be by his side, to lend a hand in whatever way he needed a hand lent, and perhaps also in some ways that he resented. My father's congestive heart failure and acute emphysema married him to a bottle of oxygen. He could no longer work and preferred to put a couple of thousand miles between his factory and the tug he experienced every morning to get up and go there.

So he sold his business for a song, refusing to consult or compromise. I tried to persuade him not to sell, mostly because it made more financial sense to retain his interest than to hastily sell off a lifetime of labour and love. His partner and best friend, Clifford Griffiths, begged him to not to go to Israel, if only because he would miss him. Dr. Zion Sasson, my father's cardiologist, warned against the trip for health reasons. "He is not fit to travel," Dr. Sasson told me. "Should he go anyways, you should know that he will never return." But once my father had made up his mind to leave Canada, he became a rock.

And so it was that in the late autumn of that year we took my parents to the airport in Toronto and bid them adieu. My three children were sad to see their grandparents go. They would miss my mother's mix of giving and taking away, of doting and scolding and disciplining and spoiling. Over the past year or so, she had taken to giving her granddaughters Hebrew lessons, and strangely enough both Natalia and Mira said they would miss those as well. They would also miss my father's infinite capacity to be charmed by his grandchildren. To them Asher was bigger than Santa Claus if only because no Santa would agree to bring them a forty-foot-high, fully mechanized Ferris wheel, which my father constructed and installed in our back yard. Even my wife, Deborah, who was not always amused by my mother's manipulations and stubborn insistence on certain routines, seemed sorry to see them go. She was in the process of saying goodbye to her own mother, who was dying of cancer, and was already feeling as unmoored as most people feel when they become aware that they are now the front line.

I was really the only one who felt relief that my parents were gone. I felt that a great burden had been lifted from my shoulders—largely because a great burden had been lifted from my shoulders. But there was another reason I felt relieved as well. Try as I might, I could not imagine burying my father in the frozen earth of some cemetery in Scarborough, Ontario. It did not even matter that the earth in this hypothetical cemetery was sometimes unfrozen. Nor did it matter that I believed that as far as the corpse is concerned, it doesn't matter one way or another. Or that I would probably never or hardly ever make a pilgrimage to the graveyard.

Somewhere deep inside me, though, I did think that my father should be returned to his people and to the soil from which he sprang and to the country he had fought for and cared about more than anything. My son Mischa, the youngest of our children, had gotten the closest of us all to understanding that this mattered to my father too. When he grew up, Mischa wanted to be either a philosopher or a logician (not both) and so he had relentlessly pursued the logic or the thinking behind my parents' decision to leave Canada. He would not get off the case and, in a fit of pique, I told him to go ask Asher, which he did. My father told him, "Your great-grandmother believed that if a man was not returned to the earth from which he arose, his bones would rattle to eternity. I have rattled enough in my life." Mischa, who neither understood my father's wry tale nor had ever considered the possibility that his grandfather would die, could not hold back his tears. But the truth is that no one in their right mind could find logic in either my father's reasons for returning or my relief that I would not have to bury him in Scarborough.

So my parents got on that plane, and all the kids cried for a while, and then everyone except maybe Mischa got on with their lives. Mischa decided that he wanted to visit Israel while my father was still alive and though he was only twelve at the time, he proposed that I take him to Israel in lieu of a bar mitzvah present. And when I said that I could not afford the trip, Mischa asked his grandfather to foot the bill. Asher agreed and Deborah suggested that we travel during the March school break in 2001. The best ticket we could find got us out in the middle of March and back on April 9. Mischa would have to miss almost two weeks of school, an opportunity he enthusiastically embraced. Nearly a quarter of a century had passed since I had last spent time in Israel. I had dropped in once in 1981, in order to sell the car that Yael had totalled, and once more when my brother was married. On both occasions I remained focused on a very small circle of family and a few army buddies who still lived there, and rigorously ignored the larger context. This time, in part because I needed to show Mischa around, I knew there would be more exposure, and as we boarded the plane I was nervous about that. Something inside me was not quite ready to put myself to the test.

—◦◦◦—

Maybe she sensed my anxiety, but for whatever reason, my mother tried to schedule Mischa and me to death. On the way to their apartment from the airport, she unfolded her plan, which included a three-day trip to the Dead Sea and to Masada; she insisted that "no child should become bar mitzvah without experiencing" these places. She would come with us on that trip, leaving my father in the hands of a Filipina caretaker since he could not travel. "Unfortunately, this is the only trip we can take together," my mother said. "But you and Mischa must also go to Jerusalem, to the Wailing Wall and to the Knesset, and to the Holocaust memorial at Yad Vashem."

"Yes, Mother," I said. Mischa laughed. My mother did not. But then she never was big on humour and certainly not on mine.

———

They were living again in the apartment in greater Tel Aviv, a ten-minute drive from the downtown core, in which they'd lived as a young married couple—the same apartment where Yael and I had also lived, and where my buddies and I had played poker on that fateful Yom Kippur in 1973. It had fallen victim to a new design and renovation overseen by my cousin Shavit. Nothing of the old haunt was left, and when I walked in, I felt as though an entire piece of my past had been papered over. There was nothing left of its history, no remnant of the nightmare scenes between my mother and her father, who had reluctantly agreed to pay the monthly costs when they had first taken the mortgage on the place. In point of fact, my grandfather Yunkl's main reason for signing her mortgage was to be rid of his daughter and her two sons when we three hunkered down in his home on Philon Street back in the late 1960s. Rather than put a standing order to pay her mortgage, Yunkl forced my mother to come beg for the money every month. And because he was paying, he thought he was within his rights to abuse his daughter. "I told you not to marry that peasant," he would yell, "but you were a headstrong girl who thought only about sex." The fact that my mother's grown children happened to be present meant nothing to him.

"I used to live here," I told Mischa. "But you wouldn't have liked the apartment back then. There was a balcony up front and one in the back for the laundry. And that building across the way wasn't there."

"I don't think I would have liked it," he said. "But I like it like this."

"Me too," my mother said.

"What about you, Saba? Do you like it?"

"I like you better, Mischa," my father said.

—⁂—

"Your father feels that no one understands him," my mother said over coffee at Joya Café. "He had hoped that you and your brother might understand that he sold the business not from under you but because it was the right thing to do. He feels that neither you nor your brother gets it that—"

"He loves his sons more than anything?" I finished the sentence.

"You are being rude."

"I am? But isn't that what you were about to say?"

Fifteen years ago my wife taught me a lesson that I kept forget-ting. It had to do with not crossing my mother. "Next time that your mother says that she has made your favourite soup," Deborah instructed, "don't say that it is a bit salty or that you don't have a favourite soup because you hate soup. Just say, 'Thank you, it's delicious.'" So when the next occasion presented itself, I tried that. I said, "Thank you, it's delicious." My mother's jaw dropped and then clamped shut. She knew she was being taken for a ride and that she didn't want to go, but couldn't quite figure out how to take control. Then she said, "Isn't the soup rather salty?"

"Everything has changed here," I said, changing the subject.

My mother looked puzzled. She always removed her glasses when she was puzzled. Reluctantly she let go of her favourite sport, which was defending my father, and went with the change of direction. "I guess you mean that the waiters don't seem like they are doing you a favour anymore."

"Yes, that and the little Arab rafter factory in the field near the apartment is gone. And so is the tiny grocery on the boul-evard. Whatever happened to the bill we racked up with the old fellow?"

My mother smiled. "I think your father paid it. But anyhow the grocer died. I saw the posters. So if your father didn't retire the debt, we'll have to retire it in the next life."

"I'd really like to get into Tel Aviv. Anat tells me I won't rec-ognize a thing. She says Tel Aviv has become like New York: not the city that never sleeps maybe but that never stops eating. She said the zoo is gone and that there are dozens of new sky-scrapers and hundreds of thousands of Russians. . . ."

"She's perhaps exaggerating a little," my mother said, not because she thought my old friend Anat, who was a very outspoken critic of Israel, was exaggerating, but because she thought Anat herself was exaggerated.

"Really? How so?"

"I don't really know. Your father and I used to go to Gesher, the Russian theatre in Yafo, just a stone's throw from Tel Aviv proper, once in a while. Then he didn't want to go anywhere so I went with my sister Talma. But now your father has made it impossible for us to see Talma and I hardly go anywhere except when he takes a nap."

Amazingly, my mother had us talking family again. And I would have pulled away again, except that I was vaguely interested to know more about this little fuss. My father had done some sort of a number on Talma's husband, Yair, most probably because Yair had not fulfilled his expectations.

Like my father, Yair was raised on a farm, from which he took a decade-long leave of absence beginning in the mid-1960s. He served in the military and then, for a short while, became a deputy minister of agriculture. By the mid-1980s, Israel's agricultural sector had lost much of its early vitality. The famous Jaffa orange was all but phased out, as were other citrus crops. Avocado had become a staple export, but had slid from its peak price point.

It was then that my father suggested that Yair become the Israeli distributor for the overhead conveyor belt systems my father's company manufactured. Yair accepted the offer and within five years had expanded his business to include products from a dozen different European companies. When my father decided to return to Israel, he assumed that Yair would find him useful as an unpaid consultant, or at least take him along to work sites. That is how my father thought he would keep himself busy. For the first while Yair played along. Then something happened, no one knew what, but my father began to feel that he was being patronized and humoured, not valued.

Soon after this breach, my father got wind of a huge government contract. He knew that Yair was up for it, and he learned that he had only one competitor, a scoundrel who knew nothing about materials handling but a lot about the Mediterranean art of baksheesh. My father contacted the scoundrel and worked out a one-off partnership agreement. When Yair found out about it, he blew his top, swearing that he would never step into my parents' home again so long as my father was alive. Though my aunt Talma was half estranged from Yair, she took her husband's side and perhaps got closer to him as a result. My father apparently insisted that his idea had been to "neutralize the opposition." But Yair did not believe a word of it. My mother, for her part, could not believe that her baby sister, the girl she had raised like a daughter, would be loyal to anyone except her.

"Have tempers cooled a bit?" I asked my mother as we walked back to her apartment.

She stopped on the sidewalk, looking old. "Not at all," she said. "I am not sure they ever will. Not in this lifetime, anyway."

"So maybe you want to move back to Toronto now?" I teased.

"I will tell you one thing" she answered, with a half-hearted giggle. "I miss your girls. Noam and Doron (Daniel's sons) are needy and need me. But I raised two boys and I always wanted girls. Anyhow, your father can never travel again. His emphysema has gotten so bad that the air, especially the thick grimy air of Tel Aviv, has become what water is to the rest of us. He moves in it, when he moves at all, only with the help of that snorkel of his. Sometimes the nozzle clogs up. And sometimes the company forgets to refill the bottle. Then he goes crazy. Once, when he came home from a very short walk, he complained so bitterly about the six stairs that he had to walk up that I called a meeting of the residents' association. 'We need to install an elevator in the building,' I announced. I knew this was no small matter because it meant that each tenant would have to cough up thousands of shekels and sign on for several years of Israeli-style renovation, known more for its fits than its starts. But as you know, once I get my mind set, it is not easy to stop me and soon this project became my crusade. And sure enough, I persuaded each resident—one after another."

"How did you manage that?"

"I gently reminded them all that your father was a war hero and that they have him to thank for their being able to live in this country in the first place."

We soon knew all about the elevator installation. On those mornings when the contractors saw fit to arrive at all, they arrived at 6 a.m. and began hammering, sawing, smoking and spitting. This drove my father out of his mind. Now he not only complained about the apartment stairs but about this upgrade, which prevented him from sleeping, waking, reading and forgetting that he could no longer engage in his favourite activity in the world, which was smoking.

"Your mother's point in life has always been to torture," he said. "This apartment is the blight of my golden years. It is your grandfather Yunkl's middle finger shoving up from the grave."

"So move," I said.

"Apparently we can't move."

"No, we can't move," my mother piped in from the kitchen, where she was showing Mischa how to peel the thick skin off a pomella. "We're committed. Your father is the only reason the tenants agreed to install this elevator in the first place. Nobody gives a damn about the elevator except him. They only agreed because they felt bad about him. . . . Just wait. It'll be wonderful. Just wait."

Though he never admitted as much to my mother, my father often fantasized about the day when the elevator would finally make its debut.

"I'll go down to the garden," he said. "I will have permanently installed a lawn chair there and a footstool which I will secure from this entire country of thieves with the help of a 100-kilo ball and chain."

It probably would have worked out just as he dreamed, except that the contractors soaked up whatever time he had left. Three years later, the elevator carried its first living passenger not down to the garden but up to the first floor to the Shiva for my father, on June 5, 2004.

—∞—

On March 30, 2001, my oldest and dearest friend, Anat Biletzky, invited me to join her and several of her colleagues from the University of Tel Aviv on a trip to the Arab Israeli town of Sakhnin in the northern Galilee. Anat was then a feisty fifty years old, a professor of logic at the university who wore her thick blond hair butch in her more militant moods and then longer and softer when she was feeling more hopeful. At the time, she was serving as the chairperson of Israel's largest human rights organization, B'tselem.

"Arab Israelis will be commemorating the twenty-fifth anniversary of Yom al Ard (Land Day)," Anat said over the phone. "And in case you've forgotten, Land Day is the day when we killed six young Arab Israelis who had the audacity to object to the expropriation of some six thousand dunams of land that they owned. We didn't think anyone should stop Israeli tractors from mowing down their villages. After all, it was for a good cause. 'The Judification of the Galilee,' remember that? You were still living here back then."

"To be perfectly honest," I said to Anat, "I have absolutely no memory of it. And it is hard to get why, given that I was reading maybe two papers a day."

My mother was waddling about in a pair of thongs, grumpy because I had refused to commit to a family dinner she claimed to have told me about. She didn't like the idea that I was about to go off with Anat and if Mischa had not been there to serve as a buffer, we probably would have duked it out. My son notwithstanding, by the time Anat picked me up the next morning, my mother and I were not on speaking terms.

Anat's friend, whom she introduced as the "other Anat"— whose last name was Matar and who also taught at the University of Tel Aviv—moved to the back seat. "You've got longer legs," she said in case I thought she had vacated out of respect for my age. Or my good looks.

We headed east to the Ayalon Highway and then pushed northward toward the Galilee. Anat Matar spoke about her son, Haggai, who had signed a petition that would be presented to Prime Minister Ariel Sharon when the school year began on

September 17, 2002. Harnessing the same voice of spirited youth that inspired the drafters of the Port Huron Document, Haggai had endorsed the so-called *michtav haShministim* or "seniors' letter," which was a stubborn refusal to abide by the status quo. It read: "We who are about to graduate from high school and are contemplating the future and the mandatory conscription, refuse to be soldiers of the occupation."

"How do you feel about your son becoming a refusenik and about the very real possibility that he will have to do some serious prison time?"

Anat Matar said she was glad Haggai had chosen to resist and had not taken the easy way out.

"Which is?"

"He could have pleaded some psychological condition and the army would have probably given him the exemption. They are far more lenient these days, mostly because they don't need the manpower. But Haggai and four others want to take a stand. They want to do community work rather than military service, and if the state won't extend that privilege then they will take it anyway. As they see things, a court martial, which will force the army to justify an unjustifiable status quo, will go some distance to end the occupation."

"In my day that would have meant a black mark for life," I said.

"Not any more," my Anat said. "It used to be that if you didn't serve, it would appear on your ID card. And that in turn would mean that you couldn't work in most respectable institutions, that you might even have a hard time getting into certain academic programs. But there was a Supreme Court ruling on the issue and it is no longer the case."

"What about the kids who bow out and don't make a fuss?" I asked Matar.

"There are lots of reasons why one kid goes for an exemption, another to trial. Far be it from me to judge," she explained, "but the army gets away with murder in this country. And when a kid puts his head on the guillotine, sometimes people wake up and smell their own shit."

We drove on to Sakhnin in the upper Galilee, arriving at just the moment when the sun and wind decided to transform the entire region into a giant blow-dryer. The blast of heat that hit us as we began the walk into town put a stop to conversation. There are no sidewalks in Sakhnin, only roads that taper off into nothingness. The voices coming from the bullhorns that amplified the rage at the schoolhouse where the rally was being held were about as inviting as the heat.

The organizers had strung a giant Palestinian flag on the back wall of the ramshackle schoolhouse. The iconography—a red triangle overlapping angry black, white and green bands— seemed ominous and told a story I did not know. Back in the old days, Arab Israelis often felt far more sympathy for Israelis than they did for Palestinians. In fact, many Arab Israelis treated Palestinians as though they were the destitute cousins with whom no one wanted to be seen. For the most part, Arab Israelis had seemed indifferent to the plight of the Palestinians.

Anat brought me up to speed: as far back as the Judification Project, but more so since the first Intifada, a large percentage of Arab Israelis had changed identity, referring to themselves not as Arab Israelis but as Palestinian Israelis, or, more and more often, simply as Palestinians. Arab-Israeli youth often hated the mayors of their towns, whom they quite correctly accused of being collaborators with the Israeli authorities.

On a block of cement that once housed a child's swing set, I perched like a crow on a fence, turning my head this way and that. The heat was mind-numbing and the anger blasting out of the megaphones boggled what was left of mine. Palestinian policemen loitered about looking tough but also making it clear to the demonstrators that they supported their cause. And then, without any warning, three surly, muscular young men, wearing T-shirts emblazoned with a mug shot of one of the 1976 martyrs, stepped up to my perch. I held tight so as not to be dislodged, but the young men managed to crowd me until I lost my balance and slid off.

Who the fuck do you think you are? I thought so loudly that it boomeranged and struck me instead: what a fucking racist thought that was. Then another idea flashed through my mind: *These are not my thoughts.* I remembered my friend Shirley Katz explaining to me why she quit being a humanities professor. "No amount of education helps to change the mindset of kids who are raised in racist environments," she told me. It hadn't really sunk in when she said it, but suddenly I realized that she was absolutely correct. None of the re-education that I had received over the twenty-five years since I'd gone back to Canada had touched the core racism I had imbibed during those years when becoming a bona fide Israeli had meant the world to me. Maybe I, and many other Israelis like me, would be better off consulting an exorcist.

I walked away from the three young men, and the heat hit me again and made me so crazy that I actually found myself wondering whether my skull was thick enough to have kept others from hearing my thought. Could it be that it was blasted across the entire city?

I looked around for signs. The two Anats waved at me to begin making our way back to the car. Apparently they had not heard my thought, which struck me as a good thing. But I couldn't avoid the fact that I had heard it myself, and what I'd heard in *Who the fuck do you think you are?* was the underpinning thought: *You guys are just fucking Arabs with no rights.*

En route back to Tel Aviv, I found it impossible to speak. Breathing was difficult and thinking impossible, at least for the first half of the trip. By the time we drove past Netanya, I had begun to understand where those thoughts came from. The last time I was in an Arab town like Sakhnin I was still in uniform. I recalled, vividly, immediately, just what it had felt like to patrol the Arab streets. We soldiers all carried personal weapons—Kalashnikovs, Uzis, FNs. Our index fingers straddled the trigger, our thumbs resting warily on the safety latch. As we moved through the town, the locals all lowered their eyes. No Arab dared meet our gaze. Had they done so we would not have reacted very generously. We were anxious young soldiers, or perhaps we were just grown children playing at being soldiers. Certainly we did not understand what we were doing and for sure we did not get that we were being scarred for life.

Many of us went into the IDF with a weighty conscience and a sense of compassion. But everyone hardened. Even the most compassionate could not resist. Hardening was not reserved for the battle-scarred; it was a mode of survival. One could simply not carry on softly, and one had to carry on. This meant that one had to get used to the fact that every Arab lowered his or her gaze. In fact one had to become blind to such things.

And at last, my mind clicked over and the thought changed. It became: *Who the fuck do I think I am?*

I went back again to Israel in the autumn of 2002, when the leader of Canada's New Democratic Party, Alexa McDonough, invited me to join a small delegation to the Middle East. I was both honoured and anxious—as anxious as I would have been had she asked to be invited into my bedroom. It was not that I felt Israel was my bedroom but that I often blushed and squirmed and became evasive when I was asked to account for this or that action undertaken by the Israeli government. And worse still, like many secular Jews, I felt alternately enraged, embarrassed or ready to kill any Orthodox Jew who thought it proper to parade himself in sixteenth-century attire or to huddle in prayer at the airport or to look right through any human being who did not happen to be an Orthodox Jew. I was just as often put out when I came across Christian evangelicals and shocked and appalled when unconscionable acts were perpetrated in countries other than Israel, but when it came to Jews and to Israel I felt personally accountable.

From McDonough's point of view, I spoke Hebrew, knew some of the players in the region, and was familiar with the customs and the history of the country—as well as having had some experience with politics in Canada. It made sense. But from my point of view, if I was going to be a useful part of her trip, I had to come to terms with the set of assumptions that powered this delegation and perhaps any Western delegation travelling to the region—I had a huge problem with the

fundamental, rights-based perspective that shaped the atti-
tudes of my travelling companions.

Gisela Dachs, a scholar and a long-time Middle East correspondent for *Die Zeit*, had addressed and named this problem:
she called it *Projectionsflache*, a German concept that translates
as "projection space." The tendency, Dachs claimed, is to see the
Israelis and the Palestinians and likewise the Israeli-Palestinian
conflict through the moral lens and the history of the outsider.
Germans, Dachs argued, see the Middle East through their own
experience with the Shoah; the British, Belgians and French
through their colonial past; the Swiss through the dormant
bank accounts that undermined the myth of their neutrality;
Scandinavians through a very Protestant sense of goodness.

Dachs's list easily expanded to include all left- and right-
wing perspectives on the conflict in the Middle East. What all
these prisms have in common is just this: people who engage
with this particular conflict are focused on their own issues,
and do not get that, in a very big way, the conflict in this region
represents the tension at the origins of the tradition from which
all of these perspectives arose in the first place. In this sense,
the conflict in the Middle East is not just another conflict. For
Westerners, whether their history, faith or feelings incline them
more toward Israelis or Palestinians matters far less when it
comes to understanding the region than whether they get what
the big stakes are.

In the two decades between Israel's independence and the
Six Day War that triggered the occupation of Palestinian land,
the liberal, egalitarian point of view was embraced by many
secular Jews and also by most progressive Arabs living outside
the region. The 1967 occupation of Palestinian lands changed

all of that. By the time our delegation was ready to go, the New Democratic Party of Canada had been hemorrhaging Jewish support over what was perceived as its pro-Palestinian stance, but it was really only old-timers like Janet Lewis, the daughter of former NDP leader David Lewis, who could still stomach the party's knee-jerk support for half a dozen UN resolutions condemning Israel. Many liberal Jews, myself included, thought that the NDP's position had more to do with the growing Muslim constituency in Canada than with the problem at hand. To our minds, it was of no use either to condemn or affirm actions taken by either side of this conflict. The only thing that would have perhaps satisfied us was the finely calibrated, nuanced ways of responding we occasionally heard from those insiders who suggested various ways of supporting progressives on either or both sides of the green line.

Dachs did not exempt Israeli or Palestinian insiders from Projectionsflache. Even as I was thinking about McDonough's offer, I was considering my perspective in roughly the same language. Where did all this leave me? To take Projectionsflache seriously, I reckoned, was not to let it destroy any hope of a resolution, but to figure out how to engage with the Middle East as both an insider and an outsider at same time. How did I pull that off ? That was the main question I had in mind as I prepared to set out on a trip that changed just about everything I ever thought about the conflict.

On January 2, 2003, I spot McDonough's executive assistant, Anthony Salloum, in the main hallway at Pearson International

Airport in Toronto. I knew that Salloum was born in Trinidad, but from a distance he reminds me of old King Farouk: he is heavy-set, sports a goatee on a swarthy Middle Eastern face, and wears tinted eyeglasses in mid-winter. We shake hands and I ask him whether he has ever visited the region. "Not as an adult," he says, radiating the kind of sensitivity and low threshold for injustice that makes him just the kind of young person who could easily have a breakdown in the Middle East. As we speak I learn that his parents are Lebanese and that he and his family lived in Lebanon for nine years, between 1971 and 1980. In the middle of my learning curve, Salloum spots two other members of the delegation. "Come meet Bill and Carolyn," he says.

I shuffle off behind him toward a sunny, silver-haired fellow just donning a well-worn jacket over his Hawaiian shirt. His ensemble is topped with a straw hat. He greets me with a warm hug.

"Bill Phipps," Bill Phipps says.

"I know all about you," I say, and Bill takes a step back in a pleasant gesture of mock surprise.

"Oh yeah? Well, waddya know?"

"Well, I know that you're the fellow who thought that the United Church of Canada could do worse than rent its own float in the Gay Pride Parade."

Bill chuckles. "Not quite," he says, "but close enough. I was the moderator of the church and I did advocate for gay rights." He gestures to the woman standing beside him, who is possibly regarding me somewhat warily. "David, meet my wife, Carolyn Pogue."

"Charmed," she says. And so am I. Carolyn is a plucky fifty-something woman of the sort that gives Canada its good name. I immediately imagine her as a righteous force of goodness back in the Crusades, blocking with her lean body the belching armies of God, singlehandedly convincing them that their convictions are really their own business and that they should leave the natives alone. She was born in Vogelin, Ontario, which I think no one but her believes exists. She is a social activist, writer and "PLAIN LANGUAGE EDITOR," as she calls herself, who advocates for "world change through word change."

"Where's our fearless leader?" I ask Salloum.

"Alexa and David are travelling in Egypt. They'll meet us in Tel Aviv," Anthony says and ushers us to the departure gate. David MacDonald was a former politician who was now Alexa's partner.

"Are y'all prepared for the descent into hell?" I ask. Bill, Carolyn and Anthony laugh lightly, perhaps because they don't get just how serious I am.

———

It is an unseasonably warm afternoon in Tel Aviv. Outside Ben-Gurion Airport we hail a cab to the Andromeda Hill Hotel in Jaffa, which I recommended in part because it is simply a gorgeous compound, and in part because it is situated in Jaffa, the only mixed Arab-Israeli neighbourhood in the vicinity. Jaffa bleeds seamlessly into the southern tip of Tel Aviv but it is far older. Founded by the Canaanites at a time before there was time, Jaffa has bustled ever since. For most of its history, it served as the region's main port and marketplace.

In 1910, a young entrepreneur named Haim Shlush and sixty-six of his best friends left the pleasures of the harbour and the stench of piss-drunk sailors to launch the city they called Tel (meaning old) Aviv (meaning spring and therefore new). Inspiration for the name came from the title of Theodore Herzl's final opus, *Altneuland* or Old New Land.

The Jaffa that Shlush and his friends left behind did not get much of a facelift until Israeli Prime Minister Yitzhak Rabin and PLO Chairman Yasir Arafat signed the Oslo Accord in 1993. For seven years after that accord, Jaffa teemed and was gentrified. Then in September 2000 the Al Aqsa Intifada broke out and Israeli developers abandoned Jaffa to its own devices, which also meant to homegrown gangs centred in the Ajami neighbourhoods to the south of the hotel and harbor.

The Andromeda Hill was not an uncontroversial choice. For one thing, it is Israel's first gated community, a fact I worried would not jibe with core NDP values. Orthodox Jews claiming that the Hill contained the remains of ancient Jewish graves had threatened to close it down, and local Arab-Israeli groups complained that a promised path to Jaffa harbour, which was supposed to weave through the compound, was never built. On the plus side was the mixed neighbourhood that surrounded it and the airy rooms that the Intifada rendered almost affordable. From some of the east-facing balconies, one could breathe in the Mediterranean Sea, which stretches out like a courtyard surrounded by exotic lands.

The compound's own courtyard is beautifully landscaped, with palm trees and an elevated planting of cactuses and lilies. An underground spring feeds open-air canals that irrigate the gardens. Sunburnt mosaic tiles lend the regional flavour I love and on the wall that divides the grounds from the Arab street below, a sheet of bougainvillea cascades down as though it was nature's own laundry, hung out to dry.

At 6 p.m., Alexa, David, Anthony, Bill, Carolyn and I head off to dinner at Anat Biletzky's apartment in Jaffa. When I asked Anat to invite us for dinner I had four different reasons in mind. First and foremost was my own love for this woman with whom I share so much. We are both outsiders as well as insiders. Both of us are Israeli-born, with Israeli-born parents who spent a stretch of decades in North America. Our relationship dates back to the early sixties and both of us retain a very warm spot for the spirit of that bygone era. To bring the delegation to meet Anat was also an opportunity to show support for the buckling Israeli left in which Anat plays a significant role. Indeed, I sometimes go so far as to imagine her as the unheralded engine that drives the entire Israeli protest movement. On any given day she whizzes about to half a dozen lefty events, bounces over to Jerusalem, where she still serves as B'tselem's chairwoman, speeds back to Tel Aviv University, parks her old Citroen, and runs off to teach a class or two on symbolic logic.

From there she might make a quick pit-stop at the cafeteria for a couple of energizing chocolate bars and then rush over to her bunker office from which she corresponds with every major human rights organization in the world. In the evening she's off to one or another event or organizing packages to send to young men like her friend Anat Matar's son Haggai, who was doing time in jail for his act of conscientious objection. Anat's schedule makes Henry Kissinger's shuttle diplomacy seem like a cakewalk.

Anat often complains about the tag team of politicians and artists and well-wishers that come through this region with the regularity of German trains. "As much as I like to meet these peaceniks," Anat told me once, "it drains me." This led me to believe that bringing the delegation to her for an informal dinner might provoke a conversation about that ambivalence, which I feel as well. Unlike me, Anat has constructed a consistent surface that never betrays that ambivalence, which only now I have realized comes from the fact that this conflict is not like any other conflict, but represents the tension at the source of Western civilization. To anyone except those who know her as well as I do, she is a perfect lefty. Her natural compassion and sense of humanity forces her to rail against injustice wherever it might be perpetrated. She cries easily and identifies with victims without ever thinking of herself as either a victim or their saviour. But just under the surface, she also carries the doubt that many of the more thoughtful Israelis of our generation carry within us, which makes us wonder whether we really own the country and the culture that undoubtedly owns us.

I also thought meeting Anat would help the delegation to think about the difference between criticizing the current Israeli government, denouncing this or that policy, condemning this or that campaign, and engaging in wholesale criticism of Israel. Criticism of that most general kind not only gets the country's collective back up, but also sets the whole project called Israel back on its hind legs. Even moderate Israelis fail to understand why people who are critical of this or that Israeli government policy or campaign would resort to wholesale criticism of Israel, and when they do, Israelis suspect that anti-Semitism is operating behind the scenes. Most of the leaders in the Middle East know this much about the Israelis. Even a monstrous man like Iran's president, Mahmoud Ahmadinejad, makes distinctions that Western leaders tend to ignore. When Israelis are attacked wholesale, the default reaction that kicks in is that we are being attacked for our "Jewishness."

Western politicians have something to learn from the Arab leaders when it comes to these distinctions. Why have they been so slow on the uptake? Could it be that when they are engaging in wholesale criticism of Israel, Western leaders are also refusing to acknowledge that in their own countries the gap between government actions and a populace that doesn't support those actions is in fact a yawning abyss that speaks to the limits of representative democracy in general?

Anat and I have discussed various alternatives to resolving the conflict. Strictly speaking, she sympathizes with the One State Solution and in fact would co-author the Olga Document, which circulated in June 2004. But she is also a pragmatist who thinks that in the short term a divorce of the sort envisioned by the proponents of the Two State Solution may be just the medicine the doctor prescribes.

At the time I was of about four minds on the issue, and basically anything that got a peace agreement signed was fine by me. I was hoping that we would have a chance to address this issue as well. What I had not taken into account was the raging Intifada, which trumped all these subjects and cast a pall on the very possibility of reasonable conversation.

⸻

Anat looks far wearier than she did the last time I saw her, back in 2001 when there was still hope that the Intifada would be short-lived. Over dinner, she describes just how impossible things have become in Israel, how diminished and enfeebled the left now is. She believes that the Israeli army is reeling dangerously close to a precipice, and that their actions will result in even more extreme measures in reprisal. The urge to write Arab culture off entirely is worming its way so deep into the heart and soul of Israeli society, she tells us, "that it is hard to imagine how we will ever dig ourselves out, how we could ever build up the trust that any peace process requires."

Anat blames the former Labor Party prime minister, Ehud Barak. In Camp David, Barak offered Arafat what Anat describes as "98 percent of 22 percent of Palestinian land" and when Arafat not only refused but did not even make a counter-offer, Barak returned to Israel and declared that Israel had no partner (*ein eem mee ledaber*), that Arafat had gone off the deep end.

Interestingly, Anat does not interpret Barak's declaration as having much to do with the Palestinians. In her view the statement was a dagger intended to tear out the heart of the Israeli left. After the collapse of the Camp David talks, Barak realized that his supporters on the left wanted him out. And so he turned on them. His *ein eem mee leduber* allowed mainstream Israelis to dismiss anyone who believed we needed to keep talking with the Palestinians.

Strictly speaking, Barak is more a man of the left than of the right, and Anat's analysis brought to my mind the old and extraordinarily intense schisms within the Communist Party. In the thirties and forties, American and European communists were at each other's throats to such an extent that to a left-winger another left-winger was in danger of becoming more of an enemy than a flagrant capitalist. To review the literature from those times is to understand the problem of the insider for whom the world has become so small that nothing but the details matters.

Whatever else it is, there is no question that Anat's anger at Barak is also a symptom of this kind of insider fragmentation. Indeed things have gotten so bad in Israel that, aside from a few dozen like-minded activists, Anat is now politically isolated. And while she always manages to convince me that she is right, she also makes me feel as though we have grown so far apart that the kind of intimacy we shared as young people can never be restored.

Anat holds that Israel is now firmly in the grip of an invidious, systemic conspiracy of lies and obfuscation. She is not, by nature, a conspiracy theorist. It is just that when one lives in Israel, it seems quite impossible to pull a single nail out of a coffin without someone hammering in three more. To the extent that Anat still holds a glimmer of hope, she thinks that the entire system must be replaced. But if that is the case then it still remains unclear what she has in mind to take its place.

"The left is hemorrhaging to the point where the core group of activists are considered 'fringe types,' if not altogether out of their minds," Anat tells Alexa. "And each time a suicide bomb goes off, fewer and fewer Israelis are prepared to speak out for peace." Even sadder than this sad situation is that the once healthy relationship between Israeli and Palestinian moderates has gone down the toilet. "Our good friends in Gaza and in the West Bank—those with whom we once made common cause—are no longer prepared to talk to us," she continues. "They say that the very act of conversing with Israelis normalizes an impossibly abnormal situation. They say that we should be focusing on our country and on our leaders."

"Your friend Anat seems terribly sad, weary, hopeless," Alexa tells me as we shuffle down the stairs of Anat's apartment building. I am thinking about her and about our relationship and about being an insider and an outsider and whether she and I would ever be able to find common ground. But I am also thinking that in the most literal sense, Barak was quite correct when he said that Israel has no interlocutor. After Camp David, neither Arafat nor moderate Palestinians want to talk with Israelis. But neither do Israelis wish to talk with Palestinians, except in language and on terms they can dictate. If both Israelis and Palestinians were prepared to back off into their own corners, attend to their own households, and leave the other alone, this wouldn't be a problem. Barak's statement becomes far more of a problem when it is understood as granting Israelis a licence to act without taking the other into account. Unilateral action of this sort tends to treat Palestinians not as frustrated with the whole dialogue, but as unable to converse because they really have no language, and maybe are not altogether human in the first place.

January 5, 2003. The road that winds down from the Andromeda Hill hotel to Yafo's clock tower is bleak. At this time of night the smells of stale fish linger in the salt air blowing in from the Mediterranean. The fishmongers along the road have closed their stalls but not before tossing out and across the narrow sidewalk a heap of assorted fish heads and tails. Balding Egyptian cats with pert, pointy ears gnaw on scraps that once held sleek ectothermic forms of life together.

We have the evening off and I have arranged to meet my parents at an upscale restaurant in Israel's Silicon Valley neighbourhood of Herzliya Pituach, on the northern Tel Aviv coastline. My plan is to stroll down through the flea market to Jerusalem Boulevard, which is Jaffa's main thoroughfare. From there I will either catch a bus into Tel Aviv or grab a cab. But I get distracted, walk past the entrance to the souk, and find myself at the Abolafiah bakery kiosk near the clock tower. The smell of pita with za'atar, a spice mix indigenous to this region, wafts over me and I decide to join a group of Israelis huddling at the bakery counter. One pita, as an appetizer, can't hurt.

Then from somewhere in the distance, a sudden silence arises—a silent scream that we hardly compute. What we hear is everything that goes through the minds of human beings who are shown how things end—not the life that they have led but the horror of themselves cut off from life. And then comes the sound of an explosion and a second one. An Israeli colonel standing in front of me turns to his date and says, *"Pigu'a, be'etsem shnaim,* a suicide bombing, in fact two of them." She asks, *"Eich yodim?* How can you tell?" and he says, "Didn't you hear the silence?" And then he says, "The explosion is a thud. It has no resonance."

A swarm of ambulances, police cars and fire engines spill into the street as from a piñata. Horns and sirens blend and another of the bakery's customers is yelling above it all. He wants to know why his order is taking so long.

I leave the line without my pita and wave down a cab. When I hop in and give him the address of the restaurant, the cabby asks me if I know that there have been two suicide bombs. "I heard," I say, "but if you don't mind, I would prefer not to talk for a moment." "No problem," he says in English, and turns up the radio. The announcer says that a few minutes ago more than a dozen people were killed in Tel Aviv's Central Bus Station, which was hit by two suicide bombers exploding seconds apart. The police and ZAKA, a motorcycle squad of Orthodox Jews who come to collect the remains for burial, have arrived to gather the shards of flesh.

My mind channels the scene. A crowd is waiting for a bus. Suddenly a young Israeli boy spots an Arab reaching inside his jacket. He wants to scream but can't find his voice. This is what horror does—it robs us of our voice, which is why the great Romanian sculptor Sorel Etrog reproduced Picasso's *Guernica* with all the mouths of the animals and men slammed shut. "Picasso was terrified," Etrog once told me. "He couldn't get close enough to death to understand that when it comes the way it did in Guernica, all the victims can do is scream without ever parting their lips."

To me it suddenly seems that the scream explodes inside the body and kills the victim even before he or she is torn apart by the shrapnel.

"Are you okay?" the cabby asks.

"I am fine," I say. "Shaky but fine."

A sports car travelling the other way smashes into a van.

"I guess I am not the only one a tad out of control," I say.

"*Nu, mu nagid, meetraglim*, one gets used to such things," the cabby says. "We eat their shit and they eat ours. It's a bad scene but we've all signed on for life. Twenty, thirty years ago, when there was an attack of some kind, everything stopped. When we heard the three beeps that announced the news, life stopped. Now nobody stops. *Normalizatzia*." He turns up the radio. The announcer repeats the earlier item, except that the body count has risen. "Police have closed down the bus station."

"How long before the station reopens?" I ask the driver.

"We've gotten pretty damn good at it. They've got these heavy-duty vacuum cleaners and high-pressure water hoses. In four, five hours no one will remember it even happened."

"Except the victims' families."

"Yes, that is true. They never get over it. I know a man who lost his only son to a suicide bombing. Once he and I were at a bar and maybe he had one drink too many but he said that one day, maybe the day after a peace agreement would be signed, he would get even by blowing up the Al Aqsa Mosque in Jerusalem. He didn't care if he died in the explosion. As far as he was concerned Islam was responsible for the death of his son."

❦

Early the next morning our delegation is whisked off to the Canadian embassy in Tel Aviv. The idea is to negotiate visas to Jordan, where we are scheduled to meet with Prince Hassan, the recently deceased King Hussein's younger brother. McDonough speaks to the Canadian ambassador about the possibility of shuttling off to Syria, where a Canadian citizen, Maher Arar, is imprisoned. By 10 a.m. we are on our way to the first of several official functions organized by the Israeli Department of Foreign Affairs. This one will take place at the foreign ministry's new home on Yitzhak Rabin Boulevard in Jerusalem.

Our host is a coldly handsome fellow who introduces himself in a whisper. I think I hear that his name is Ari or Uri, but can't get myself to ask him to repeat it. In his early forties,

Ari strikes me as flawless as a mannequin. He is tanned but not too tanned, tall but not daunting, squarely built but not a box. I picture him pausing at his closet this morning, considering a dozen starched white shirts and half a dozen identical and perfectly pleated grey trousers. After some thought, he chooses this shirt and these trousers for reasons that seem crystal clear to him but would befuddle nearly every other male in the world. His hair is light brown and cropped; his features are chiselled, his chin lightly cleft. He walks briskly and never glances back to see if we are following. The grey halls smell of wet plaster and fresh paint.

At the door to a small conference room, Ari stops and enters but does not hold the door for us—David MacDonald does that. We take our seats around a new wooden table that smells of varnish. Except for a photo of the just-then-installed foreign minister, Benjamin Netanyahu, the walls are bare. Only now do I see Ari's subzero blue eyes.

We all expect him to begin by addressing the Intifada and the conflict, laying out the official government position. But he does no such thing. Instead, and for the better part of an hour, he delivers what an Israeli friend later calls *ha-khavila*—the package—but which in Hebrew slang also means a "dump." We get stories about destroyed temples, an abridged version of the Crusades, scenes from the Spanish inquisition, Torquemada's expulsion, the Hep-Hep riots, the Kishinev pogroms of 1903.

Clearly the old Sabra firewall erected to keep Diaspora history apart from the history of Israel has been entirely demolished. Ari's message is that Jews were always victimized and that they are still being victimized. But he never actually says any such thing. What we get is only the facts. Everything else he leaves to us.

What I find confounding is just how unfamiliar he is to me. It is perhaps the first time in my entire life that I am in the presence of an Israeli I cannot place. In some ways there is nothing unfamiliar about him. I know for sure that he was born in Israel and that he hails from neither a kibbutz nor a moshav nor from anywhere south of Allenby Street in Tel Aviv. I figure that, like the current mayor of Jerusalem, Ehud Olmert, Ari was born in a small town like Binyamina, near Haifa, where many of the old militant Irgun members moved after the War of Independence. I could of course be wrong about the specific town, but not very wrong.

But who is this man and how does he fit within the model of the Sabra? Surely there is no direct line linking him to the good old right-wing followers of Vladimir (Ze'ev) Jabotinsky. Jabotinsky loved language and literature. He was a passionate writer who translated Edgar Allan Poe into Hebrew. He spoke half a dozen languages and retained such disgust for the old "passive" Jewish Diaspora that he could not help but struggle with it all the time, internally and in his public addresses.

But Ari does not struggle. What strikes me about him is just that lack of internal struggle. For Jabotinsky, the tension between the New Jew and the Old Jew was omnipresent and ubiquitous. It was expressed in every thought the old militant had and in every action he undertook. But Ari does not struggle. Somehow he has managed to synthesize everything. In fact this is what I am finally getting about him—that he is a seamless, self-satisfied synthesis of the past and the present.

What was Netanyahu thinking when he hired Ari, whose manner militates against the very sympathy for Israel's situation that he should be interested in eliciting? We would have been putty in almost anyone else's hands. Certainly a man modelled on a Mandy Patinkin or a Saul Rubinek could easily have got us feeling terrible about the innocent victims of suicide bombs. Had Netanyahu hired even Adam Sandler he could have easily conjured forth the image of a parent who learns that his child was in a café that just went up in smoke and scattered flesh.

But Ari will have none of this. He does not want or care to elicit compassion. In fact he manages to elicit nothing but our rage. It occurs to me that this is one of the main features of the new synthetic man that Ari embodies: he treats everyone but his own kind as "no partner."

My thoughts, becoming in equal parts aggressive and analytic, go something like this: Ari is definitely a bright enough guy. His English is flawless and for some reason I am convinced that, unlike Netanyahu, he has picked it all up in school and not from having lived abroad. The flawlessness of his English makes it impossible to detect the person behind the voice. There is an anonymity about this fellow that is quite unbearable.

There is nothing messy about his thinking. Stubbornly, he keeps all things discrete. He suffers only (it seems) from an excess of hygiene, which means that he is just the kind of man who is perfectly prepared to address any subject as long as it is not in relation to any other subject. This man is rational and analytical to his core.

Ari has begun winding things up. For a moment he turns to the current conflict between Palestinians and Israelis and he has no problem asserting that all Palestinians are either actively or potentially terrorists. "Speaking personally," he adds, stunning me for a moment, he says he does not blame them. But I don't think he's speaking personally in the way the former minister of defence Moshe Dayan did when he said, "If I were an Arab, I would most certainly be a terrorist." I think Ari means that he believes that terrorism runs in the Arab bloodstream, that it is in their DNA, and that they can no more be blamed for that than a cobra can be accused of snaking around. He does not say as much, only insinuates it. Nor does Ari make the connection between the Intifada and the failed Oslo Peace Accord, whose every condition Israel summarily ignored. Nor does he say anything about Ariel Sharon's infamous march on the Temple Mount, which some claim triggered this uprising. He says nothing about the checkpoints or about the occupation's illegality. He does not ignore such issues—he simply does not raise them, refuses to make the connection between any of them and the Intifada.

When he finally stops talking, Ari turns to Alexa and asks if she or anyone else has any questions. Mercifully, no one does. He then wishes us an enjoyable stay and leaves the room.

A security officer in uniform ushers us out the back door, which leads into a parking lot. We all take a breath, except for me—I prefer to inhale as much smoke as I possibly can. David MacDonald comes close and, in a hushed tone, says, "I don't wish you to take this the wrong way but I have got to say that this Ari fellow seemed more like a Nazi than anyone I have ever met."

Many months later I asked MacDonald what he meant by his comment. "Until I met Ari," he said, "I honestly thought that Israelis were just like us. There was something about his manner—brusque, self-important, not interested in clarifying anything for us. But I think I understand him a little better now. I think I know how he came to be who he is. If you are constantly being attacked and spend a lot of time thinking about your enemy then a great deal of his hate must rub off on you."

I could not have agreed less. To me it seemed that Ari would never allow himself such an emotional indulgence as hate. In fact he did not have much use for any kind of emotion at all. Aside from whatever else hate is, it is also an emotion, a glue of one sort or another. People are held together by the bonds of hate just as much as they are held together by ties of love. What is so alarming about Ari and his kind is that they are not interested in any opposing idea or point of view precisely because they experience themselves as the final synthesis of all the correct ideas. To me Ari seemed to want only to embody the cold and impersonal hand of necessity; he wanted to be a destiny that cannot be stopped.

———

In Jerusalem the next day we meet Ehab Shanti, a thirty-something Palestinian Canadian who serves as the United Nations Development Program's (UNDP) communication officer for the West Bank. For the next few days, Shanti has us booked into monkish rooms at the Augusta Victoria Hospital compound on Mount Scopus. By the time our taxi arrives, he has everything, including a light supper, all set out.

Ehab is a Palestinian who was raised in Canada. But it seems that when he is in the Middle East, he succumbs to his Palestinian identity entirely. He welcomes us not with "hello" but with "*marhaba*" and a smile. McDonough had met him when he was in Ottawa, and asks him how he's doing. He cannot seem to contain his displeasure with the Israeli authorities. He tells us stories of brutality and then shows us an album filled with photographs—a wrinkled old Arab at a checkpoint, a hundred Muslims with their hands up. Alexa and David and Bill and Carolyn and Anthony look on with appreciation, as though these photos somehow represent high art. But I see mostly sentimentality and the urge to fetishize a culture that needs to get over itself.

The photos *are* decent snapshots of indecency. But as art they are stuck in the old colonial impulse that Edward Said called Orientalism. The scenes they depict are shocking but they don't take the viewer anywhere that he or she has not been before. They trade on a morality that is somehow also kitsch. I find myself wondering about all the Arab geniuses— the men who invented algebra and introduced written language and democracy before the Greeks ever dreamed of it. What does Ehab want us to see in these photos? Surely he wants us to feel the humiliation that he feels, that the Palestinians feel when they are treated like stray dogs. But I am having a hard time feeling these things in the same way that I have a hard time experiencing the plight of Canadian Aboriginals through touristy soapstone statues and drum circles. I want to ask Ehab why there are so few Palestinian poets of the stature of Mahmoud Darwish (who has since died, in 2008 at the age of sixty-seven); whether he thinks Palestinian artists might recall that the human need to return home is not the kind of thing that can really be satisfied by re-confiscating real estate. A man needs a house, but the artist's mission is to suggest that a home is far more important and can be realized independently of politics. If Palestinian creativity bends to the Israeli will, then and only then will the Palestinians really have lost the struggle.

I also want to ask Ehab about the need to get over the melancholy that Orhan Pamuk calls *hüzün*—which is also depression and the surrender to the linearity of time. If it is true that a culture that was once an empire cannot become an empire again, does it follow that it cannot be great again? If that were true, then maybe I would understand the melancholia, maybe I would understand that all that was left to nurture the spirit is the memory of an irretrievably dead culture. If there was no way for Palestine to become whatever Ehab and his cohort want it to become, then maybe kitsch would be acceptable. But I don't believe that. Does he believe that?

Ehab speaks in a rich, nasal voice that has a distant-hunting-horn quality to it. It is as though he has allergies, or maybe it is just that he feels constantly chased. He is balding early and his high forehead, shiny skull, and elongated neck remind me of Nefertiti, who, I later learn, is one of his big heroes. He tells Alexa that he has fallen in love with a Palestinian woman and that they plan to be married in a "traditional ceremony." He tells us all that his uncle is, or was, the mayor of Tulquarem and he has invited us to Nablus for lunch tomorrow. "My uncle will take you on a tour of the town so that you can see how the occupation feels from where we live. I want you to understand just how the Israelis are killing our spirit. I want you to get that they are entirely committed to turning the West Bank cities into ghost towns. I want you to ask yourself whether there are any alternatives to suicide."

It rains all night.

The sun rises on Mount Scopus. The rain is gone and the air is crisp and carries the scent of cardamom or *hel* as the locals who brew it into their coffee call it. For some crazy reason the entire courtyard outside our hostel has been tiled in porcelain. The tiles have collected the water and the cold has transformed it into a sheet of ice. David MacDonald steps out, slips, and manages to avoid serious injury only because he is really Fred Astaire. But the jolt is enough to make him rethink the day. He decides to hang back, do some catch-up reading, make a few phone calls and rest.

Ehab arrives in a sedan followed by two dark grey armoured SUVs. All three vehicles fly both the Canadian flag and the United Nations flag. He is wearing dark shades, and barks commands into his cellphone, then motions the SUVs to double back toward the road. He asks about MacDonald and McDonough tells him that David will not be joining us. Ehab asks why, and by the manner in which she responds, the rest of us understand that there is some stuff here that we are not getting.

En route to Nablus our motorcade passes through several checkpoints, but is never held up. From inside the SUV one might even imagine how it was that President George W. Bush could claim that the roads are free and clear and that Palestinians can move about more easily than Bostonians during the massive reconstruction of South Boston. But no one in our delegation is suffering a similar delusion, perhaps because we only need to glance through the tinted, bulletproof windows to see the endless lineups of overloaded taxis, trucks, and private vehicles that are forced to eat our dust. Did Bush not look out his window? Or maybe when his forty-car entourage was travelling in the West Bank, the Israelis cleared the checkpoints.

I find myself comparing Ehab's approach to the checkpoints with the way my old Canadian friend Syd Nestel reacted to such things. In the mid-1970s, Nestel lived in Israel and did a lot of driving to and from work. Often he would encounter a checkpoint, always on Israel's side of the Green Line. Most of the checkpoints were temporary, set up after a bomb scare. Israeli soldiers invariably directed Nestel's car to the fast lane reserved for Jewish Israelis. Just as invariably he refused and joined the Arab queue, which was often backed up halfway to hell. When Israeli police attempted to persuade him to join the line for cars with Israeli licences, he refused. To Nestel it seemed that Israeli Jews had to suffer, too, rejecting the privileges they were offered, or there would be no solving the problem. Sometimes Israeli authorities reacted aggressively and threatened to arrest him. But Sydney is as stubborn as can be. Nonetheless, he eventually packed up and left the country, worn down and worn out.

On the dusty road into Nablus City, our motorcade hits a traffic jam and comes to a dead halt. Alexa, Anthony, Bill, Carolyn and I get out of the car and begin to make our way into town on foot. Ragamuffin Palestinian children swarm us. Many have things to sell—matches, misshapen chocolate bars, Israeli army issue paraphernalia. Alexa, Carolyn and Bill hand out candy, miniature Canadian flags and pins like those our diplomats wear on their lapels. The children take the candy and return the icons. I leave them mobbed by the children, and walk toward a crowd that has formed some fifty metres up the road, where I see several Israeli soldiers surrounded by a group of angry young Palestinians.

Nearby, two burly, unshaven Israeli labourers lean on the muddy fender of a Massey-Ferguson. In Hebrew I ask them what is going on and they mutter something reluctantly. As best as I can make out, the turmoil has something to do with a bad map showing that the security wall, which they are here to erect, can only be constructed if a power line is removed. "I don't know what the fuck they want from us. Our boss asked if he could move the wall closer to the schoolyard and got a go-ahead from the mayor's office," one of the Israeli labourers says.

An elderly Palestinian man speaks to me in broken English. "Our big fat mayor is a shtinker"—an Israeli collaborator— "and everyone knows it. If you put the wall over there," he says, pointing at the schoolhouse, "it'll block out the sunlight in the classrooms and it'll cut the playground in two. Our kids are going to say that we kissed Israeli asses and they won't come to school. Anyways they don't go to school."

Meanwhile, the circle of angry young Palestinians surrounding the soldiers is tightening like a noose. The crowd is smouldering and could easily become enraged. Driven by some very deep character flaw, I decide to take matters into my own hands. I push my way through the crowd and discover that several European types are also baiting the soldiers. One scraggly-bearded Dane dressed in army-surplus denim tries to insert a flower into the barrel of the soldier's weapon. "Let's sit down right here and talk about things," the Dane says. The soldier is not amused and tells the lad to fuck himself. I ask the Dane if he thinks he will win a stuffed animal if he gets the flower into the barrel. He puts the flower down.

"What is going on?" I ask the officer in charge. "*Azov*—let it be," he says, and then also to the Dane who is still playing with the barrel. The soldier asks the Dane, "Is yours long like this one?"

"Sounds like you fucked off during English class," I say to the soldier. The soldier smiles and I know I have him. "Let's get the fuck out of here," I say and the three soldiers and I start pushing out through the crowd. "*Y'alla*," one of the soldiers yells and the crowd, sensing that the pressure is being released, loses interest and soon disperses.

"Our orders were to protect the contractors," the officer tells me. "Their boss is a complete asshole, said something about a power line, which does not exist, and paid off the mayor to allow him to take a shortcut through the playground. When the locals started to complain, the mayor came down and told them to go home. They yelled at him, said that his mother was a whore, which she may have been."

"How did you manage to get yourself swarmed like that?" I ask.

"When things started to heat up, we called for help. It will probably arrive tomorrow. Fucking army. I don't get why we are protecting these contractors in the first place. They are earning a million shekels a minute. Why don't they pay for their own goddamn security?"

Bill and Carolyn, who have been watching from a distance, now come toward us. They can't stop smiling. "Did you see how he got the soldiers out?" Carolyn yells. Bill gives me a hug.

"Look, he's just a kid," Carolyn says, pointing to the soldier she would have maybe loved to squeeze like his mother.

"Wouldn't you prefer to be playing soccer or something?" Bill asks the officer, who turns away in disgust.

Suddenly the tension lets go in me and a torrent of impossible-to-control blather erupts. For the next half hour all I do is rant. I go on and on about fat contractors bribing overweight mayors, an army that is out of control, corrupt politicians and ridiculous legal systems. My Canadian friends do not get what I am talking about, but they are glad to indulge me. Later on Bill Phipps tells me that he did get how anxious I was when he saw me pushing my way into the crowd. "To be sure, I am far too old to die," I tell him.

—⁂—

We meet Ehab Shanti's relative in a piazza near the town centre. He is wearing a dowdy three-piece suit and worn patent leather shoes. "You can see that the Israeli occupation is a form of transfer," he tells us. The Israelis have made it impossible for normal economic activity to take place. Business people just leave. They leave and leave and there is more unemployed. And more angry militants. There's more violence and the Israelis come in and smash us and still more merchants leave. It is a vicious circle and it never stops."

We lunch at a local dining hall—hummus, mounds of beef and lamb skewers, tabouleh salad piled high. The centrepiece at each table is a bottle of Johnny Walker Black Label. Ehab struts proudly between the tables. "This is our tradition," he tells Alexa. "Even if an Arab is starving, he will honour his guests."

I don't really get how this tradition is possible and would have much preferred that the food be distributed to thinner people. But no one asks me what I would prefer, and the food is tasty.

Filled to the brim, we head off for an unpleasant walk through the streets of a refugee camp called Balata. It is from here that many of the most militant Palestinians hail. (After the Intifada more than five hundred residents of this camp and its surrounding area will be dead and three thousand wounded.) We meet a portly Italian psychiatrist named Giovanni, who wryly lectures us on what he calls "the thickness of Israeli skulls."

"I have an old Palestinian friend," he says, "who, not so long ago, got terribly worried about his boy. The *bambino* is the sweetest thing, *dolce*, really. Then he turns fourteen and his moods go up and down like Carmen's libretto. At a family supper the boy throws a rock at his older sister's head for disobeying him, and he almost kills her. Papa is worried that the boy maybe gets into bed with bad people and that they maybe prepare him to meet his God—tickets gratis in a belt full with explosives. Thank God, I get to the boy first. I convince the boy to move to Italy, where I arrange it so he stays with my relatives."

These situations are very common and Giovanni doesn't have enough relatives to go around. He tells us that he pleaded with the Israeli authorities to allow him to open a clinic to which parents like his friends could turn for assistance. The Israelis were all too happy to oblige. But when it came time to open the clinic, the Shabak (Israeli homeland security) insisted on bugging the place.

"You cannot bug the place. In a minute everyone will know it is bugged. And when everyone knows, then no one will come except someone who will come to kill me," Giovanni argued. The Shabakniks shrugged and said that whether anyone comes or not is not their business. Anyone with nothing to hide would still come. Giovanni tried to explain that the people he wants at the clinic do have something to hide but also a good reason to talk. So he abandoned the project and now he wants to leave town but hasn't yet persuaded himself to do so.

"I am the only doctor in the camp," he says.

At most Israeli checkpoints our drivers slow down just long enough to wave their special-issue UN documents. Sometimes soldiers pop their heads through one or the other of the back windows to ask us for ID. Mostly they back off once they spot the diplomatic passports. But the next day, when we visit Jenin in the northernmost sector of the West Bank, the octane level is so high that soldiers are prepared to take no chances. One young soldier collects our passports and disappears into a make-shift hut. Our drivers pull to the side. We stand around the car observing a dusty IDF soldier atop a Merkava tank, working an endless queue of Palestinian taxi drivers. Suddenly McDonough shouts out, "Did you see that?"

"Yep, I did," an exasperated Bill Phipps responds.

"What are you talking about?" I ask.

"Didn't you see it?" Alexa exclaimed. "The soldier in the tank was approached by that Palestinian taxi driver, the one walking back to his cab now. Over there—do you see him?"

"Of course I see him."

"Well, he walked over to the tank, handed the soldier his ID. The soldier flipped through it and then dropped it into the sand. Look at the driver. He is pissed as hell."

"It is annoying," I say, and mean also that I do not find it alarming. "Maybe the kid is pissed off as well. Maybe one of his friends got killed in a suicide bombing. Maybe he has not slept for three nights, who the hell knows." Even as I say these words, I realize that I am sounding like an Israeli apologist, which is an impulse I resolve to keep in check—if only because I do not feel any compulsion to apologize for anything that the Israelis are doing. Most of the time I feel as though I am living in exile in my own birthplace. Is this not what so many Sabras feel—that they are émigrés in their own land?

———

Ramallah, the capital city of the Palestinian Authority, is a bustling metropolis. We drive past Chairman Arafat's head-quarters, called the Muqatta, which literally means "abbreviated," as in the mystical numerology governing the opening lines of each of the suras of the Qu'ran. Following a series of suicide bombings back in September, the Israeli cabinet authorized a direct assault on the Muqatta. Yasir Arafat, it is said, has not left his headquarters since.

Our first visit is with Dr. Mustafah Barghouti, who would soon mount an unsuccessful campaign to become president of the Palestinian Authority. Mustafa Barghouthi, not to be con-fused with Marwan Barghouti (the head of Fatah's Tanzim, the organization's military wing, and imprisoned in Israel), is a remarkably handsome man in his late forties. Trained as a phy-sician, he is the chairperson of the Palestine Medical Relief Program and also the editor of the *Palestine Monitor*. He speaks softly even when he addresses intractable issues like suicide bombings, which he calls "a profound cultural psychosis." He tells us, "Many Palestinian intellectuals and writers agree with me about this issue. We write about it and speak publicly against such acts, which are not only terrible politics but explicitly against the Muslim tradition."

As I listen to him I think about how many of my Israeli friends would refuse to believe him. "Why is it that we in the West don't hear more about the internal resistance?" I ask him, and he cites Edward Said on Western deafness. Barghouthi, a champion of democracy, has also described Arab leaders as tyrants.

But at this moment, he is most distressed by the Israelis. He walks us to his office window and bids us look out into the lot where a half a dozen bullet-riddled Red Crescent ambulances are parked. "The truth is that so long as Israel is occupying us, they are obliged to provide medical services, which include ambulances. But they don't. Instead they shoot ours full of holes. Palestinian men have died at the checkpoints. Our women have gone into labour and have lost babies because they were detained at checkpoints."

Our next stop is with Steve Hibbard, who leads the Canadian mission to the Palestinian Authority, and he takes things even further. Whereas Barghouti was careful not to pronounce on the general mental health of Israelis, Hibbard has no such reservations. Lean, wizened and elderly, Hibbard talks to us about his frustrations with hard-headed Israelis, who he claims are mostly insufferable, and who have thwarted several Canadian peace initiatives.

McDonough asks Hibbard about Arafat. "For many years I made a point of meeting with the chairman every week," he says. "But the last time we met, Arafat could not stop repeating a single phrase. 'The Virgin Mary is crying for my people,' he kept muttering."

"What's that about?" Bill Phipps asks.

"Can't really say," Hibbard responds. "Maybe it had to do with the last Israeli incursion into Bethlehem after Palestinian militants took hostages into the Church of the Nativity. The Israelis eventually foiled the kidnapping, damaging the icon of the Virgin Mary in the inner courtyard."

"Do you think he's losing his mind?" McDonough asks.

"Can't really say," Hibbard says again. "When the Israelis raided the Muqatta, besides turning the entire compound into rubble, they confiscated a huge number of secret documents belonging to the chairman. When they left, Arafat had his tailor make him a jellabiya with dozens of inside pockets that he now stuffs with all his important documents and letters. So he actually looks rather more robust than he is. But I can't really say. Maybe he is losing his mind. Couldn't really blame him if he was."

The next morning we take a cab to the Allenby Bridge and cross over to Jordan. Another taxi picks us up on the other side and in a few hours we are in Amman, the capital. That evening we are invited to dinner at the Canadian embassy, the regal home of Ambassador Jordan Roderick Bell. Cocktails are served by exquisitely attired East Asians. An entirely separate staff of attendants ushers us into the dining area and hovers over us even as we muster our best table manners. Bell, who has twice been the Canadian ambassador to Israel, once to Egypt and now Jordan, exudes a sense of ownership over the position and the residence. "Given the way Svend Robinson behaved last time he was here, we probably should not have invited you," he says snarkily to McDonough. His tone and manner remind us how arrogant Canadian Liberals have become. This is the first time since we arrived in the Middle East that I am reminded that our delegation belongs to Canada's third party, but also that Liberals have been inbreeding and that the various clones have all cultivated a *l'état c'est moi* attitude.

David MacDonald asks Bell about the protocol for meeting Hashemite royalty. "I think you are expected to laugh at every one of their jokes," Bell says, laughing.

———

For all intents and purposes, the Wihdat Refugee Camp is a suburb of Amman. A great majority of the refugees were born in the West Bank and are allowed to come and go as they please. They don't even have to maintain a home in the camp unless they wish to take advantage of the tax freedoms extended only to its residents. In fact a great many able-bodied younger men and women have left the camp, which is now top-heavy with single mothers, the elderly, and widows caring for young children who have been abandoned.

We visit a classroom where the students are learning English. They all seem to have been freshly scrubbed and dressed, their hair combed and parted to the left—perhaps because they have been told that we represent a social democratic party. As we enter, the instructor, a tired middle-aged woman dressed in a black hijab, signals the children to stand. "Good morning, Miss McDonough," they declaim in high-pitched unison and in a manner that brings *The King and I* to mind.

From here we are ushered into a computer room where a dozen young women face old monitors, earnestly typing. The whole room, even the ceiling, has been painted the blood-red colour of Coca-Cola ads. Hung on the walls directly behind the computer monitors, Coke's banner and logo provide the only decoration. Carolyn Pogue asks one of the instructors whether the commercialization of the room does not distract the children. "On the contrary," the teacher says. "We love Coke and are very grateful to America for helping our children get educated."

At the infirmary, the queue is endless. Overweight mothers bounce unhappy-looking children on their laps. Benches threaten to break, medicine cabinets and shelves are mostly bare or lined with the basic first-aid supplies. Though it is still before noon, the doctor and nurses look like they could use a vacation. By the desperation painted on patients' faces, we realize that the medical staff can offer little more than temporary stopgaps to terminal diseases.

At no point during our walkabout do we come across a washroom. By the time we are back in the huddle of our cars, our bladders are ready to burst. "Next stop is the palace, and before we do anything else, we make a beeline to the john! Is that clear?" McDonough commands with a giggle. As we drive past commercial buildings with names like the First Palestinian Bank of Jordan, we dream of toilets.

Two huge East Asian sentinels swing open the fortress doors of the palace. An oversized cat, evidently one of the survivors of the "dead cat caper" in which a palace cook tested various poison recipes for the one best fit to kill a king, scampers across the marble floor. In seconds our host, former Crown Prince El

Hassan Bin Talal, the late King Hussein's younger brother, enters. "Normally I do not suffer fat cats," he says, "but there are exceptions." He lets loose a belly-laugh to which we all try to respond but cannot quite do so without losing control of our bladders.

At fifty-six, Hassan's face still retains hints of the muscular jaw and flared nostrils of the Arabian stallion he once was. He is as short as a jockey but also thick, square, and fitted to the chessboard life of the royal court. He would have looked perfect in military uniform but has chosen a milder, less aggressive persona. On his official website, for example, there is only the slightest whiff of the prince's interest in power. Where one expects photos of Hassan as a warrior, what one gets is Hassan in scuba-diving gear, Hassan playing solo squash.

But like his late brother, Hassan does have something of that Napoleonic small-stature-big-ego thing going. The boom of his voice makes it clear that this is a man who is larger than life, who does not need to converse but only to hold forth. In the streets of Amman it is said that the short Hashemites have had the ceiling height in all their palaces lowered in order to make these descendants of the prophet Mohammed appear like a taller dynasty.

For most of his life Hassan was the crown prince, heir to the throne of Jordan. Throughout this little kingdom, created by the British in the aftermath of the First World War, there are still photos of the late King and his brother, arm in royal arm. But in 1999, King Hussein returned from cancer treatment at the Mayo Clinic with a list of accusations that he served upon his younger brother. In an official letter he accused Hassan of meddling with the armed forces, scandalizing the royal family and creating around himself a cult of personality. From conversations with senior Jordanian journalists, I later learned that it was not these accusations but the objections of the powerful Bedouin tribal leaders that was the decisive factor in Hassan's fall from favour with his brother. In 1970 Hassan had been instrumental in the Black September massacre of Palestinians who were encamped in the south. Yasir Arafat managed to escape, but very few Bedouin leaders in Jordan were prepared to forgive Hassan.

For his audience with us, he is wearing a perfectly pressed short-sleeved shirt, a cravat, a pair of elegant black pleated dress pants and American loafers with tassels. His nails are superbly manicured and his thin moustache elegantly trimmed. A pretty young South African woman who introduces herself as his "aide-de-camp" follows him around, and then invites us all to step into the garden, in which, she informs us, the royal family houses every known plant in the kingdom.

Hassan seats himself at the head of a wrought iron table inlaid with gorgeous mosaic tile. He tells us that as moderator of the World Conference of Religion and Peace he has been kept very busy doing interfaith work, which he says has become "most necessary since 9/11, which has persuaded so many Americans that all Muslims are terrorists."

I suddenly realize that the connection between our mission and the Prince is through the Very Reverend Bill Phipps, who is big on interfaith. I find myself listening more intently, even as I, like the rest of our delegation, am dying to pee.

The prince received a master's degree from the college of Christ Church, Oxford, and he lists at least a dozen committees, conferences and foundations that he has recently founded. "We must remind Westerners that we are part of the Abrahamic tradition," Hassan says. "Miss P., do make a note to send copies of my very good book on Christianity in the Arab world to their hotel."

His aide-de-camp makes just such a note.

If this is so, I want to ask, why it is that Jews are prohibited from purchasing land in Jordan. But then I am a guest here and do not feel I should say anything that might upset things, especially not before the bathroom intermission, which is entirely in His Highness's hands. Desperate, I pass a note to the aide-de-camp and she interrupts the prince, who grants us our moment.

The washroom I am directed to is wallpapered from floor to ceiling with a collage of clippings that all have to do with Ronald Reagan, to whom the resource-poor Hashemites owe far more than this pot to piss in.

When we get back, tea is served and Prince Hassan takes the occasion to complain about criminal activity, including incest and sodomy, among the Bedouin tribes. He tells us that on numerous occasions he has tried to intervene on behalf of a victim, usually a woman who was raped by her father or brother, sending Jordanian police to make an arrest. But they almost never succeed and often the consequences for the victim are dire.

Many years ago I learned this lesson from Anat, who once told me a story about a group of well-intentioned Israeli human rights activists who tried to intervene on behalf of a young woman living in a small Arab village in Israel. The woman had been raped by a family member and either she had complained to authorities outside the village or these authorities had got wind of the violation by other means. The man responsible was arrested and brought to trial. But the villagers did not take well to the arrest, accused the raped woman of being a whore, and banished not only her but her entire family from the village. "When such interventions occur in Jordan, the tribe sometimes reacts terribly," Prince Hassan tells us. His point has to do with the very nature of tribal life, which is the idea that everything gets dealt with inside the tent and in the shadows. The light of consciousness and of language is the enemy of the tribe.

Later that day we meet with a Palestinian banker who tells us that so long as Arafat is in power, Jordanian Palestinians will not support the Authority. "The monarchy has been good to us and we do not intend to help Arafat, who is wholly corrupt. Let the Israelis deal with him as best they can. Allah only knows we have enough problems of our own."

We stay the night in Amman and return to Tel Aviv the next morning.

On Monday, January 13, 2003, the delegation meets with the Labor Party leader, Amram Mitzna, who is stumping in the general elections to be held some three weeks later. "If we cannot reach an agreement with the Palestinians," Mitzna tells us, "then we should act unilaterally." If Barak is right and Arafat cannot or will not sign off on a peace agreement, Mitzna argues, then Israel should withdraw from the West Bank and from Gaza according to its own timetable, on its own terms, either in exchange for concessions or not.

His chief adversary, the Likud leader and current prime minister, Ariel Sharon, will later come to accept Mitzna's idea, but he is fighting this election from the opposite side of the fence. In Sharon's view, Israel should stand firm. "We have already been there, gone there too many times, and we got precisely nothing for our efforts," Sharon is quoted as saying.

Salloum was unable to get in touch with Mitzna's press secretary in advance, so we have been forced to wing it, and decide to try to speak to him after a speech he is giving in a hotel that evening. When it comes time to head out, Carolyn and David stay back at the hotel, while Anthony, Alexa, Bill and I take a taxi to the event. After a brief Q&A we make our way to the front and I introduce Mitzna to Alexa, who speaks with him briefly. Then I ask him, more candidly and in Hebrew, if he could explain why he is such a staunch advocate of the two-state alternative. His response shocks me.

"I might not say this to everyone," he replies, "but I understand that you were in a reconnaissance unit and so are one of us. I have lots of reasons, but you will understand this one I think. So long as we are occupiers, we are bound by certain international conventions and rules. When a suicide bombing occurs inside the Green Line we have little choice but to put our boys in harm's way. But if a terrorist trained and based in the newly established State of Palestine should hit a target in Tel Aviv or in Jerusalem or Haifa or anywhere else in Israel, we would be within our rights to treat the attack as a declaration of war by a sovereign nation. No longer would we be forced to deploy infantry. Our air force could do the job just as well."

Mitzna and I shake hands and we part. As we walk out of the hotel ballroom, I wonder how non-Israeli advocates of the two-state option would feel if a day or a year or five years after an agreement is signed Ramallah awoke to the sweet smell of napalm?

That evening we meet with the Israeli historian Benny Morris, who in *Righteous Victims* exposed the dark underbelly of Israel's first war of independence ("an atmosphere of ethnic cleansing prevailed throughout the war," he writes). Over supper in a West Jerusalem fish restaurant, Morris, who accompanied Ehud Barak to the failed Camp David meetings, complains about the mercurial Chairman Arafat. "As long as Arafat is in charge," he tells us, "there is no hope of negotiating a peace agreement. Arafat was given the chance of a lifetime when Barak offered him something like 96 percent of the land he had been asking for."

In his book, Morris writes that Arab leaders "kneel at the shrine of Saladin, the Kurdish Moslem warrior who beat back the crusaders. I could see President Hafez Assad on his death-bed telling his son Bashar not to succumb to the Zionists who will be gone just as the crusaders are gone." To us, Morris spoke anxiously about the 1.2 million Arab Israelis who, as I had learned a year earlier on the visit to Sakhnin, no longer see themselves as Israelis first but as Palestinians. Morris thinks that Israel's first prime minister, David Ben-Gurion, made a terrible error by not ridding Israel of all the Arabs. "They are an extraordinarily dangerous fifth column," he says. Morris supports the two-state solution as perhaps the lesser of evils. "I think of myself as a man of the left," he says.

The next day we meet with a high-ranking IDF officer who paints yet another terrible morning-after scenario. With the aid of charts and maps, he points out that should a Palestinian state come into existence, there is a good chance that the Hezbollah leader Hassan Nasrallah would be in Ramallah the following day recruiting soldiers for his army from the vast pool of unemployed Palestinians. "What the Israeli army fears is the rise of yet another military force in the region. Nasrallah, we think, would probably not strike at Israel," he says. "But he would do all in his power to destabilize other Arab states, including Jordan. To Nasrallah, the Hashemite Kingdom of Jordan is a collaborationist kingdom set up by colonial imperialists."

As I was listening to this officer another reason why we might not wish to sign a peace agreement occurred to me. What would happen if some radical settler saw in the inevitable confusion an opportunity to blow up the Al Aqsa Mosque? I should not like to be on this planet if that happens.

Major Daniel Beaudoin is the deputy head of the foreign relations branch of the Coordinator of Government Activities in the Territories (COGAT). His department is responsible for liaising between Israel and the various agencies providing humanitarian aid to the Palestinians in Gaza and in the West Bank. I wake up at the Andromeda Hotel excited about meeting him. I am itching to talk to a sympathetic Israeli about the stuff I have been thinking about this place and its future. I know very little about COGAT and even less about Major Beaudoin, but I harbour some hope that maybe we can have a real conversation about the checkpoints and about the soldiers who were surrounded by inimical Palestinians. I want to ask someone why the IDF is not training its people better, why it is not possible to treat Palestinians in a manner that will not transform them into terrorists.

After breakfast, which Alexa, David, Carolyn, Bill, Anthony and I take by the hotel pool, we make our way by taxi to one of the many IDF trailers that serve as headquarters while the flashy new building in the Kiryah area of Tel Aviv is being completed. Inside, two fold-out tables are configured in a T formation. At one end sit three Israeli officers, two female lieutenants and Major Beaudoin, whose scalp reflects the fluorescent lights above, giving this movie-star-handsome man an ethereal aura. A dishevelled colonel in his fifties, probably representing Army Intelligence or IDF public affairs, sits at the head of the table. As our delegation enters, Major Beaudoin looks up, nods a welcome, and then quickly returns to a discussion with his colleagues. They are planning the meeting with us, speaking Hebrew among themselves and apparently assuming none of us will understand.

"Do any of you even know anything about Canadians?" the colonel asks. "All I know is that they tend to be very respectful and prefer to avoid tension. But if this is so, then what say you all that we get through this meeting as fast as possible? I, for one, have an important meeting later this afternoon."

When we have all taken our seats, the major looks up. "Shalom," he says. "My name is Major Daniel Beaudoin. I was born in the Belgian Congo. My mother is Israeli and my father is a Catholic and French. So maybe I have a little more distance on the situation in the Middle East than others who have experienced the conflict from outside of the region." Beaudoin's boots are as brilliantly polished as his scalp, and there is a slight scent of the mercenary about him. But unlike Ari, with whom we met a few weeks earlier, Beaudoin feels no need to lecture us, which is a good thing. "I know you've been touring in Judea and Samaria and so I thought that rather than talking to you, we might begin with your questions."

Alexa McDonough opens the discussion. She thanks the major for taking time out of his busy schedule to help Canadians understand the Middle East. From there she turns to the checkpoints, relating the incident of the soldier who, from his perch atop a tank, dropped the Palestinian passport into the sand.

In Hebrew, Beaudoin mutters something like "again with the same old shit." And then to McDonough, he says in the most ingenuous way, "Ma'am, to be perfectly honest, I was not at all expecting this kind of question. It seems to me that there are so many more interesting things we could talk about. But if you insist on it then I must say that the IDF is a very large institution in a country that has universal conscription. Unfortunately, when you can't handpick soldiers you sometimes end up with a few bad apples. Did you perchance get the soldier's name? No? Oh now, that is too bad."

A few bad apples? To me that old chestnut translates as a senior officer's way of evading responsibility. I am tempted to interrupt. One bad apple is enough to rot the entire basket, I want to say, but say nothing instead.

"Major Beaudoin," McDonough continues. "We met with several high-ranking Palestinian officials who gave us hard evidence about numerous human rights violations, including ambulances held up and minors being arrested and locked up without trial. Could you explain?"

In Hebrew, as if he is conferring with his colleagues, he asks: "What is this, am I supposed to carry on a debate with her? I thought we would talk about COGAT and about how we are trying to get aid to the territories."

In English, he says, "There is no excuse for bad behaviour. We are trying our best. There have been some incidents when explosives have been smuggled out of the West Bank in the back of ambulances. But then I am not an expert in such things."

"Could I?" I interject.

"Have I answered your question, madam?"

"I am not so sure you have, but go ahead with David's question."

"Yes, David?"

"Major Beaudoin," I begin. "For the moment I am less interested in the way Israeli soldiers are acting toward the Palestinians, and more interested in the relation between you and your soldiers."

Beaudoin gives the dishevelled reservist colonel a what-the-fuck-is-this-guy-on-about look. "I am not sure I understand what you mean, sir."

"Well, Major. When we got to Jenin, three of your soldiers were surrounded by maybe fifty irate Palestinians. And for a while it seemed to me that the lives of your soldiers were on the line. So maybe you could just let us know how long do you actually train your people before you deploy them into hostile conditions?"

Beaudoin in Hebrew: "Things are getting out of hand. Someone find out who this guy is." In English: "I don't think I can answer your question, David. How long we train our soldiers is secure information."

"Well, that is interesting. But what would you say if I told you that these soldiers said they were never trained at all and that they resented the fact that they had been ordered to provide security for a corrupt contractor? And what if I told you that soldiers at all the checkpoints are far less professional than they could be?"

"I think we had better go to the next question. I am not

sure you are asking something. Sounds to me like you are accusing us."

"What about the kids, Major?" Carolyn Pogue asks. "Your kids, but also the Palestinian children. The wall that is being built—don't you think it will make young people feel like they are in jail. Do you have children, Major?"

"As a matter of fact, my wife and I have young boys," Beaudoin replies. "And as you all probably know, raising boys is a handful, can even be a pain in the ass. Not only are they totally rambunctious, but their demands are nonstop. My wife, who has been a—how do you Canadians call it—a 'stay at home mom,' does all the hard work in our family. I loaf around this office while she works herself to the bone. Every morning she has to take the kids to school, keep our home in some kind of order. She picks them up and then she has to chauffeur them to karate and to music lessons. It is nonstop.

"Before the Intifada broke out," Beaudoin continues, "my wife would treat herself, perhaps once every couple of weeks, to dinner with a few of her girlfriends. This was the only thing she did just for herself. They would all go out for supper at a local Persian restaurant. This was her replenishment, the few hours that were only hers. And then the suicide bombings started and now my wife has become so anxious and scared that she does not go out at all except when she absolutely has to. So you tell me, who is the victim here—them or us?"

Beaudoin's story moves Carolyn. "Your kids, the Palestinian children. Everyone is suffering."

"We are doing our best, madam. And I can assure you that things in the territories are getting better, security at checkpoints is getting more efficient."

As he begins to list improvements, I can hold myself back no longer.

"You know, Major, a while ago I was reading an account of a Jewish diplomat who, in the early years of the Second World War, visited Eichmann in Berlin," I begin. "The meeting went very well, the diplomat wrote. Eichmann reported that things in the territories occupied by Germany were indeed getting better: the trains were not quite as efficient as Germans would have liked them to be, but things were improving. The only weird thing about the meeting, wrote the diplomat, was that for the entire time, Eichmann was sitting and he was standing."

The veins in his forehead swollen to capacity, Beaudoin turns to McDonough, interrupting me. "Madam," he stammers, "we are prepared to listen to a lot of criticism here, but when someone compares us to the Nazis then as far as I am concerned, this meeting is over."

The room breaks into chaos. Suddenly everyone is talking at the same time. David MacDonald is whispering something to Bill Phipps, McDonough says something to Anthony Salloum and to Carolyn Pogue. In Hebrew, Beaudoin asks one of the female officers who has been busy on her laptop whether she has figured out who I am. She has not. But it is finally McDonough's voice that cuts through.

"Major, David did not compare you to the Nazis. He was just pointing out that from our point of view, things in the territories did not seem like they were improving at all. What we saw was entire villages and towns being hollowed out as a result of Israeli policies."

Bill Phipps provides back-up. "If you think that David drew

a comparison maybe it is because you are feeling guilty." By now, Carolyn Pogue is sobbing.

Beaudoin consults with his group in Hebrew—should they go on or should they take this opportunity to adjourn? His team thinks we should continue.

The major opens part two of the discussion with a modification of his previous statement. "Perhaps you did not understand me," he says. "I was not saying that everything in the occupied territories is fine but only that Israel is doing all in its power to improve conditions."

"What proof do you have of that?" I ask. "As far as I can see, Israel is not at all interested in improving conditions in the territories. And not only that, but the Israeli military courts are acquitting dozens of soldiers who have been charged with criminal behaviour."

"Excuse me," the reservist interrupts. "Could you tell us what it is that you are interested in, because we don't understand what it is that you want?"

"I'd be very glad to tell you . . ." At this point I revert to Hebrew. "Look here," I say. "I was born here and served my time in the military. It seems to me that you have far less control of the army today than we did back them. And it seems to me that Israel has learned very little about how one might run an occupation. As you don't have a clue about how to manage the territories, then you should either get a manual or get out of there."

My switch to Hebrew sets the room aflame. Beaudoin squirms and the female officers come alive. Clearly they are taking pleasure in watching the major lose control.

I carry on in Hebrew: "Look, if you guys have more bullshit that you are planning to feed my colleagues why don't you just go ahead. I'll wait outside." And I get up, get out and light up.

Obviously I overreacted. But to what?

Beaudoin struck me as a man made of the same mould as Ari from Foreign Affairs. They, who have become absolutely comfortable with themselves and with the old Jewish identity and with the new macho one, have taken over the country. And that means I am now entirely outside of the loop.

A few minutes later the delegation pours out of the trailer. McDonough looks at me and smiles. "Not the most politically astute move you have ever made," she says.

The next morning we visit Neve Shalom, the only mixed Arab-Israeli village in Israel. Halfway through the tour, McDonough's cellphone rings. It is the foreign ministry. She puts the phone on speaker and invites us all to listen in. The woman on the phone tells us about our next meeting, which is to be with Supreme Court Justice Barak. Someone will meet us downstairs. And then she pauses. "But Mr. Berlin is not welcome," she says.

It is McDonough's turn to pause. "Let me make sure I understand what you are saying. We are scheduled to meet with Justice Barak to discuss issues relating to freedom of speech, and you are telling me that Mr. Berlin is not welcome because he spoke his mind yesterday?"

No answer comes over the phone.

"Well then, I think it is better if you cancel our meeting and also cancel all the rest of the meetings you have scheduled. Thank you for everything," McDonough says and hangs up.

January 15 is my father's seventy-seventh birthday. Earlier in the day my parents and I have made arrangements to meet at a restaurant in Tel Aviv. I get on a bus and cannot help noticing that my mind is more concentrated than it has been at any time since we arrived in Israel. The question of the conflict is all I want to think about. What is it, this conflict? Terrible as it is, it suddenly also seems like an enormous distraction—a way for both Israelis and Palestinians to avoid having to deal with their own internal mess. So long as the conflict goes on, neither the Palestinians nor the Israelis have to worry all that much about their own militants or about who they themselves are or what it is that they really want out of life.

But if this is so, then, could it not be that the "existential threat" that both the Israelis and the Palestinians are forever railing about is really no more than the fear that we will fall apart en route to discovering who we really are? Could it not be that all this existential business is really just the expression of fear—or the absence of courage to face the inward abyss that all human beings who seek out their own identity must face?

To be sure, there are a thousand seemingly impossible obstacles in the way of peace, but none of these need be impossible unless we happily or not so happily define them that way. "Impossible" in this sense means that we all can continue to treat ourselves as righteous victims of the conditions we create.

Maybe it is too much to ask of these two anxious peoples that they put aside their fear and distrust. In this mood they will certainly not find any immediate or perfect solution. But would it not make sense for the moment to forget about a "final status agreement" and try for an interim agreement, perhaps a ten-year ceasefire that would grant each side the peace of mind necessary to rediscover their centres? Could we not just put the big problems, the core issues — Palestinian refugees, Jerusalem, the settlements, final borders, security and Hamas — on hold for a decade or so, go with a really detailed and strong negotiated interim agreement that would provide both parties with the time and the space to put their own houses in order and learn who they really are?

I look out the window of the bus and wonder: Would the Palestinians agree to such a thing? Chairman Arafat would probably prefer it if only because it would free him from the impossibility of selling out the old dream. There are of course many Palestinian leaders with a huge personal stake in the state. They would probably have to go before any negotiations of a different sort could begin.

What of the Israelis? I ask myself. Same problem. There are many Israeli leaders who have invested everything in the possibility of a final status agreement. And there are many others, as I have discovered, who prefer the conflict over any kind of compromise. There are also those who simply accept the conflict if only because it holds Israelis together and keeps them from each other's throats. But there are still others, perhaps many others, who would welcome an interim solution, if only because they believe that time heals wounds and sometimes even points to a future that cannot be perceived while the conflict is raging.

To strike out for a negotiated interim agreement we would have to find the courage to admit that we who have been fighting each other for so long could not now — or even in the foreseeable future — negotiate in sufficiently good faith to establish a final status agreement. But an interim agreement

would mean a suspension of hostilities, and the present generation would not have to suffer because of our inability to make
progress. With an interim agreement, a thousand and one prac-
tical issues, life-enhancing issues, could be negotiated right now,
even as the really big ones were put on the back burner. A negotiated interim agreement would create an opening for the occupation to end and for both Palestinian and Israeli society to grow
to maturity without yet having resolved the core issues.

To negotiate such an agreement would require extraordinarily skilled mediators who were neither Israelis nor Palestinians.
Such mediators would have to be sufficiently powerful and
knowledgeable about the region to really understand what
terms and conditions can and cannot be sustained. To me
these mediators should demand a huge financial bond from
each side to be put into a trust and forfeited if the interim
agreement were violated.

Needless to say, the power of an interim agreement is only
as great as the depth and expanse of the issues it settles and only
as binding as the punitive measures that are triggered in the
event that its terms are violated.

Could a legal system that would replace the antiquated and
largely inadequate Jordanian legal system currently operating
in the West Bank be fashioned and deployed? What about taxa-
tion? Should the larger settlements, if they were left in place
under an interim agreement, pay taxes to the Palestinian
Authority? What about the checkpoints? To the extent that an
interim agreement would allow them to exist, would we not all
be better off if they were manned by professional customs and
border guards rather than young and inexperienced Israeli
soldiers? What about the police force? Could a combined

147

Israeli-Palestinian police force be deployed? And should there not be an oversight board capable of holding police accountable?

According to Dr. Barghouthi, the Red Crescent ambulance service has become unable to render proper services to the constituencies living in the West Bank. Should Red Cross ambulances be introduced in their stead? Many more hospitals, trauma clinics and social services must be created in the West Bank. What is for sure is that the wanton real estate grabs need to stop. In any interim agreement worthy of its name, title and ownership of everything from water wells to land must come under strict laws. The security wall, which has been designed and built with very little concern for the Palestinian populations enclosed behind it, needs to be rethought and redesigned. Over time, Palestinians should be allowed to work and study in Israel, and Israeli students wishing to study in the territories or to meet with colleagues at various academic departments should be encouraged to do so.

These are my racing thoughts as I ride the bus into Tel Aviv to meet my parents.

───── ∞ ─────

From the window of the restaurant I can see my mother and father coming toward me. My father looks pale and drawn. It is January 15, 2003. This will be our last meal together.

FIVE

Asher Dies

can trace my un-naming of my father to a boyhood trauma. It is difficult to explain why I carried such a childish resolution forward into adulthood. Perhaps, as my wife has suggested, my anger never abated because my father never acted like a father: our relationship simply hardened into a contest of wills. Even as he grew older and more needy, and I became a father myself, and less dependent, I never retreated from my position of childish anger, which was as intransigent as King George's stutter.

And if I am honest, between us two when I was grown, we treated the fact that I had no name for him mostly as a matter of indifference, sometimes even as a kind of intimacy, as though nothing stood between us and we were seamlessly father and son.

But all of this changed in the fall of 1998 when my father had a heart infarction so seismic it could have set records. I arrived at Toronto General Hospital's ICU, as I had done in the past when his heart had given him grief, with two hot corned beef sandwiches wrapped in silver foil. This was the tradition he had launched on that Passover so many years before. Like him, I too had bought the sandwiches at Moe Pancer's, allowing conscience the upper hand only with regard to the side of the brisket from which the beef was sliced.

"It's a bit lean," my father said, after I cranked his bed to sitting position. But then, instead of removing the tubes and the catheters, and the foil from the sandwich, he simply sat there and stared into space. "*Mah eenyaneem,*" I asked apprehensively. "Are you feeling all right?"

For a long time he did not answer and when he did, he still did not turn his head my way. "I've known a lot of pain in my life," he said, "but the thing that has hurt me most of all is that you have never called me Abba or Dad or anything else for that matter. It has hurt me terribly and I can't understand it. For the life of me I can't."

I was speechless, as only those who have seen a ghost can be. I'd always believed that he lived too deep inside himself to notice that when I called him to join us for supper I did not say his name or when I phoned him or came to meet him at Mr. Donut for a French cruller, I always began the conversation *in medias res*.

My impulse was to resort to that famous children's trick where you close your eyes and believe that you can't be seen anymore. But I didn't close my eyes. All I did was nothing. The ball, which I could not even dream of returning, stayed in my court. A month, a year, a thousand years passed us by, and then he said, "Well, that's the way it is," and reached for the sandwich.

The issue never came up again, but I promised myself that I would find an opportunity to nail that old ghost to the door and begin again. But I didn't. Over the next decade, my father became weaker and his heart and lungs served him less life than ever. As that happened, I grew ever more sympathetic to him, like Cordelia for her maddened and dethroned Lear. My desire to be done with this inability to call him anything, to understand it, to get past it, became a kind of obsession. And yet I could not. And I did not. By the time my mother called to inform me that my father was in a coma in a hospital in Israel, it was too late.

—◦◦◦—

"Why did you wait so long before you called?" I asked her. "Did you really have to wait until he went into a coma?"

"Zafi, he's done this before. You know that. He's been hospitalized and then he's rallied and it was as though it never happened. I didn't want to disturb you for nothing."

"But all you've ever done is disturb me for nothing. Why should this time be any different?"

"There's no need to be rude. I didn't think you or Daniel should come sooner. Your father would have just assumed that you'd come to pay your last respects, that he was sicker than he knew. He's always believed that people, even his nearest, hide things from him. But anyhow, now he is in fact sicker than he knows."

"So, what hospital is he in?"

"Meir in Kfar Saba. It's not the best hospital, but the paramedics in the ambulance insisted."

"Can we get him transferred?"

"I don't think so. The doctors say he can't be moved."

"I'll be on the next available flight."

"Okay. So we'll see you very soon."

"Raychool?"

"Yes, Zafi."

"I'm sorry I was rude."

"*Lehitraot*, see you soon, Zafi," my mother said.

Meir Hospital, on Tchernichovsky Street in Kfar Saba, a small city in Israel's centre, is a sickly place. Its beige brick patina is blistered and pockmarked; the once friendly goosebumps of protective whitewash have eroded. The rows of windows, which have been collecting soot for decades, are thrown open perhaps only to mock the cooling units that broke down long before anyone can remember. Throughout this tenement-like space, the thick June air moved so rarely as to justify the feeling harboured by many inmates—that they have been abandoned as much by earth as by heaven itself.

In 1956, when Meir Hospital first opened, it was hailed as a breakthrough facility on an international scale. Designed for tubercular patients with severe ambulatory and respiratory problems, the hospital installed, instead of the usual bleak staircases and train station lobbies, a host of colour-coded ramps that wound languidly from one floor to the next. The original long-term patients found it easy to maintain independence. They took solace on the banks of a man-made pond dug out in the main courtyard. To their rambunctious grandchildren, wheezing grandmothers and grandfathers would point out the monster goldfish that swam beneath real lily pads floating about in the artificial pond. Sometimes wild ducks with red-tipped beaks would fly into the open-air pavilion. The children shooed them away from the fish and then followed a trail of webbed feet and quacking as though the ducks were vengeful pipers of Hamelin.

But then, in 1957, only one year after Meir opened its doors, a pharmaceutical cure for tuberculosis was discovered and everything imploded. Soon the hospital was closed, its magic dissipated, its windows boarded up. And thus it remained for five long years, until 1962, when the government decided to reopen the facility. Except this time it would not be the jewel in the crown but a regional centre in a region about which no one cared. The half-million people that Meir now served were mostly Arab Israelis and a bouillabaisse of new immigrants from Morocco and Yemen.

Who would have guessed that it would be here, in this medical soup kitchen somewhere in the Middle East, that my father, who owned factories, drove Cadillacs and flew business class, would queue up for his final kick at the can?

⁂

Dr. Smorzik's pulmonary ward is on the third level at the end of a purple ramp. His office is on the right-hand side just as one pushes through a set of creaking double doors. A round-faced, rather pleasant-looking secretary sits behind a counter that in most other institutions would serve as a barrier against the deluge of humanity clamouring for her boss's attention. But in the maelstrom that is Israel, nothing protects the poor man, for whom I feel sorry even before we meet.

My mother, who happens to be one drop in the deluge, stops yelling at the secretary when she sees me come through the doors. We hug for a long time and then she runs her fingers through my hair.

"You look exhausted," she says.

"It was a long trip."

"Let me introduce you to Dr. Smorzik, he's the head of the department." Before I can object, she pulls me into the office and waves the doctor down. "This is my son, Dr. Smorzik. He has just flown in from Canada to be with his father."

Turning to me: "You see that the skin on the doctor's cheek has no pigment? You know why that is? It's because this right-eous man used himself as a guinea pig for some new drug. The mark is one of the side effects that prove the main point—that he is the best. Isn't that so, doctor?"

"Yes, Mrs. Berlin," the doctor says. "But Mrs. Berlin, I . . ."

"Just one more thing. I need to talk to you about the trache-otomy. Our friend's son Mandy does transplants at the Ichilov Hospital. He says that a tracheotomy could be lethal. Zafi, you go ahead to your father's room. I will be with you in a moment."

"Charmed to meet you, Mr. Berlin," Dr. Smorzik says, shaking my hand heartily.

The hallway to my father's room seems to have taken its cue from Dr. Smorzik's mottled face. The varnish on the old floor has rubbed off and shines only where yesterday's soup has dried on it. Up and down the corridor there are deep grooves, like streetcar tracks, and orderlies, their white gowns billowing in their wake, run wheelchairs along them in Kafkaesque fashion. The doors and the thresholds to the rooms are scuffed, the walls chipped and scratched.

I pass a depressing little dining area near the nurses' station. A half-filled vat of cauliflower soup with the ladle leaning to one side stands on a stainless steel planter as though it needs to be watered along with the fake mums in the vases lined up along the linoleum's edge. The walls are awash with religious icons: one kitsch photo of the Wailing Wall reads *"Azov otee yom ve-e'ezovhah yomayim."* Abandon me for a day and I shall abandon thee for two.

"Asher Berlin?" I ask a nurse with high Slavic cheekbones.

"Room 7," she tells me. Her nametag reads "Erena." She points without looking up from her oversized appointment book. "At the end of the hall."

"Sweet Mary mother of God, what has He done to you? One might have expected Him to hold off for a bit. After all, He'll have you forever, so what's the fucking rush?"

I am not talking to my father but to the lump of melted wax that I am not even absolutely sure is the right lump. Room 7 has four lumps, and this one is my best guess. I notice that the lump to the right has a rumpled plastic bag beside it. There's some stale pita on the bed and a bottle of arak. My lump never drank arak in his life, so that couldn't be him. I feel more comfortable knowing that my chances have increased by a percentage point.

The taste of airplane food is rising at the back of my throat and I swallow it. Sweet mother of God, why? Who can love this thing that does this to men? But then again, you did, lump. You loved the circle — the very idea that everything that goes around comes around. You thought it was right, this shitty idea. You said it was a thing of beauty, this crap.

"You look like that one over there, yes?" A male nurse, standing behind a pushcart loaded with syringes and gauze and thick plastic bags filled with saline, calls out to me as he points to the bed across the aisle.

"Thank you, Mr.—?"

"Arkady, my name it's Arkady," Arkady says.

"Of course," I say. "I know my father. I am just warming up on this one. Don't you think I know my own father?"

"Your mama, she told me about expectation you."

"She what?"

"She say you come soon. I ask Mrs. Asher, where your children, why they don't come see dying father? She look so sad. Maybe you come two weeks before, no? She say to me, you very busy man and she look very sad."

"And you said?"

"No, I say nussing. She say you too busy. What she tells you, yes, that I love father like he was my papa?"

Before I answer, Arkady's mobile phone rings and he draws the silver cell from a burnished leather holster he wears on his hip. In a single seamless flick of the wrist, which he undoubtedly learned from John Wayne, he prepares himself for the showdown. But instead he says, "Hellow, Zaryosha? How are you, my cupcake?" Arkady looks at me, muffles the speaker with his palm. "Shee so, so beautiful," he mouths and rolls his eyes around their sockets and brings the cell to his breast in a swoon.

"Do you want to know what my mother said?"

"Okay—one minute, please. Cupcake, hold me for one minute. Okay?"

"She said you talk all day with your cupcake and that you don't like to work very much."

"Yes, yes, I know she like that. I know she think I am too much in love with my cupcake. But in Israel everybody must be on phone anyways. She maybe doesn't know so much about new Israel."

I am beginning to see him. The bulbous nose is rising from the miasma. His dentures are gone. I have never seen him like that. He was always too proud—would not have been caught dead without his teeth. And his comb-over? The lock falls limp over his ear like a rotting husk of corn. "Sweet Mary Mother of God," I repeat. "It's been less than two years since I saw you last. . . ."

My mother is suddenly by my side. She gives me half a smile and then bends down to the lump.

"Asik," she says. "Zafi is here. He's come to see you. Aren't you glad to see him? Of course you are. He just got off the plane. Oh, you're all sweaty." She takes a towel from the bed table, wipes his brow, unbuttons the pyjama top and wipes his chest.

"Does anyone visit? Aya? Lela?" I ask

"No, he doesn't want anyone to see him like this," my mother says, as though the lump has made that very clear.

"But does his family know he's here?"

"I am sure they do."

I do not say anything, but I had called Lela from Toronto. She had no idea that her brother was in the hospital and was shocked when I told her that he was in a coma. She said, "Your mother always thought she owned him. . . . But I should have known when I called and got the machine. All year, Asik has been threatening to die. He kept asking when Saba Gershon died. At first I said that I couldn't remember. But then he took out his stupid calculator and so I told him. I said that Saba Gershon was the same age as you are. He was seventy-eight when he died. But he had cancer and you don't. Asik said that seventy-eight seemed like a perfect number. When next would two numbers come consecutively? Eighty-seven is backward. Eighty-nine, then? No way he could hold on for that long, he said. Seventy-eight years is enough."

My mother is mumbling something but I can't make out what she's saying. I am losing it, capable only of furtive glances at his blistered lips. I look around for a bottle of water and find one on Arkady's wagon. The catheters have frayed my father's nostrils.

"I am going to take a taxi home," I tell my mother. "I don't think I've slept much since you called. When was that? Two or three nights back?"

My father suddenly has four blurry limbs and they are all blue and black, swollen like eggplants. My insides are burning and my ears plug up as though we are about to land. All I can think to do is sit on his bed. I might lie down and sleep with him, but my mother doesn't let me do that. She hands me the key to her apartment and kisses my forehead. "I've made the bed in the little bedroom for you. There's salad and yogurt and coffee beans for the Bodum. I'll be home in a couple of hours but don't worry, just sleep as much as you need to sleep."

For a moment I just stand there, hoping against hope that Kafka was right when he said that the stillness of death is good for thinking.

—◦◦◦—

"You are lucky," says Arkady the next morning. "I never have papa."

"Did they make you from the earth of Mother Russia?" I ask.

"My papa was big cheese in cheese shop but before I was born he run from home."

Dr. Smorzik and three interns are doing the rounds. He leads them into room 7 as if he were a museum tour guide.

"This is Asher," Dr. Smorzik says of the lump.

"And this is son of Asher," Arkady tells Smorzik. "He come from Canada."

"Yes, we've met. You look better," the doctor says to me.

He removes from a bleached, knee-length white coat a toolbox of medical equipment that he places on the table at the head of my father's bed. With his thumb and forefinger he pries open my father's eyelids, notes that the left has no pigment, that the right is hazel. He peers into my father's ears.

"How is he, doctor?" I ask.

"Nothing has changed," Dr. Smorzik assures me. "He is stable, nothing dramatic, nothing at all. Your mother is not here?"

"She should be here any minute." One of the interns pulls on my arm ever so gently.

"*Adon*, sir, could you please wait outside for a while?"

Dr. Smorzik draws the curtain around the bed as though it were a bathtub.

As I am being ushered out I start to feel rage boiling up like Etna. What is this fucking place anyhow? The staff has lost my father's dentures, his chin is collapsed, his embouchure bunched at the neck. He looks like a head of garlic. The man who was my father would never have stood for such things. He was too proud and too private, too prudish. When he'd had a couple of beers, he might piss on a wall but never in my life have I seen him naked. He was the kind of guy to comb that single lock of hair across his scalp to conceal a receding hairline, as if people saw only what he wanted them to see. He would never be able to stomach what he has become in this fucking place. The rage turned against him, as I looked back at the body in the bed, surrounded by white coats.

"Abba, Father, lump or whatever the fuck your name is, you told me that you could be trusted, that I could rely on you, but you never came through. I joined your goddamn army and fought the wars that you could have prevented. And you never even bothered to find out how things stood. Did you really know or care whether I or my kid brother was alive or maybe hostages? Well, I can tell you that we both died in the war. Both of us were dead and you killed us. And now it is your turn to die. What is it that you would have me do? What more do you want? Why are you looking at me that way? Why are you lying there like that? Shall I get you a corned beef sandwich and tell them to cut it on the fat side? Is that it? Is that what you want?"

It seems to me that my father's bloated face stops bloating for a moment and that he has stepped out of his catalepsy. His toothless mouth moves. I am sure of it. His lips part and I see a faint smile break through, like a cold, midwinter sun.

My mother says, "*Bo Zafi, neelekh neeshte koss café.* On the beach, let's go and have a coffee on the beach."

<hr />

The next morning the alarm clock in my mother's room beeps. In my somnolent haze I think the beeps are the alarms for a war.

"I am making coffee," my mother says. "Shall I make you some eggs?"

I am awake now. Maybe.

I jump in and out of the shower and walk the coffee down the stairs where I can smoke. Minutes later my mother shows up and we are off to the hospital and near the end of the day to the country club at the beach. This was our routine for a week: we would drive to Meir and then in the late afternoon we would drive to the beach to relax. She'd sit at the café and read. I would jog and then join her, usually for a plate of fresh shrimps and a tall glass of arak.

Ten days have passed since I first arrived and Arkady has still not given up chatting on his cell even as he adjusts the oxygen valves for his most critical patients.

"How's Zaryosha?" I ask with unmistakable sarcasm, which Arkady mistakes for amicability.

"She zo zo beautiful. But I no see her anymore. Because of Anna. I cannot do something with that cupcake."

Arkady bends down to lift up a bed that is now empty and for the first time I notice the gold cross around his neck.

My old army buddy Benzi comes to visit around lunchtime. I complain about Arkady, and Benzi tells me that the entire Israeli health care system has been taken over by Russians.

"Do I need to worry?"

"It's a good immigration mostly," Benzi says. "But some of the Russians are wily as Stalin. Recently some Russian nurse got someone's papa to sign his estate over to him. This Arkady fellow may not have designs, but when he says he doesn't have a papa and that he loves Asher, maybe he means that he loves your papa's money even more."

"I can't quite see it happening. I mean, my dad's in a coma."

"But you never know," Benzi retorts. "Today he is in a coma, tomorrow he is up for long enough to sign over his will. I am not serious, Dave, but *Yediot Aharonot* [the country's most popular broadsheet] has been running a front-page story about some gruesome murders and unheard-of deceit foisted by a new Russian immigrant couple upon another new Russian immigrant couple."

Arkady's ginger hair is brushed back and greased. His wooden cheekbones have been inserted under button-size blue eyes. My friend Benzi suspects that Arkady is one of the 300,000 imposters who got the rights of a new immigrant by learning to say a few words in Hebrew—shalom, bar mitzvah, Mogen David wine, things like that. "And then they get here, join the army and spray paint *zhid*, dirty Jew, on the side of Merkava tanks."

But Arkady does get some things done. Even though he has no idea where they put my father's dentures, he seems to have taken a shine to the man and I am grateful for that.

I fall asleep on the chair by my father's bed and dream. I am in a raft and it has been raining for days inside the hospital. I realize that this is summer in Israel so it could not be raining. I search the ceiling pipes, many of which are exposed. The plumbing is suffering from constant cuts to the health budget. I rail about the health care budget, carry a sign that says MAH EEM HA MAYEEM— what's with all the water. I decide the best place to protest is at the bottom of the man-made pond, which is covered with the corpses of dead goldfish. I stop doctors and patients at random: "I am doing a survey, so if you can answer just this one question: why should my father, who sacrificed so much for this damned country, get such shit treatment?" I am getting angrier and almost wake myself up, but I don't. Where is the janitor? Is there a janitor in this dream? The floor tiles have become as slippery as ice and I am slipping. I am trying to hold on but I am slipping. I begin circling down the ramps—one ramp, two ramps, three ramps. It occurs to me that maybe there is no end to these ramps. A young man wearing Dr. Smorzik's white coat passes by.

"Pardon me," I ask. "I seem to have missed the door. Can I smoke in here maybe?"

"You must be new around here," he says. "Only dead people think there is a door."

I wake up. I am in a haze, and my head is throbbing. I strain to look up at the ceiling. It is not raining but there is liquid, a thick mucus splashing onto my sandals. I trace the floor and realize that the flow is coming from my father's fingertips. They have become faucets. Horrified, I realize that his skin has shut down and is leaking its fluids. What do I do? Is his entire body leaking? Will the level rise and wash him out to sea?

Arkady arrives and swaddles my father's hand in gauze. When I get up, I notice that they have done a tracheotomy.

"Who the fuck authorized that?" I scream at Arkady.

"Speak to Smorzik," he says.

"You've been a good son," Benzi tells me. "You can't blame yourself."

"Yes I can."

"But it won't help."

"It might."

"What do you think you did wrong?"

"How long a list do you want?"

"A short one will do."

"Well, when I was a kid, I invariably took my mother's side against him. She demanded that he toe the line but somehow, even as a kid, I knew he was not a toe-the-line kind of guy. But I felt sorry for her when he didn't show up for dinner. And I felt sorry for myself and for my brother when he came in drunk. But how could he have survived without drinking? He had ambitions—to open up a factory, to design things. But every-thing he wanted to do needed some capital. And she wanted the pittance that he was making to pay for a better home and maybe vacations. At the very least they were both equally wrong, probably should not have had children in the first place. But I never saw it from his point of view. And then I ran off and joined your fucking army, despite him. And I never, ever called him Dad. Not once. How's that for starters?"

"And what did he do to you? He let your mother take over your life. And he filled you up with love of his country. What did he expect? I am sure that he wasn't the least surprised when you enlisted."

"I am quite sure that he was entirely beside himself."

"Anyhow, I think that you not calling him Dad was just your way of letting him know that he wasn't acting like much of a father. I think that many of us feel that way about our fathers. I mean, his entire generation was so self-absorbed and absorbed with each other and with creating this country they didn't have time to worry much about their kids. And we all thought that. You were maybe a little more strident than most of us. But then

Kibbutz
Kids
✗

again I know at least two other Sabras who don't call their parents Abba or Eema or anything at all. And, of course, almost all the kibbutznikim call their parents by their first names. In fact, the whole idea of kibbutz education was all about biology not mattering."

Benzi and I are sitting outside the hospital looking at a dozen rabbinical students facing west and chanting. He is in lecture mode and I am feeling strangely receptive. He can tell me whatever he wants.

"Where is mama?" a scrubbed, cheery Arkady says as he fiddles with an empty bag of glucose.

"I convinced her to take the morning off."

"So maybe I tell you something about papa?"

"About his condition?" I say anxiously.

"Something maybe you don't know—your papa, he dream in Russian."

"What are you talking about? My father doesn't speak Russian."

"He do. I hear him in the sleep. First time maybe when he come to hospital. I am on night shift."

I am dumbfounded.

"What did he say?"

"Your papa, he is a war hero. He says he gives you name of best friend who killed near Jerusalem. He loves Israel, but he loves his son much more. He say he move out from Israel because he wants son not to be soldier. He says he could not live if bad happens to son. I maybe hear him say that he thinks you were war hero like him."

I can't get my mind around this idea at the moment. All I can think about is whether this nurse has some plan up his sleeve and that I am missing something. How dare he know more about my father than I do? He has no right.

Dr. Smorzik and three interns are doing rounds again. Smorzik asks me how I am doing.

Arkady interrupts, "He is angry because tracheotomy."

Dr. Smorzik looks at me and says, "It will make it easier for your father."

"But doesn't the law state that the family has to agree? Isn't there a consent form we have to sign?"

"It had become impossible for him to breathe," the doctor says. "There really was no choice."

—⊗⊗⊗—

I had my reasons for not calling you Dad. But my mother, your wife, did not help. I agree with you there. "Abba lo heegiya, Dad has not arrived," she would say. "Abba doesn't give a damn." Especially in her Jewish period. Remember her Jewish period, when she decided that the only thing that would hold us together as a family was Sabbath? "Ever since I've come from work," she would say, "I've been cooking and cleaning for the Sabbath and Abba lo mageeyuh. He just doesn't give a damn. It is Friday night and we are supposed to eat together, like a family, but Abba is a goy, a peasant . . ."

It was my birthday, and then it was Daniel's birthday, but Abba became a person who does not arrive. Whenever you came home, I thought: This couldn't be Abba because Abba does not come home. But then who were you?

You couldn't be Dad or Father because fathers were named Ward and they wore suits and taught their boys to pitch a ball. They spoke English for chrissakes. You would come home smelling of whisky and you didn't speak at all. And I couldn't call you Asher or Asik because your wife often called me Asher or Asik. It was a slip of the tongue, of course, but it was one of those slips that a person should be shot for.

It always began the same way. Your wife would say, "Go change your clothes. I can't stand the smell of machine oil and Ajax and whisky." She would say you smelled like a goy. The Sabbath food and the Sabbath tablecloth and our clean clothes smelled Jewish. Your smell was the smell of the enemy.

I was glad you were home but your smell made me think of danger. You would start touching her at the table, calling her baby or bubele or whatever, and then her tears would become impossible to contain. She would cry and you would try to comfort her. Then she would explode and you would get up and pretend to leave, maybe even open the door, and she would chase you and scream. "You are disturbing the fucking neighbours," you would say. "We'll be evicted again."

Before Danny and I knew it the two of you would make your way into the bedroom and shut the door. We would have to listen to your sex. Okay. It was a small apartment. Maybe you had no choice.

But what about us? Who were we? The goddamn Greek chorus?

There was this one Friday night. It began the same way as always. You came home late. Your wife began to weep, soon uncontrollably, bending over her plate to prevent bits of half-chewed chicken from spraying. You joked in that warped Moshavnik way that you had, saying to us, "Ma asseetem la?" (What have you done to her?) No one moved. You looked at us, your boys, and you noticed that neither of us could hold your gaze. Your wife's sobs faded. You put down your fork. Your face had lost its glow, which was probably only Canadian Club.

"Heevanti, I understand now," you said after a while, fixing your eyes on your wife. "Heesatet et ha'yeladim negedee. You have turned the children against me."

There was a brutality in your voice that I had never heard before. You had never laid a finger on any of us. But suddenly I realized that you could. Then you said that the jig was up, that it was over, now that you got her plan.

"What would you like me to do?" she sobbed. "Tell you that I have brainwashed my little children and that I turned them against you? How stupid can you be? Where were you when I was turning your children against you? Wasn't it your absence that turned my children against you?"

"Your children? Your children? With my little pinky I could crush your children into nothing."

And we, your children, sat there frozen, horrified, thinking that this was what you were about to do.

I realized that all the promises you made to us that never happened, all the bullshit stories that you told, had very little to do with me or with Daniel; they had to do with you and your wife. I don't think you didn't care about us. I am sure you did. But I am also sure that both of you were warriors and in that theatre Daniel and I were the chorus. The woman you married and loved, you also hated and wanted to destroy. And you were prepared to threaten to kill her children to get back at her.

—◦◦◦—

The phone beside my bed rings. It is 3:45 a.m. and I decide to ignore it. The answering machine picks up.

"Shalom, this is Erena from Meir Hospital. I think you should get yourselves here soon as possible."

I run to interrupt the machine.

"Hello, Erena. . . ."

"Yes."

"Is he still alive?"

"I can't say anything, but I think you should get here as soon as possible. Shalom."

There's a creak from across the hall. My mother, wearing the remains of the night, peeks into the room. Her face is sombre.

"Who was that?" she asks, as if there were any doubt.

"They want us at the hospital as soon as possible."

She turns back into her room. Dutifully, mechanically, she shuffles like an old diva making up her face for the final curtain. It is five minutes before the curtain, five minutes before she must face her leading man, but she will take her time, make them wait for her. My mother must put on her face.

I slip on the clothes I left on the floor, brush my teeth, pour boiling water to make a cup of coffee, and then go downstairs to smoke. I wish the camera would leave me alone. I wish I could just act as though there were no audience. I so much want to feel everything that I can feel pushing from the other side, madly trying to get in. But I don't have the power to raise the curtain. I want the curtain just to rise on its own without me doing anything.

And then I realize that it is this very anxiety, this thick smog that floats about, that I can't get off. This is how I create and re-create the viciousness of the circle in which I can hardly breathe. I want to breathe different air.

Three cigarettes later my mother emerges from the doorway.

"I will drive," I say.

Erena meets us in the hallway.

"He died at 2:30 a.m.," she says. "I am sorry."

My mother walks in front of me into the room. I see the corpse and it has been covered with a crisp, white sheet. I do not enter the room; I let her have her moment. She is as white as the sheet. And then she pulls it back, tears streaming down her face.

"*Nu* Asik, *ha rikood shelanu nigmar*—our dance is over," she tells him.

"No. No. No—" that is all I can think. I can't help it. My tears are now flowing unchecked. My mother pulls a chair up beside the bed upon which my father once lay. She holds the corpse's hand in hers. It is the same hand that not so long ago was leaking. And she is looking down at the floor. For a long time she just looks down at the floor. And then she gets up, covers the corpse, smiles the most painful smile I have ever seen, and walks over to me.

"This is for you," my mother says, handing me a sealed envelope.

"What is it?"

"It is from your father. He left it for you, made me swear that I would not open it. I will sit here for a while."

I take the envelope and go down the purple ramp that ends at the foyer. I drag myself outside and find a crumpled cigarette in my pocket. Someone offers me a light and I take a drag and another one. The cigarette is wet and breaks off at the filter. My nose won't stop running and my head hurts, my hands are trembling and my vision is totally blurred. But still I manage to open the envelope.

It says, "Zafi, *shmor al ha-medina shelee ha-ktana.* Abba."

Zafi, take care of my little country. Dad.

—✇—

Death did not end things. I walked away from my father's grave feeling as though his unnamed spirit was now inside me and that neither of us would rest until I got to the bottom of it.

The tension that had always been there between my father and me broke suddenly, and was gone. I found myself wondering not just about him and me, but about his generation, the Sabras, and mine. If once I had asked myself who was that masked man whose passion had named me and then unnamed me, and whom I could not name, now I was wondering about an entire generation of parents who had emasculated the generation to whom they had given life. I realized that there was no clause in their pioneering spirit that required them to nurture those children—the nation they had conceived. It was not their mandate. They were not the guides. They made the necessary process of individuation almost impossible. In fact, in their naivety, they thwarted it and this has had profound consequences, not just for me but for Israel.

SIX

The Disengagement

When the plane lands at Ben-Gurion Airport on June 14, 2005, there are still six weeks to go before Israeli soldiers are scheduled to clear the Jewish settlements in Gaza. Everything I had read about Ariel Sharon's disengagement plan before I got on the plane painted a sober portrait. The Israeli press was filled with heart-rending cries of distress. Several senior Israeli leaders, including its Supreme Court chief justice, Aaron Barak, had cancelled speeches on the grounds that the country was about to enter into a civil war. Young Gaza settlers were threatening to commit suicide rather than be evacuated. Many of those young people, and their settler parents, had always thought of themselves as Israel's front line, its new pioneers, and they argued, quite correctly, that they had been manning the barricades in Gaza all these years at the behest of the Israeli government. More controversial was the declaration from YESHA (the settlers' leadership) that the twenty-one Jewish settlements in Gaza would be destroyed in order to further the political ambitions of a corrupt, treasonous man—Sharon. Israelis who supported the disengagement had no stomach for such declarations, and Sharon's supporters were calling the Gaza settlers *ohley heenum*—parasites and racist scum.

At the airport's baggage claim, employees in favour of the disengagement are wearing sky-blue bandanas wrapped around their foreheads in support of the government position. Representing the opposition , a very young seminarian, sporting a beard so emphatic it looked like he might have rented it, hands out brochures and orange baseball hats imprinted with the protest movement's slogan: A JEW DOES NOT BANISH A JEW. The anti-disengagement forces have stolen the orange of the Ukraine's Orange Revolution as its team colour.

"*Teelboshet loveshet teelboshet*, a disguised disguise," sneers a handsome, elderly woman just behind me. She and I are so taken aback by the exuberance of this young man that we back up into half a dozen tourists who stand there paralyzed, either taking in the scene or reconsidering their entire trip to the Holy Land. A group of Christian clerics openly stare at some Brooklyn-born rabbinical students wearing orange running shoes and orange baseball caps under black, broad-rimmed *streimal*. Religion, they are undoubtedly thinking, is supposed to be more serious than this.

I am in Israel to write about Operation Main Event—the code name the Israeli military has given to the campaign as a whole. But it soon becomes clear that the simple act of deciding which act in this multi-ring circus is the main one will probably take up more than the eight weeks I plan to be in the country. "Just keep your head above water," I mutter to myself. And then I spot my friend Gidi Netzer, who has come to pick me up.

"Read how the Sharon family is selling out the Jews," a young sidelocked settler says to me as he stuffs a brochure into my pocket. I head toward my friend, Colonel Gidi.

"*Azvu oto be'nouach*. Let him be. Let people breathe," Gidi instructs the settler with a smile, then navigates me away through the crowd. "Everyone is pretty hot under the collar," he adds.

"Is the entire country like this?" I ask.

"Pretty much. The disengagement is driving us all crazy."

In his late fifties, Gidi is wearing what he always wears, what he may have been born in, what his closet is for sure bursting with—a dark blue denim work shirt that he half tucks into a pair of worn jeans. His wispy white hair, to which an unobtrusive knitted skullcap is pinned, is far longer and more dishevelled than one might expect from a man who makes his living as a consultant on international terror. A pair of cheery blue eyes, a button nose and a round chin graced with two-day stubble makes Gideon seem like the perfect welcome wagon, something between a Macy's Santa and Snuffleupagus. At the moment to me he also seems like the single still point in a raging storm.

"David, you wouldn't believe how much shit is going on around here," he says as he unlocks the trunk of his car and throws my baggage inside. We climb in and he drives off toward my mother's apartment in Ramat HaSharon. En route I notice that the billboards that once advertised various products are now plastered with mug shots of the prime minister labelled ARIEL "THE BULLDOZER" SHARON. Rubber-stamped on Sharon's forehead is the word *BOGED*—traitor.

"How long will you stay?" Gidi asks

"Until it's over. So, are you going to give me the lowdown on the disengagement?"

For Gidi, the question acts like a corkscrew. Within seconds he is bubbling over. "You know I am actually too old to be conscripted into the reserves, but I've been called up anyway. I'm to play the babysitter. I am supposed to chaperone officers, move the furniture around so they don't walk into things, clean up after them. I'm supposed to calm down the settlers, make sure none of them get violent, maybe tell them bedtime stories about how great life after Gaza will be. The IDF wants me in civilian clothes, but I am to be Brigadier General Gershon HaCohen's right-hand man. Many years ago Gershon served in a unit under my command. Now he's in charge of the entire disengagement campaign. He is probably the best man for the job, but the army still thinks I should be there to hold his hand."

He goes on. "The worst thing is the Israeli politicians. They are all driving me out of my mind. I told them that it was crap to deploy Israeli soldiers against Israeli civilians. If they had to use the army, which I don't think they do, they should put the soldiers in police uniforms. They should make sure that the settlers believe they are being evicted by the police and not by the army. Otherwise we violate the very idea of the IDF as a people's army. To send in the military is to risk alienating and traumatizing the best young settler kids. David, just imagine that you are an eighteen-year-old boy born in one of the Jewish settlements in Gaza. You've never known any Israel that did not include Gaza. All your life you've thought of yourself as a real patriot. You've maybe lost a father or a sibling or a friend in the skirmishes with the Arabs or in the shelling of your village. When you turned eighteen, you've always planned to volunteer for a commando unit or become a pilot. And then Israeli soldiers arrive at your home and they drag you and your eighty-year-old grandfather out of the house he built with his bare hands. How do you feel? Would you not become half crazed by it all? For the rest of your life would you have anything more pressing upon your mind than rage? But the politicos aren't paying attention. Sharon wants to prove that the entire country supports his plan. He is insisting on the army because the army is the people and the people are the army. They certainly won't be after the campaign."

As a religious nationalist, Gidi occupies a unique position within the maelstrom of Israeli politics. On the one hand he truly believes that God promised the land of Israel, whose borders extend as far as Jordan, Iraq, Lebanon and Syria, to the Jewish people. On the other hand, he thinks that the good Lord never said when this real estate would be ours. Gidi feels the urgency of these convictions in his belly, but he also believes that the state is the final arbiter of such things.

"What can I tell you, David? This is the worst assignment I've ever had and I have had a lot of shit assignments over my forty years in and out of the army. This disengagement is a hundred times worse than the one from Yamit." He's referring to the Israeli settlement established in northern Sinai after the Six Day War, which was handed back to Egypt in 1982 as part of the peace treaty. "At the very least Yamit was handed over to Egypt as part of a deal," Gidi says. "But here we get nothing for all our trouble. In fact no good can possibly come out of this one. Nothing will change except maybe the terrorists will get a better shot at our towns. I don't know if you know this, but

I think of many of the settlers as my children. Many of them were in fact my soldiers and I personally helped found two of the Gaza settlements. So, all told, I am sick to death about things and worried to death as well."

Gidi's cellphone rings.

"Yes, yes. Tell the general that I will come see him as soon as the Sabbath is over." He gives me a what-did-I-tell-you eye-roll and carries on talking until we pull up in front of my mother's apartment.

Gaza is a stretch of land forty-five kilometres long and five and a half kilometres wide. It borders on Israel to the north and east. The Mediterranean forms its western border and the Egyptian-controlled Sinai Peninsula butts up against it on the south. To get what all the bluster is about, it helps to know a little history, which in this case begins in 1947 when some 800,000 Palestinian residents were displaced by the Arab-Israeli war over Israel's independence. Roughly 100,000 to 200,000 displaced Palestinians, mostly from Israel's coastal plains, took refuge in Gaza alongside a handful of indigenous Gazans, some of whom claimed to hail back to the pre-Christian era. On May 14, 1948, when Israel declared independence, Gaza came under Egyptian rule, where it remained for the next thirty-odd years. Eight UN-registered refugee camps were established during this period. The largest, Jabaliyah, sits on a paltry three square kilometres and is home to more than 90,000 refugees. Jabaliyah is considered the most densely populated area on the planet.

In 1958, Egyptian president Gamal Abdul Nasser conferred upon the Palestinian population in Gaza the status of a discrete "entity." Though this designation did nothing to ameliorate conditions in the camps, it did confer a symbolic political independence on the Strip. In Nasser's pro-Soviet, pan-Arabic entente called the United Arab Republic, Gaza became a rallying cry.

On June 6, 1967, at 7:45 a.m., the Israeli minister of defence, Moshe Dayan, issued orders to General Yitzhak Rabin to "complete the conquest of Gaza," which Rabin summarily undertook. Initially Gazans treated the Israeli troops as if they were their Moses come to free the Gazans from the Egyptian pharoah, but by the early 1970s they viewed Israel as an occupier. In the meantime, the ruling Labor Party approached the secular kibbutz movement with an offer to establish several military/agricultural settlements in Gaza. The kibbutzim refused, but another faction, the religious Zionist Bnei Akiva movement, took up the offer and over the next three years established two Jewish settlements, Kfar Darom and Netzer Hazan, in the heart of an Arab population in Gaza that was growing ever more hostile.

In early 1978 the right-wing Likud coalition became the government of Israel. On its watch, the Jewish settlements in Gaza flourished. By late 2003, when Prime Minister Ariel Sharon announced that Israel would be evacuating the Strip, there were twenty-one Jewish settlements with a total population of about seven thousand—small islands in an ocean of Arabs comprising 1.2 million people, more than half of whom were under the age of eighteen.

By 2003, the occupation of Gaza in general, and the Jewish settlement project in particular, had become an albatross for

Israel. To the settlements, the government was delivering heavily subsidized water supplies, export relief and, at an annual cost of some 450 million shekels, security, including checkpoints, patrols and escorts for the settler population. The number of civil servants in Gaza on the Israeli government payroll—mayors, deputy mayors, assistant deputy mayors, assistants to the assistant deputy mayor, liaison officers, religious leaders, social workers—was many times the national average.

As a result of the escalating conflict with the Palestinians, Jewish Gaza had become an increasingly traumatized community. The government psychologists and social workers I interviewed there described a "mini-holocaust" of mental health problems, especially afflicting the young settler children. Communities were plagued with pre-teen bed wetters. Teenagers suffered from a dizzying array of mental health problems: severe agitation, ADD, tantrums, nightmares. One psychologist working in Neve Dekalim, the capital city of Jewish Gaza, told me that he had developed dozens of strategies to get around the Orthodox leadership, which prescribed a one-pill cure—prayer. "I tell the rabbi that we are taking the kids to the zoo and then I get children to talk about what is bothering the animals." Another psychologist told me that she takes teenagers from the settlements on tours of the Israeli Institute for the Blind: "They have a room that is all black and which is supposed to give guests the experience of being blind. More often than not, the kids can't manage it for more than a few minutes. To manage they would have to rely on their feelings but they don't want to get anywhere near their feelings." Another government psychologist told me, "If you believe the Orthodox leadership, the entire Strip is one big summer camp." Every Israeli professional with

179

whom I spoke complained bitterly about the rabbinical leadership of the settlements, and the blind eye they turn to the realities facing the settlers in order to maintain the illusion of "settlement."

By the time Sharon put forward the plan to withdraw from Gaza in 2003, 60 to 70 percent of Israelis supported the campaign. This, of course, did not mean that Israelis were prepared for a bloodbath. Nor did it mean that the Israeli population would line up behind any blueprint proposed to them. In point of fact, the number of Israelis supporting the disengagement was more or less the same as the number supporting a withdrawal from all the occupied territories. In both cases, the actual numbers could only be gleaned in the context of a particular plan and at a particular moment in time.

To try to make sense of Sharon's decision to withdraw from the Gaza settlements at this particular moment is to enter a rat's maze. After all, he was largely responsible for the settlement project in the first place, as the program's chief architect and main advocate. Indeed, cynical Israelis argued that Sharon suddenly embraced the idea of withdrawing so that he might successfully postpone an impending trial in which he and his two sons were charged with illegal solicitation of electoral campaign funds. But though many Israelis thought the campaign financing allegations had merit, very few actually believed that Sharon, a seventy-eight-year-old warrior who had put his life on the line for the country so many times, would risk Israel's future in order to save his own skin.

Most did believe, however, that Sharon's decision had something to do with the so-called "mutiny of the pilots." Some months before Sharon announced the Disengagement Plan, more than a dozen senior fighter pilots refused to report for reserve duty to protest the alleged brutality of General Dan Halutz, then the Israeli Air Force's commander-in-chief. The pilots claimed that Halutz was bomb-happy. On numerous occasions, the general had ordered that double and triple the prescribed payloads be dropped on targets in Gaza. When the pilots argued that the risks of collateral damage were too high from such a campaign, Halutz dismissed them and went so far as to publicly declare that he still slept "like a baby." Sharon, who considered several of the pilots personal friends, worried that if the mutiny were successful Gaza as a whole might become off-limits for the IAF.

The Israeli political commentator and TV personality Immanuel Rosen told me that the idea of disengaging from Gaza was sparked not by Sharon nor by any member of his team but by a journalist. According to Rosen, Sharon got the idea during an intermission in talks with Vladimir Putin in November 2003. "A whole bunch of Israeli reporters tagged along with Sharon on the trip to the Kremlin," Rosen said. "Arik was melancholic. Everyone and his uncle had come forward with some grand political scheme to end the Intifada. 'What would you do if you were the leader of the governing party?' Sharon asked the Israeli press. Someone said 'Get out of Gaza,' and that was that." In a now famous interview, Sharon's closest associate, the lawyer Dov Weisglass, declared that "the Disengagement would put all the other schemes [to end the Intifada] into formaldehyde."

When I interviewed Weisglass in his office on Lilenblum Street in south Tel Aviv, he dismissed the prime minister's personal motives. "Sharon would never put his own interests before the country's. In fact," Weisglass said, "the idea of withdrawing from Gaza began taking shape in Sharon's mind in 2002, when the young King Abdullah of Jordan wrote to the US president, George W. Bush, begging the president to intervene on behalf of the Palestinian people. On the twenty-fourth of June of that year, Bush gave the famous speech that reversed the world's priorities. 'I want a road map to peace,' Bush said. 'The first thing that needs to happen is that the terror must stop. Only then can we talk about negotiations.' For Sharon, this was his wettest dream come true."

Weisglass told me that Sharon was prepared to do anything to make Bush's "road map" a reality: "Critics of the road map both in Israel and abroad argued that the plan was nothing more than a strategy for stalling the peace process ad infinitum and that Sharon's government had bought into it only as a way of maintaining the status quo, avoiding the question of the occupied territories entirely. It did not take very long before Sharon understood just how vulnerable and unpopular the road map was. Everywhere he travelled, critics, including most leaders of the European Union and Russia but also large numbers of Jewish communities in the United States, argued vehemently that Israel has no business in the occupied territories. Sharon needed to do something to persuade the world that this was not Israel's intention. The main idea of the disengagement was to support the road map."

Many of Israel's most astute political analysts, including Ron Pundak, who co-authored the Oslo Accord, argued that the Palestinian Authority president, Mahmoud Abbas, should be credited with Israel's withdrawal. "Failing to cooperate with the moderate, secular Palestinian leadership," Pundak argued, "would result in Hamas taking the credit and soon enough in a Hamas takeover of the Strip." When I asked Weisglass why

Sharon dismissed the possibility of coordinating the disengagement with Abbas, he leaned back in his chair, inadvertently calling my attention to a series of chummy photographs that hung on the wall behind him (one featured Bush putting him in a mock chokehold). "There is no one amongst the Palestinian leaders with whom Sharon could have negotiated," Weisglass said. "Abbas's support extends to maybe one half of the population of Ramallah and no more. Besides, Sharon was not worried about a Hamas takeover. There were, after all, over forty thousand Fatah police in Gaza. And unlike the Palestinian police in Judea and Samaria, these guys are permitted to carry arms in public. Against such force, Sharon believed, Hamas could do nothing."

When I thought about the disengagement as the first move toward an all-encompassing interim agreement or as the first stage of a comprehensive withdrawal from all the occupied territories, including the West Bank and parts of the Golan Heights, it seemed like a good idea. But when I thought about it as a final concession, aimed at preserving the occupation of the West Bank, it seemed like an absolute disaster. And no matter how I turned things around in my mind, no matter how many people I spoke to, I could neither firm up my own thinking nor understand how it was that so many Israelis, many of whom knew less about Sharon's intentions than I did, were yet able to take sides decisively.

—◆◆◆—

A couple of weeks after arriving in Israel, I published a piece in *Haaretz* called *"Seret Sagol"* or "Purple Ribbon." In it I proposed that Israelis trade in both the anti-disengagement orange banners and the blue-and-white Israeli team colours and go with a colour at once more demanding and more contemplative—purple. My argument was that Israelis do not know enough to take an informed position and that as a result we should not do so. To take sides for or against the disengagement was simply a bad idea. Better to sit on the fence. Why was that so difficult? Why did so many Israelis, who neither trusted Sharon nor believed that he had a game plan, still play his game? The answer, I wrote, is that it is a matter of national character: To a great majority of Israelis, refusing to take a position risks appearing innocent—or worse, stupid. On the newspaper website, the piece received dozens of "talk backs" and for days afterward I got phone calls from Israeli writers and journalists, many of whom agreed with my formulation of the national character. For a moment I actually believed that a purple ribbon movement might arise out of the blue. I could not have been more mistaken.

On a beautiful morning in mid-July, I set out to join two Israeli photojournalists, Miki Kratsman and Eldad Rafaeli, on a trip into Gaza and then back across the border and on to Netivot, where the first monster protest rally against the disengagement is to be held. Riding with my window down on the early morning bus into town, I inhale the mesmerizing perfume of the crisp, clean morning air, and I am lulled into optimism about what the day will bring. Despite everything I know about the faulty design of this campaign, and despite the fact that there is so much talk about a civil war, it is a new day and I am excited and hopeful on the bus. But the day will eventually become unbearable.

Thoughts about the weeks leading into America's current war in Iraq knock at the back door of my mind, but I am reluctant to answer. Shouldn't I be more cynical? More realistic? The weather is just not letting me go to dark places. It is almost as though it has taken sides, giving me no choice but to think happy thoughts. Why should I not go with the majority of Israelis who support Sharon? Is not a partial withdrawal better than nothing? So what if there is a civil war? Maybe only a real confrontation between seculars and settlers will settle matters, and if it has to happen, why not now?

Somebody's grandmother in thick horn-rimmed glasses is sitting near me reading *Haaretz*. I can hardly help peering over her shoulder, reading the back page only and, I think, discreetly. At the next bus stop, the woman gets up, folds her paper and hands it to me without a word. A quick perusal takes the morning's exhilaration down a notch. The paper's editor, David Landau, has obviously decided that the disengagement is a good idea and that the paper does not need to maintain any distance from Sharon's position. The editorial page reads like propaganda and I don't like being pushed around. Is the fix really in? Are we on a path from which there is no turning back? Thankfully I remember to look up in time to realize that we have arrived at the train station on Haifa Road. I push the stop button and get off the bus. A moment later a car pulls up and, although I have never met Miki Kratsman, I somehow know that Miki is the one who's driving and Eldad, whose shoulder-length dreadlocks are truly impressive, is the passenger already in the car.

Argentinian born Miki steps out of the car to greet me. He is heavy-set and rather dishevelled. His Hebrew is tinged with a South American accent. We exchange pleasantries as he clears some room for me in the back seat and he introduces me to Eldad. "Eldad and I have been trying to capture the anti-disengagement period, a process we call *ha'netisha*, the voluntary abandonment of the settlements, which is the phase before forceful banishment," Miki tells me, as he shifts the car into gear and drives off.

"Do you really think there is no alternative to the use of force?" I ask. "What if instead of bulldozing the settlers out of Gaza, we invited their leaders to Jerusalem, thanked them for holding the fort, maybe decorated them with a couple of Order of Israel medals, and got them to buy into the new agenda? If it worked, we'd be saving the couple of billion dollars that this campaign will cost."

Miki may be sensitive, but he evidently doesn't get my worry, or simply does not suffer fools. He looks into the rear-view mirror as though I may be just the kind of person he doesn't suffer. "What is it that you have been drinking so early in the morning?" he says with only half a smile. "Who in the world wants to reward those pigs? They've been *ohley hinam*, freeloaders, since they first settled in Gaza. We've been subsidizing their water supply, paying through the nose for their security, granting them huge tax breaks, and for what? So they can go beat up on some poor Palestinian workers? In an hour you'll see for yourself how they live—in unabashed luxury right next to entire Arab communities living in shacks with no running water." Miki says that YESHA wants Sharon to hold a referendum—if the nation votes to accept the disengagement, YESHA said, they would accept it. But an editorial in *Haaretz* blew off the demand. Miki paraphrases from memory: "There is no more justification for a referendum now than there was a justification for a referendum back when the settlement movement dismantled the country's social programs and forced the occupation down our throats. The settlers did not hold a referendum asking us whether we wanted to become occupiers. They didn't ask us whether we were prepared to give up the welfare state for the sake of the settlements. Why should we grant their demand for a referendum?"

We drive through the Erez checkpoint at the north end of the Gaza Strip, down through Dugit and Elei Sinai, secular settlements from which most of the inhabitants have already left. Some settlers have taken the government financial packages. The seasonal workers and recent Russian immigrants to Israel who came to Gaza looking for employment have moved on as easily as they came. And yet it is clear the entrenched settlers do not make a distinction between itinerant workers and anyone else: to them, betrayal is betrayal and it does not matter who is doing it, and they have spray-painted swastikas on the exterior walls of abandoned matchbox-size homes. We make several stops to document these empty houses. On several filthy living room walls the words *bogdeem* (traitors) and *sonei Yisrael* (despisers of Israel) are brushed on in paint as thin, drippy and red as the blood Charles Manson's cult members used to write "Helter Skelter" on the walls of the Tate mansion. Miki and Eldad shoot kitchens littered with half-eaten cans of tuna, sardines, broken bottles of Galilee vodka. There's a child's bedroom with a dozen decapitated doll heads strewn about. At another stop, we walk into a field of shrivelled tomato plants where a wrinkled Arab man is dragging greenhouse structures to a huge pile near a flatbed truck. "I will miss the Jews when they are gone," he tells us. "They were good employers for nearly forty years." The photographers snap a picture and wish the man well.

In front of houses in the new ghost town of Peut Sadeh, dozens of black Mercedes-Benzes, plundered from Lebanon during Israel's eighteen-year occupation, appear to have been abandoned. Disgusted, Miki mentions the obvious: because the occupation as a whole violates international law, no one here has bothered much with the rules, including the Israeli laws prohibiting war-time pillage. A wind blows through the streets, bringing an air of the Wild West to this place where, not so long ago, entire swaths of humanity lived by their own rules, in a self-contained bubble in which every man is the law and respect for other men must be negotiated anew at every corner. I am reminded of my time in the Sinai oil town of Abu Rodez. At eighteen, just before I was drafted, I got a job driving young women who cleaned house and performed off-the-menu services for the criminal types who lived there. The oil town was a Disneyworld of drugs and prostitution, a perfect place to experience the savage side of life. In large regions of Gaza, the same black market mindset prevailed, except that in Gaza the intoxicating substances are heavily laced with religion.

Kfar Darom, where we go next, is the amygdala of Jewish

Gaza, a dark, self-enclosed settlement formed around a hard core of religious fanaticism. From our IDF sources we'd learned that Kfar Darom has the most intransigent settlers in the Strip and will probably be the last to be evacuated. If there is too much violence at the beginning of the disengagement, Miki explains, the nation will lose heart and Sharon will be forced to abandon the campaign. Miki had called ahead, arranging with the rabbi for a visit to the yeshiva. As we drive past the sentry at the town gate, Eldad tells us that he is willing to bet that not a single settler has yet abandoned this site. "If anything, the population here has grown. Probably everybody's blood relatives are arriving to help man the barricades," he says.

"So, why are we bothering with this place? Aren't you guys supposedly only interested in 'abandonment'?" I ask.

Miki smiles sardonically. "Compared with this place, everywhere else is child's play," he says. "Here the stakes are magnificently high. Here, we're not talking about leaving a house or a town, we're talking about whether God will or will not abandon his most faithful. All the settlers will be looking to Kfar Darom. They will be watching and praying that the Messiah shows up here. The fate of the entire project and maybe the entire Orthodox tradition is to be decided right here."

He parks near the synagogue and, as soon as we get out of the car, a steely-eyed seminarian points his M16 at us and demands that we leave the way we came. "Strangers are not welcome," he says, even as he introduces himself as Shimshon. Some of the settlers may think all of this evacuation stuff is a big game. Not this guy. He has no use for three anthropologists who are here to chronicle the extinction of his species.

Miki informs Shimshon that we have an appointment with the rabbi of the town and God's warrior agrees to phone his fearless leader, who soon arrives, already smiling. "You can't blame the kids," the rabbi says cheerily. "Your presence here makes them feel as if the place has become a public zoo. Unfortunately, I can't let you go into the yeshiva. I know I said I would, but things have changed. Isn't that what Arik said? Things have changed? But you can shoot from the back door. You've brought zoom lenses, have you not?"

The prayers are shrill. Perspiring yeshiva boys are huddled in pockets, cardio-genuflecting and then resting up from the exertion. The young men in this room do not display the pallor and bad skin of the young men who attended the Volozhin Yeshiva in TK CITY, founded by my relative, Rabbi Naftali Tsvi Yehuda Berlin. Here the boys lift weights and shoot from the hip. "We are preparing for the advent of the Messiah," one bronzed student tells us as he walks us back toward the car.

"What will the Messiah do with my kind of Jew?" Eldad asks, amused.

"You will be destroyed," says the boy.

Speeding along the Strip's main highway, the three of us are feeling listless. A few more hours in this madhouse and we too might go crazy. From the apartheid highway we can see the back road reserved for Palestinians. Beat-up mini vans—taxis that might just as well be bow-legged camels—trail off into nowhere. Miki says that most of the same vehicles, which never get through the checkpoint, will be here tomorrow and the next day and the day after that. Eldad, who is perhaps feeling as though he's been browbeaten enough for one day, shoots back.

"Do you really think we're treating them worse than the Egyptians did?" Miki replies that he's not sure.

⸺

We arrive in Netivot less than two hours before the first settler-organized protest rally is scheduled to begin. Netivot was built in the mid-fifties as one of a string of small towns whose purpose was to develop the Israeli countryside and to spread out the immigrant population, which tended to cluster in the big cities on the Mediterranean coast. Dour, half-vacant strip malls line both sides of the street. Signage is mostly in Cyrillic or Hebrew with bad spelling mistakes. From tenement balconies, posters declaring that Sharon is a traitor have replaced the usual strings of wet laundry. We drive into the only plaza that seems vaguely alive and park at a kebab joint that turns out to be filled with probably half of the photographers in the country. Some are leaning on serious chrome motorbikes. Others are sitting on folding chairs guzzling beer and munching on skewered lamb. Everyone has an open laptop, and seems to be clicking through their set of disengagement shots.

Miki introduces me to a photojournalist whose name I do not catch but who tilts his laptop in my direction and clicks on a file titled EARLY FRAMEEM (Israeli-speak for frames or shots). He scrolls through pictures of young settlers wearing yellow stars like those the Nazis forced all Jews to wear. "I missed those," I say. "What happened to them?"

"When the settlers co-opted the Nazi insignia the entire country went berserk. Turns out that even in the disengagement there are rules. You can threaten to launch a civil war or claim you are going to drown all your children in the Gaza Sea, but you can't use certain icons—not at least without paying the royalties," he says.

Ten or fifteen minutes go by and then many of the cameramen begin revving up their bikes. Miki, Eldad and I pick up three shawarmas, three diet Cokes, and leaking tahini, head for Baba Sali Square, where the action is supposed to be.

⸺◦◦◦⸺

When the Moroccan-born Kabbalist Yisrael Abu-Hatseira, known as Baba Sali, died in 1984, his son Baruch built a tomb, erected a synagogue adorned with a pristine white cupola and tiled a plaza at the centre of Netivot to commemorate his renowned father. According to articles published in the Israeli press at the time, the construction of the square had less to do with the dead father than with the son's masterful attempt to bury his criminal past. Baba Baruch, as he is now called, emerged from the criminal netherworld to become a devout, respectable and worshipped Kabbalist. The extensive negative media around this public metamorphosis did not stop thousands of Orthodox Jews (who strictly avoid the media) from becoming his devotees. Entire yeshivas make annual pilgrimages to Netivot.

Today the square is set up for a rally at which a hundred thousand anti-disengagement protesters are expected. Merchants have erected portable kiosks and are selling blessed bottled water, photos of Baba Baruch in gold-plated frames and other talismans. There's a huge stage and an extensive loudspeaker system throughout the plaza. A row of Johnny-on-the-Spots divides the square in half—men go to the left, women to the right.

The rally is set to begin at 7 p.m. But it is now fifteen minutes to seven and while the sizzling day has begun letting off steam, there is still no sign of the crowd. There are probably no more than three dozen scraggly beards loitering about. Someone turns on the mikes and the voice of one of the organizers booms out: "The Sharon family is engaging in every criminal act known to man. They will stop at nothing in order to prevent our supporters from reaching this holy site. Already the Sharon family has forced bus drivers to surrender keys. They have illegally confiscated licences, set up roadblocks, threatened passengers. But nothing they do will stop our supporters. Our people will come. They will come in taxis, in private cars, on foot if they have to. They will come from all four corners of the country, because they must, because they, like all of us, know that a Jew does not banish a Jew."

Cut to the protest's main theme song: "Yehudi lo megaresh yehudi"—a Jew does not banish a Jew.

Miki and Eldad scuttle back and forth like crabs in the sand. Miki is shooting black–and–white images of disappointed and apprehensive people, pressing passing moments with the stamp of eternity. Eldad is less interested in the eternal, and more in capturing the kind of drama he can sell to editors. He climbs up on the stage and shoots the empty square. I notice another photographer snapping interactions between ushers and a few religious women who have mistakenly sauntered onto the wrong side of the square. A few young Chabad students march in carrying signs in English. THE NATIONS OF THE WORLD EXIST ONLY BY VIRTUE OF ZION, one sign says. Another, addressed directly to God, reads POUR THY WRATH UPON AMALEK—which in this case does not mean that God should eradicate doubt, as moderate Jews interpret the phrase, but more literally that God should kill all the Arabs, past, present and future. Many of the signs coming off the buses display a photo of the saint-like face of Menachem Shneerson, the Chabad rabbi. Clearly the rabbi, who is dead, but whose students expect him back any day, has been brought along to add heft. On one sign, the caption under his photograph reads ALL GENTILES SHOULD LEAVE THE HOLY LAND LEST THEY PERISH.

"I don't believe Rabbi Shneerson said such nasty things," I say to one of the young Chabadnikim

"For sure, Shneerson said that."

"What makes you so sure?"

"My friend Tsidkiyahu got him on video."

"I thought the second commandment decreed that Jews weren't allowed to make videos?"

The young Chabadnik screws up his face. Evidently he does not think I am an authority on graven images.

Within the hour the predictions have come true. Tens of thousands of protesters arrive carrying tents, pallets of kosher canned food, jerry cans filled with water, and cases of Carmel wine. By nine, as dusk begins casting shadows, Baba Sali Square is a solid block of bodies and the noise has begun endangering the eardrums. The stage has filled with dignitaries, including current and past members of parliament, a smattering of generals, and a dozen rabbis decked out in robes. The very proud mayor of Netivot struts about, shaking hands.

Then, as if lifted by the gravity of the full moon, a sea of skullcaps forms a wave that foams against the stage. Apparently Sholom Ber Krinsky, the leader of the Degel Ha Torah Party, or maybe the ninety-five-year-old Yosef Sholom Eliashiv, the supreme head of Lithuanian Jews and the greatest living authority on the Kabbala, have just arrived. From where I stand it is impossible to ascertain who the exalted personage actually is. All I can see are bodyguards surrounding a figure dressed in a glittering gold mantle and a Pope-like triregnum. Then comes a burst of electric energy. The crowd yells "Rentgen, Rentgen, Rentgen" ("Rentgen" in Hebrew means X-Ray). Yaakov Yisrael Ifergan, known as the "X-Ray Rabbi" because he is said to be able to detect illness better than any magnetic resonance imaging technology, has arrived. An overheated young man screams out to his friend in Hebrew, "Did you see Rentgen at last night's *hilolot*, all night vigil?"

I can't quite make out the answer but I am beginning to see that this is a world I do not get. What I know is only what Israeli scholars like Yoram Bilu, Anat Feldman and Boaz Huss have written, and what they have written is basically that Jewish immigration from North Africa brought with it an entire sub-culture devoted to the supernatural. In Bilu's view, it was the disaster of the post–Yom Kippur War era that unleashed such forces in Israel. If I understand him correctly, it was not only the anxiety of the post-war loss of centre that opened the door to marginal and sometimes criminal elements in Judaism, it was also the sudden vulnerability of the Zionist dogma. By the fall of 1995, only weeks after the November 4 assassination of Prime Minister Yitzhak Rabin, Israel had become a madhouse of the black arts. Minyans of rabbis across the country gathered in synagogues lit by black candles and sanctified by the intermittent blowing of ram's horns. Holy men in cloaks engaged in occult rituals, leading to a huge black market in herbs and flasks to cook them in and vials to store the resulting potions.

By the late 1990s, orthodox seminarians were busily prostrating themselves on the graves of their loved ones. They were attending all-night vigils in Beer Sheba, getting their amulets blessed by rabbis in Netivot. Ten rabbis had gone so far as to lay the *pulsa de nura*—the curse of curses—on Ariel Sharon, the anti-hero of the disengagement.

For the most part, the crowd gathered in Netivot are members of the religious Zionist movement whose origins go back to Rabbi Abraham Kook. It is therefore not surprising that the various seminaries and sects of Judaism represented here have an abiding interest in the esoteric side of their religion. In fact, Rabbi Kook's teachings centred on the Kabbalistic notion that Jews contain the sparks of the Messiah and that in their devout undertakings, which include settlement of the Holy Land, they are bringing about the Messiah in the same way as labour brings about a newborn child.

For an hour and a half the speeches grow steadily fiercer, full of allusions that either go over my head or make me sick to my stomach. The venom is perfectly clear, though one would never know it from the stone faces of the Israeli journalists and TV cameramen covering the event. Anyone looking at them might assume they have their ears stuffed with iPod buds and are hearing music that blissfully obscures what their equipment is recording.

At some point the mayor of Netivot reminds the audience that the protest is not a religious event, that "Israelis from every walk have joined together against the disengagement." But this is a lie. Ninety-nine percent of the crowd is religious Zionists, a fact underscored poignantly by the total absence of women on stage. A Norwegian reporter who has been in the country long enough to speak Hebrew feels sufficiently unnerved by all of this to turn to me and say that as far as he is concerned we are witnessing an event no better than a brown-shirt rally in the mid-1930s. "I cannot understand the indifference of the Israelis," he says. "Why would they let this crap go? One would think they would have learned from the Rabin period."

At the next lull in the noise I tell him that many Israelis feel like he does but don't know what to do about it. "Neither did the Germans, until it was too late," the Norwegian says.

"There is a difference between what we are witnessing and the Nazis," I insist. "This is not a nationalistic movement, but a movement that is chthonic, related more to the land than to the people or to the idea of the people. When you pay close attention to the Gaza settlers, you realize that they would prefer to stay put even if the Palestinians took over the Strip—that their conviction and the mitzvah is about land per se."

My Norwegian colleague isn't buying this distinction. Perhaps it is too subtle, but my sense is that given half a chance most of the settlers would not care whether they lived under Israeli or Palestinian rule, as long as they could stay, which is not the way nationalists think.

It is nearly 11 p.m. before the rally comes to a close. The MC steps up to the mike to inform the crowd about what comes next. "We are now planning to march for twenty kilometres or so until we reach Gaza," he says. He asks the crowd to do an about-face and proceed in an orderly fashion toward the road just behind Baba Sali Square. "Once we are organized, the march to Gush Katif in Gaza will commence. Soon we will be with our brothers."

Miki flags me down. "We've got to get out of here," he calls breathlessly. "In a few minutes it won't be possible." A moment later Eldad appears and the three of us jog to the car.

By the time we arrive at the next intersection, the lights of Netivot have dimmed and we are enveloped in a plasma-black night of the sort one gets only in the desert. We've hit the military cordon and the IDF won't let us go farther. The only choice we have is to wait where we are or take a back road to Jerusalem. It is not clear why the IDF has set up camp here, but dozens of military command cars, jeeps and trucks loaded down with communications devices kneel like camels waiting to be mounted. TV cameramen are setting up equipment; photographers, including my two friends, negotiate on their cellphones with newsroom editors in Tel Aviv, Berlin, London and New York. Some have already zapped entire photo albums of the protest across continents and oceans. Editors text them back: how long should they hold space on the front page? Is there going to be a real confrontation? No one can say.

The photographers keep up a constant cynical rap. One curly-headed fellow tells us that CNN's Wolf Blitzer is in the armoured car parked at the intersection. "He and Christiane Amanpour are calling the shots. Nobody will do anything unless it works for the *Situation Room*." That shouldn't surprise anyone—after all, we are all operating by Jewish business ethics.

Miki's car radio is tuned to Galatz, the army network, whose announcer is saying: "Is the government planning an ambush? Will the settlers be allowed to march on to Gaza? The entire world is breathlessly awaiting the answer."

"Right on," Eldad says, boxing with the desert air.

An hour goes by, interrupted only by the intermittent cackle of transmitters and the sound of the photographers' Harley-Davidsons retracing the route back to Netivot, then returning with more pictures of the crowd. There are moments when I feel as though I am in a foxhole awaiting the enemy, or that I have made a pact with the enemy and that the crowd moving toward us is being led by a pillar of fire.

Another hour goes by and finally we hear the din of the multitude. Distant noises and lights come at us the way the first ominous pebbles signifying an avalanche skip down a slope. Lone stars and planetary formations are lining up for what looks like it may be Armageddon. To the fifty thousand Israelites marching toward us, chanting, pushing perambulators, on their cells describing the events to friends in Brooklyn, the road to Gaza seems clear. But very soon they will be put on notice by teenagers who have become an ad hoc reconnaissance unit. They have zipped ahead of the crowd, caught sight of the army, and circled back to inform their elders.

The crowd comes around the last bend toward us. Miki, Eldad and five dozen other photographers run forward, drop to their knees and begin snapping hard. A thousand flashes press this exodus with a stamp of eternity.

Then, like skeletons rising from the dead earth, a seemingly endless phalanx of soldiers springs up. I can't tell where they have come from, where they have been holed up. The road is suddenly walled off, as are the fields for a kilometre on both sides. As far as I can see, young men and women in khaki or black uniforms, carrying no weapons, are linked arm in arm as in the old children's game of Red Rover. The scene is absolutely biblical.

The crowd hits the wall of soldiers and the rabbis in the lead take out their cellphones and put in the call, either to God or to their lawyers. "Is this hold-up legal? We have a permit. No, we did not explicitly say we would leave Netivot but this is a free country and we are allowed to stroll."

The walkers bringing up the rear have not yet got wind of the military barricade. Tens of thousands are still chanting, and then a voice comes over a loudspeaker the military has set up on the roadside. "This is the IDF Southern Command. Please listen carefully. Your march is illegal. Please take your belongings and head back to your cars and buses. The protest is now officially over."

A hushed murmur ripples through the throng. Parents pull children close by their scrawny, elastic arms. For a moment the protesters hesitate: you can feel them thinking that they maybe ought to do as they have been told. It occurs to me that the protesters were never warned that they might encounter resistance. Some of the older people look genuinely scared, perhaps suffering flashbacks from other marches, forced ones under far less opportune conditions.

I remember asking my father the question that just about every other Jewish kid on earth asked his parents: why did so many Jews go to the concentration camps like sheep? "Because they had too much respect for the law," my father answered. "Even when it wasn't their law, even after they had been abused by the law, even after the legal system as a whole was blown out of the water, still they believed in it." This is the price they paid for being People of the Book. Years later it occurred to me that the trauma experienced by Jews who either lived through the Holocaust, or simply learned of it, could be measured not only in pounds of human ashes but also in the pain Jews feel when they are forced to acknowledge the fallibility of the law, which is also the fallibility of the rabbinical establishment that stands for the law. Perhaps this is why so many Israelis treat rules, even those rules they have generated for themselves, as though they were there to be broken.

A few turbaned, pistol-toting *noar hagva'ot* (hilltop youth) now push at the line of soldiers with the bravado of neighbourhood bullies and the cameras focus in their direction. Over the years these young men, who model themselves after biblical heroes, have taken up the lives of hermits, or live in packs that roam the Judean desert. A cadre of black-uniformed soldiers moves forward in perfect synchronicity, looking like they could tear beating hearts out of squirming bodies. These soldiers are unarmed because their entire being is a weapon. With a handful of perfectly executed martial moves they have the cubs from the Judean desert hogtied and in the back of a paddy wagon in a nanosecond. I find myself laughing as these incarnations of Judah the Maccabee and Joshua Ben Nun, these bearded Samsons, are arrested, but I feel like crying as well. Moments later the rabbis in charge are ushered through the IDF line and whisked away. Negotiations have begun in earnest.

At about 3 a.m., the crowd begins gliding forward like a tired old reptile. The army will not permit the protesters to proceed to the Kissufim checkpoint at the entrance to the Gaza Strip, but reroutes them to the religious village of Kfar Maimon, a few kilometres away, where arrangements have been made with the village administration. Anywhere from twenty thousand to fifty thousand people will spend what remains of the night outdoors. Miki wants to drive to the checkpoint; the intersection is still blocked so he drives the car into the field. We go cross-country for a while then cut back to the road. At 4:30 a.m. we get to the checkpoint to find that the area is hopping. Dozens of folding tables on both sides of the road are piled high with bottled water and food. Thirty or forty well-groomed, colourfully dressed settler teens are manning the tables. A line of soldiers keeps them from blocking the road, which is congested with a steady stream of vans and flatbed trucks making their way into Gaza from Tel Aviv.

Just as we arrive, these young settlers get the phone call informing them that the Netivot crowd has been rerouted. A loud boo is followed by screams and sobs. Someone blows a ram's horn. The volume on the speaker system is cranked up, playing an old speech by Prime Minister Sharon. "*Din Netzarim keDeen Tel Aviv* — the fate of the Gaza settlement of Netzarim is identical to the fate of Tel Aviv," he declares over and over again. Teenagers scream relentlessly at the soldiers:

"You are worse than the Nazis!"

"When the judgment day comes you will be not be able to deny that you knew, you will not be able to say that you were only following orders!"

The soldiers, who are not that much older than these kids, stand in front of them stone-faced. Miki, Eldad and I are suddenly exhausted and head back to Tel Aviv, driving through another beautiful dawn.

By mid-afternoon Miki and I—Eldad has a photo shoot in the city—are back in Kfar Maimon. Yesterday's crowd has been sealed in by a combination of barbed wire and soldiers. No one can leave except in the direction of Jerusalem. I find myself overcome by a melancholia that has to do with the experience of seeing so many Jews behind barbed wire. Once again I think about the Holocaust, but more specifically about the failure of history and of historical memory to penetrate into the hearts, to circulate in the blood, of these kinds of Jews. No one seems to have learned very much from the experience of the Holocaust. What is the Jewish response? This? Is this state, where Jewish soldiers are forced to restrain tens of thousands of Jews behind a barbed-wire fence, our response? Is this state, where young settlers call soldiers Nazis and soldiers stand frozen in front of them, the Jewish response to the Holocaust?

No one seems to know what I have been told by friends at the Shabak (homeland security): early this morning several rabbis were dragged off by Israeli police and badly beaten. But in any case the rules of the game are now clear. Anything goes except shooting; if shooting begins it will be a whole new game.

In the shade of the palms in Kfar Maimon, young men and women are huddled around an American kid with a golden voice, golden locks and a golden right hand that picks at a Gibson guitar as well as the best of them, giving a full-throated workout to the repertoire of the Singing Rabbi, Shlomo Carlebach.

Over the speakers the insistent theme—"A Jew does not banish a Jew"—is repeated with the relentlessness of a muezzin, only interrupted from time to time by a reminder from the organizing committee to "preserve the sanctity of the site by keeping male quarters separate from female." There are announcements about a singalong at the main stage and one about a lost dog and a lost child who awaits his parents at the big tent.

Nearer dusk the mood begins to darken, mostly because it has become clear that the army does not intend to budge. A couple of hundred young Orthodox men have built a contraption that resembles a catapult that they are now moving closer to the village gate. I find this show of bravado as pathetic as the earlier confrontation between the hilltop youth and the IDF. Who do these gladiators think they are? Do they really believe they can smash through the gate, that the army would sit by and do nothing, that God will provide cloud cover or a pillar of fire, that He will part the waters? Are these the delusions that faith produces? Needless to say it doesn't happen.

Meanwhile Rabbi Hanan Porat, one of the founders of the settler movement, begins to perform on the main stage. I push my way through a crowd of un-deodorized humanity to get a better look at one of Israel's most notorious former parliamentarians. Porat leads several hundred yeshiva *bukhers* (students) in song; several dozen more dance a phlegmatic version of the hora. When a young man grabs my hand and tries to draw me into the dance, it dawns on me that I have lost contact with Miki and that I am the only one around here not wearing a skullcap.

"Are you Jewish?" a young man who introduces himself as Hezi asks in English.

"I don't think it's your business," I reply.

"Not my business? If you are a Jew then it's my business."

"Okay, Hezi, I have a question for you. It's about your anthem. You know the one about a Jew not banishing a Jew."

"You like it? It's catchy, no?"

"Catchy, yes. But if a Jew doesn't banish a Jew then who does a Jew banish? And if he doesn't banish anyone, why aren't you singing 'a Jew doesn't banish anyone'?"

"To say the truth I haven't thought about this so much," Hezi says, looking like he was just hit over the head by a box of matzohs. "But you stay here. I will go to find the rabbi. He knows about everything very much."

"Okay, I won't move. I will stand right here and wait for the rabbi."

"Okay," Hezi says and darts off to find his pinch-hitter.

The rabbi Hezi drags back wants to know my name. I hesitate and then say David. The rabbi tells me he has friends in Toronto.

"So do I," I tell him.

He says, "Hezi tells me that you want to know if a Jew doesn't banish a Jew, then who does a Jew banish? Is that right, Reb David?"

"Right."

"It is a good question."

"Not the best, Rabbi, but at the moment it's the best I can do."

"So let me understand, Reb David. What you really want to know is if a Jew doesn't banish a Jew then who does a Jew banish?"

"Yes, Rabbi. Should we maybe repeat the question one more time?"

"Not so necessary. Not so necessary at all. I understand the question. You want to know if a Jew doesn't . . . This is a good question. Rav Shimon over there—Rav Shimon, come, come. This good Jew has a question. And you too, Rav Tsadok ben Yerukhmiel."

And so it comes to pass that a dozen rabbis join the huddle. They chat and genuflect and argue with each other in their own way. They also happen to be in my way. I spot a hole and formulate an exit strategy, at which point I crouch and manage a clean getaway. I dust myself off, straighten my shirt, and walk off into the sunset, never looking back at these wise men all heartily engaged by my good question. Several hours later the army disperses the crowd. The protest is over.

⊗

A few days later, my mother and I are at Teatron Gesher, the Russian theatre in old Jaffa. It backs onto a cobblestone square that separates it from the hustle of Jerusalem Blvd. There's a kiosk selling falafel in the square and a café where early arrivals can usually find a table, order lattes, beer and a sandwich they can eat while watching the overweight, overdressed, mostly Russian crowd gather for the show. My mother, who has been feeling unusually lethargic, has invited me to the theatre to distract herself.

We sit at the café watching a bunch of suburban-looking young Israelis taunting a beige Labrador to whose collar an orange kerchief is attached.

"Settler dog," a young man yells.

"Stinking settler mutt," a chorus responds.

Someone kicks the Lab in the stomach. The dog yelps, her ears flatten out against her head. She cowers and slips away looking as though she can't believe someone could be so cruel. Neither can my mother, who gets up with difficulty and beckons me to come along.

The entire country has broken out in a rash of orange or blue. The orange team is out in great numbers tonight. Young settlers carry signs that claim that to leave Gaza only means that the terrorists' shells will find it easier to hit Sderot, Ashkelon and Tel Aviv. Most orange pamphlets do not mention the concept of Greater Israel, although the one orange video that I pick up begins with a panorama shot of homes in Jewish Gaza over a musical score featuring a song called, "Fear not, for the lord thy God is with thee."

The stores around my mother's apartment in tony Ramat Hasharon show a distinct distaste for anything capable of unnerving the customer. A Nike cross-trainer with an orange sole has been removed from the display rack at the shoe store. Our local juice guy is selling only grapefruit juice and lemonade. "The settlers have spoiled orange for me," he says.

At major intersections across the country, settler youth are giving away pins and buttons as though this whole business is happening at a sports stadium or at a theatre near you.

"I wish your father was still alive," my mother tells me. "He would show me how to cope with all this madness."

⁂

In the autobiography he published in 1989, Ariel Sharon wrote that he understood very well how difficult it would be for settlers to leave their homes. But the settlers and their leaders don't believe he cares one bit. Arieh Elya, the assistant mayor of Jewish Gaza's capital city, Gush Katif, tells me that in the past, Sharon was in the habit of showing up in Gaza whenever it suited him, sometimes as often as twice a week.

"The sentry would ring me up to say 'Fatso is on his way up, make sure the bourekas are hot.' Sharon would come in, slap everyone in the room on the back, and proceed to polish off an entire tray of bourekas [savoury pastries, often cheese-stuffed]. Invariably he would tell me the same story: 'You know, Elya, your destiny depends on how many kids you can make. So how come you are here rather than at home making kids?' Since he announced the disengagement, Sharon has not visited us once."

Daily reports of irate commuters who threaten to "personally tear off the arms and legs of the next settler who so much as tries to tie an orange ribbon to the retractable antenna of my Porsche" appear in the press. No one mentions the Palestinians.

—∞∞∞—

By the beginning of August, two weeks before the disengagement campaign is set to begin, the country has gone quite crazy. Nerves are stretched to the breaking point and no leader finds a way of calming the collective jitters. It seems to me that no one, including Prime Minister Sharon, can now stop the army from rolling into Gaza on August 15. And so it is strange that an old-time moderate like Rabbi Yoel Bin Nun, who has kept to the sidelines all along, suddenly feels the need to step up to the plate. But he does—and what he does is borderline criminal. In an interview he gives to *Haaretz*, the rabbi predicts an apocalypse comparable to the two events that led to the destruction of the Temples and to exile. The battle for Gush Katif, the Gaza settlement bloc, "will be our Stalingrad and our Masada," he says. His words are echoed in mass rallies held in Rabin Square. "The only way I will leave Gaza is in a coffin," one religious Zionist leader announces to an enormous crowd.

The level of anxiety reminds me of the countdown to the 1967 war, except that no one is calling for the emergency evacuation of Jews to America and as far as I know the government has not yet begun preparing mass graves. But then again everyone is predicting that something, somewhere is going to blow. What no one foresees or could foresee is just where the eruption will occur. And indeed, had any of the latter-day prophets been asked to guess where the crack would appear, I venture that none of them would have guessed the sleepy Arab-Israeli town of Shfaram in the lower Galilee.

Set among rolling hills and famous for its amazing gelato, Shfaram was perhaps the last place in the country where one would have expected the disengagement fever to catch fire. But on August 4, 2005, in Shfaram, the two billion dollars and six months invested in preparing for the withdrawal almost went up in smoke.

The tragedy began to unfold a day earlier, when nineteen-year-old Eden Nathan-Zaada, an AWOL Israeli soldier, dressed in full IDF uniform but with sidelocks and a large crocheted skullcap, boarded a bus in Haifa bound for the Arab-Israeli town of Shfaram. The driver, a fifty-six-year-old Druze Christian Arab, Michel Bahus, was surprised to see a Jewish soldier, especially an Orthodox one, get on his bus. Assuming the soldier had made a mistake about his destination, Bahus asked Nathan-Zaada where he was bound. He shrugged and said that he knew what he was doing, walked to the back of bus, where he loosened his boots, and, in imperial fashion, stretched over the entire back bench. From time to time the driver, who had navigated this route twice a day for the past twelve years, contemplated the unlikely soldier, wondering what the young man was up to. When Bahus finally pulled the bus into the Shfaram terminal and embarked on his once-around, checking for forgotten packages, purses and jackets, he found Nathan-Zaada curled up in the back seat, asleep and heavily perspiring.

Under the driver's gaze, the lad struggled back to consciousness and sat up, rubbing watery eyes, looking washed-out, confused and dehydrated. Bahus helped him collect himself, ushered him to his feet and off the bus. When he noticed that Nathan-Zaada was wobbly, Bahus offered him a lift to a nearby hitchhikers' stop. En route Bahus stopped at his home, where he introduced Nathan-Zaada to his wife and son and offered the soldier a snack. Zaada refused, claiming that he would not eat anything that was not kosher. He did accept a glass of cold water from Bahus, who then drove him to a major intersection where he might catch a ride.

That evening, Bahus called his dispatcher at the Egged Bus Terminal in Haifa, reminding him that he had requested the next several days off work so that his family could celebrate his nephew's marriage. But the dispatcher had forgotten about Bahus's request and refused to excuse him. The disappointed driver hung up and called his brother to arrange for him to pick him up when he got to the Shfaram terminal. But the next day the bus did not arrive at its final destination.

At 2:05 on the afternoon of August 4, Eden Nathan-Zaada again boarded the bus to Shfaram at the Haifa station. No passenger I spoke to remembered whether Nathan-Zaada acknowledged Michel Bahus, who had treated him so cordially the day before. What passengers recalled was a sombre-looking soldier, dark, dreamy, side-locked, unusually dishevelled. They remembered him taking a seat near the driver. He carried an army-issue M16, which he placed on his lap. On Sheik Amid Farid Street in the town of Shfaram, Bahus signalled and pulled the bus toward the curb. Nathan-Zaada, who had written in his twelfth-grade yearbook that "most of all I enjoy butchering people in the computer game Grand Theft Auto," began fumbling with the safety on his automatic rifle. Then he aimed the gun at Michel Bahus's head and blew the driver's brains out. After that he turned on two sisters, Haza and Dina Turki, twenty-three and twenty-one respectively, and shot them in the chest. Fifty-five-year-old Nader Hayak was next. Twelve Israeli Arabs were also seriously injured before two local Arab police officers were able to wrestle Nathan-Zaada to the bus floor and into handcuffs.

Within minutes a huge and maddened crowd, mostly young Druze, descended from the adjacent hills, boarded the bus, and beat the boy-soldier Eden Nathan-Zaada to death, tearing him limb from limb. According to one report, only the arm handcuffed to the seat remained undisturbed.

When I visited Shfaram several days later, witnesses, including Bahus's brother, spoke about a getaway car that had followed the bus from Haifa, parked behind it for the duration of the shooting, and drove away only when it became clear that Nathan-Zaada was trapped. Over coffee at a Druze-owned restaurant across the street from where the massacre occurred, the owner described the driver and three passengers of the getaway car in great detail, citing the model and emphasizing that it sped off in the direction of the radical West Bank settlement of Tapuach, where it turned out Nathan-Zaada had friends from the outlawed Kach movement.

"Israeli police dragged me in for hours of interrogation." Bahus's brother told me. "They claimed that I was one of the instigators of Nathan-Zaada's murder, which is a lie. Many other Shfaram citizens were dragged in for intense interrogations. But the Israeli police did not follow up on the getaway car. Nor did they investigate who it was that filled Nathan-Zaada's mind with such hatred."

From Israeli sources, I had learned that a military helicopter had been summoned to the scene, that the pilot had considered landing but was ordered to let events unfold as they would. "Perhaps some politician felt it would be better to let the Arabs have their revenge than to chance that the entire Galilee explode," a senior police officer told me. "Perhaps the government was thinking only of how to save the disengagement." According to Shfaram's mayor, Orsan Yassin, it was thanks to him that Shfaram settled down as fast as it did after the incident. "I single-handedly saved the disengagement," he claimed. "Sharon was very pleased."

Sharon's team went into damage control mode, immediately contacting the mayors of all the Arab-Israeli villages in the area. Somehow settler leaders, including Rabbi Hanan Porat, were mobilized to declare that Nathan-Zaada had acted alone. A statement read: "His actions were abominable and the religious Zionist community shares the pain and the terrible sense of loss that Nathan-Zaada has inflicted upon innocent families." Sharon, for his part, publicly condemned the shootings as an act of "Jewish terrorism," and promised that "Arab families of these victims will be treated in precisely the same way as Jewish families of Arab terrorism." He vowed to change the Israeli law that automatically compensates Jewish targets of Arab terror but does nothing for Arab victims of Jewish terror. Sharon swore that the Knesset would pass an amendment allowing the victims of Jewish terrorism to be entered into the annals of the nation, but in the end Sharon did nothing of the sort.

A major controversy erupted over where the murderer Eden Nathan-Zaada would be buried. The mayor of his home town refused him a place in the local cemetery. Nathan-Zaada's mother wept on public television, claiming that for the past several months she had been begging the IDF to locate her son, who was both AWOL and agitated beyond recognition. Sharon agreed to a military burial, though not one with the usual fanfare.

⚬⚬⚬⚬

Near the end of August 2007, soon after the second anniversary of the murder, I returned to Shfaram to interview Bahus's widow, a solemn, sympathetic woman with heavy eyelids and a great reluctance to stick her neck out. When I asked her whether she had received any financial compensation from the Israeli government, she shook her head and begged me to wait for Michel's brother to arrive. As we waited, her handsome seventeen-year-old son came out of a room in the back, shook my hand, and immediately returned to the room. "He never goes out anymore," Mrs. Bahus said in English. "Before Michel was killed my son thought maybe he would go to the Israeli army. Now he doesn't wish to go anymore."

When Michel's wiry brother, arrived, he told me, "The mayor has not kept his promise to build a monument in the city's main park. The bus company has helped the family but the Israeli government did not allow us to put Michel's name on the website honouring victims of terror. Shfaram Mayor Yassin is a bad man, nothing more than a *shtinker*, a collaborator who likes to kiss Israeli ass."

Later that day I paid a visit to Mayor Yassin, who carries his many hundreds of pounds rather gracefully. Yassin repeated what he had earlier said, publicly—that he single-handedly saved the disengagement and that Ariel Sharon knew that and had thanked him for it. "My connections to the PMO are so tight that the moment I demanded that Israeli police release some Shfaramites charged with the murder of Nathan-Zaada, they were set free." The relative neglect of the town by the federal government, the discriminatory practices against Arab-Israelis in general, are, in Yassin's view, due to the fact that Israeli Arabs do not like to pay federal taxes. "I tell Shfaramites that if they want Israel to treat us fairly and equally then we must pay up just like Israelis do. Plus, I tell them that it is not only them that are mistreated by the Israeli government. Every Israeli, whether Jewish or Arab, is equally mistreated."

—∞—

On August 13, 2005, two days before the curtain is scheduled to rise on the disengagement, there's a glitch. My friend Gidi tells me over coffee that he has been contacted by several rabbis who have demanded an emergency meeting with Field Commander HaCohen. "They tell me that there are not enough female soldiers to go around and that they won't have male soldiers dragging out their women." Gidi looks like he hasn't slept in weeks. He complains bitterly about the bureaucrats running the show and about the lack of understanding of the settler population. "HaCohen checked the numbers, and worried out loud that the new recruits will be at a disadvantage both professionally and emotionally. But he was raised in an Orthodox Jewish family, has relatives living in Gaza, and understands everything about the need to maintain this community's integrity. So he picks up the wireless and sends out the call to HQ to recruit female soldiers."

On the August 17, two days late, at 3:30 in the morning, Operation Main Event begins with a seemingly endless convoy of buses and jeeps and trucks and command cars and armoured vehicles making their way from the Re'im military outpost, nicknamed Tent City, toward the Gaza border. The sun seems unwilling to rise. "Your dream state is over," Sharon has told the settlers, and to many of the fifty-five thousand soldiers who are being transported into the Strip this means that the nightmare state is about to begin.

Very few commanders have been briefed on the specifics of their mission. This is not because they are fresh off other tours but because Brigadier General HaCohen likes it this way. As he sees things, rigid descriptions of the enemy, briefs delivered in army jargon, timetables, fixed battlegrounds and theatres are things of the past. As far as he is concerned, a good soldier is one to whom the enemy is not known in advance but defined in the heat of a battle. "The less we insist on orders with line items that begin with phrases like 0800 hours, the more efficient we will be, the sooner we will be done with the campaign," HaCohen told me. "Commanders have to be ready to leapfrog from one site to the next at the drop of a hat. And they have always to be figuring out who they are opposing and never allow themselves to apply a strategy that is worked out in advance.

The idea is to play in an infinitely open field and stick to as creative a game plan as possible."

The settlers, on the other hand, have opted for maximum inflexibility and a unity of style and language. Again and again they spit out the same stock phrases:

"Your soldiers will not be able to say you didn't know."

"You are no better than Nazis."

"Who dares challenge the King?"

One rabbi or student prays and provokes the soldiers and becomes enraged and is carted off in precisely the same way as his neighbour and his neighbour's neighbour and his neighbour's son. The entire bloc of settlements acts and speaks as a single mind, using the same script, as though the resistance were not a matter of individual will but destiny.

En route to Gaza, a soldier interviewed on Israeli television says, "I was feeling so bad for these people that I almost cried. But then we encountered them and I almost immediately felt that they were not human, but androids or rubber puppets that had no real feelings. Their screams had not one iota of individuality to them—they were all using the same phrases, the same three gestures. And my empathy ran out very quickly. I hardened like steel and that made my job a lot easier."

In late afternoon of August 17, my old army buddy Ben Zion drives me to the Eshkol Media Centre a few kilometres away from the Kissufim border crossing to Gaza. We talk about the settlers' inhumanly wooden uniformity. "When you put all the sacred books together," Benzi says, "what you get is not only a whole bunch of Jewish learning, but a single model for living, an über-character that kicks in when Jews are scared. More than anything else, this über-identity requires only that one learn to be comfortable with replication and rote: rote dress, rote eating, rote thinking, rote life. The Jewish ability to put individuality on hold is part of the secret of survival. But really that happens only when there is fear. Without fear things fall apart and all the Jews who have put themselves on hold blow their pent-up stuff as if there is no tomorrow."

At the Eshkol Center, Benzi drops me off near the tent set up to accommodate the thousands of journalists here to cover the events. He wishes me luck and asks me once again whether I would not be happier watching the whole thing on television. "Nah," I say. "There is something about truth on the ground that even your flat screen TV can't deliver."

"Which is?" he asks.

"Girls," I say, pointing to two pigtailed young American women wearing vests emblazoned with "Israel Project."

Luckily for me, one of the pretty young women comes right up to me and offers a helicopter tour of the region and lunch in Jerusalem. I smile at Benzi, who drives off very impressed. The young lady tells me she is from the US midwest as she hands me a press bag and a red baseball cap on which PRESS is written. She begins to explain why the occupation of Gaza is entirely different from other occupations, such as the French occupation of Algiers. But when I tell her that I did not support the bulldozing of Arab homes in Khan Yunis, the Palestinian town bordering on Neve Dekalim, the capital of the Gaza settlement bloc, she smiles her pretty smile, walks away and offers the free helicopter ride to a younger and far better-looking

Australian reporter. I go into the press tent and register for the buses, which I am told leave for various Gaza settlements every half hour.

—※—

On the bus to Neve Dekalim, I share a seat with a young, earnest German journalist.

"What do you think when the settlers call the soldiers Nazis?" I ask him. "I think maybe all this is Germany's fault."

"For sure Germany hasn't helped," he responds, as though I was being serious.

I'm thinking about the fact that there are so many soldiers here and that the settlers have given up their arms. The actual evacuation, I'm sure, will be more an act of theatre than anything else. But there are other questions on my mind. The stakes are very high.

What about the aftermath? Hamas and Fatah are both planning a takeover once the settlements have been evacuated. How will that work? What about the young seminarians who are about to find out, again, that the Messiah is not coming, that the rabbis who promised that God would intervene actually lied? Will a new, more aggressive leadership replace the discredited one? I imagine that on the morning after the evacuation, the more belligerent and pragmatic religious leaders will take power—those who called on Orthodox soldiers to disobey orders, who tried to persuade the settlers not to give up their weapons, who said that that the Messiah wouldn't arrive. And secular Israel will probably pay little attention and for sure take no responsibility.

We disembark at the main gate of Neve Dekalim, and make our way to the town's main synagogue, which my friend Gidi called the settlement's Stalingrad. It is here that Brigadier General HaCohen has scheduled the Main Event's main event. "This is the most critical operation of his critical operational theory," Gidi told me. "If he breaks them here, they will come apart like artichoke leaves without the stem."

HaCohen, whom the settlers called Gershon haMegaresh, a term intended to conjure *geroosh Spharad*, the expulsion of Jews from Spain in 1492, learned the tricks of his trade at a military academy headed by Brigadier General Shimon Naveh. Naveh taught him the principles of "operational theory" as these were first conceived by the Russian military genius Mikhail Tukhachevsky. One of the main tactics of operational theory is to strike deep behind enemy lines and cut off necessary supply lines, thus breaking the enemy's spirit.

Dozens of leaders of Israel's settlement movement are now arriving for the showdown. The candelabras in the great hall of the synagogue are lighted as they usually are only on the Jewish High Holidays. Incandescent candles are everywhere but most particularly around the *aron kodesh*, the cabinet in which the Torah scrolls are kept. In the aisles, many hundreds of young settlers are praying, not to the god of peace but to the god of war and vengeance, calling out for the Messiah. They can see him. He rides upon the *merkavah*, a chariot of fire made of ice and blue sapphire and other heavenly substances. "Do not hide your face from me in my hour of need," a multitude of voices shrieks. "Do not hide your face from me in my hour of need." Sweaty bodies melt into sweaty bodies. The sight of human grief is overwhelming. Over and over and over again, the supplicants repeat, "Do not hide your face from me."

An elderly rabbi with bent shoulders walks up to the altar and announces that the afternoon service will now begin. The synagogue walls rebound with the Shma Yisrael, "Hear Oh Israel, the Lord is our God and the Lord is one." Hanan Porat, the founder of the settlement movement, marches to the back of the hall where HaCohen is leaning against a post. Porat offers HaCohen a skullcap and a talit and enjoins him to the inner circle. "Come pray with us," he says. HaCohen refuses, politely at first and then more firmly. Porat leaves him standing and returns to the congregation. Very soon the ark is opened and a dozen scrolls adorned in gold and silver are revealed. The movement's glitterati approach the ark: a member of parliament, a judge, a wizened rabbi. Each removes a scroll and circles the podium, where the reading then takes place. After that the scrolls are returned to the ark and the service winds down.

HaCohen, who is visibly distressed, waits until the last prayer is complete. He then raises his hand, a thousand bulbs flash, and he lowers it. When I spoke to him later, HaCohen said that he'd been thinking, "If ever the Messiah planned to arrive, this would be a very good time to do it." But the Messiah did not arrive. Instead, every window in the synagogue bursts open, as do the front and back doors. In a strategy HaCohen's teacher called swarming and which, HaCohen later explained, "aims to overwhelm not only the body but the spirit," hundreds of soldiers pour into the synagogue. The rabbis cover their heads with shawls, their students lock arms. Dozens of younger seminarians fall to the floor and tuck their heads into their laps as they have done a hundred times before when they were being shelled from the neighbouring Arab towns.

The soldiers are unfazed. They go about their business coolly, breaking arm locks apart, lifting splayed bodies by four limbs, dragging squirming and crying and praying boys off to the buses. The soldiers remain detached and work with extraordinary efficiency as though they were being paid by the piece.

Finally, it is the rabbis who must go. Soldiers encounter them one by one, cordially implore them to make their way out on their own feet. With some fifty soldiers behind him, HaCohen himself steps in to assure the rabbis that the game is over. He succeeds, and a line of lemmings covered by prayer shawls and muttering prayers to their god shuffle out as though they were walking to their deaths.

A queue of buses with spray-painted windows stands ready, displaying signs reading "Men" and "Women." The buses are loaded one after another. Sometimes the younger men get so crazy that soldiers are forced to handcuff them. On one occasion, I noted a nurse injecting a hysterical young woman with some sort of sedative. But soon enough the buses begin to leave and I feel as though an entire chunk of history is being put on the shelf. As the last bus moves out, HaCohen walks back into the synagogue, takes in the empty space for a moment, and turns off the lights.

The remainder of the evacuation is a piece of cake. When news comes that the main synagogue at Neve Dekalim has fallen, the spirit of the entire bloc breaks, just as HaCohen had predicted. Threats such as those made in Rabin Square—"that the only way we will leave Gaza is in coffins"— are swallowed along with the ill-conceived pride that had made them so satisfying in the first place.

I hang around for another day, take the press bus to stubborn Morag and to Gadid, where one female settler tells me that she had packed all her belongings except her dead husband's military uniform, which she had cut into pieces and nailed to every window of her home. In Kfar Darom, where Miki, Eldad and I had been confronted by Shimshon, the young lion with the M16, I join a group of several hundred foreign and Israeli reporters to watch a sitdown performance that could have been inspired by Verdi's *Aida*. Forty or fifty young men from the settlement have been joined on the roof of the synagogue by dozens of infiltrators from the West Bank. For several hours they fill plastic bags with ammonia, whitewash, paint and boiling water, which they heave down at the soldiers. The day swelters but the thousands of soldiers and journalists loitering below chat, amble across lawns that only á moment before had belonged to the most righteous. Every few minutes another truck filled with water bottles and ice cream bars arrives and smiling female soldiers distribute snacks and rumours. There is one about a young settler woman who doused herself in gasoline and set herself alight. There is another about the settlers' weapons cache that was broken open and looted.

Around 3 p.m. the army hauls in a crane followed by a flatbed truck upon which sits a huge birdcage. An engineering unit arrives and fastens a welded ring to the cage and to the chain slinking down from apex of the crane. Two dozen soldiers enter the cage, which is then raised slowly but still swings wildly out of control. The crane operator lowers the cage and then raises it again, this time to the roof where it is finally set down. Immediately the soldiers swarm out and within minutes a third of the young firebrands have been corralled, handcuffed and thrown into the cage as though they were rodents. The cage is lowered to the ground and the detainees are pushed into waiting buses and driven out of the Strip. This rooftop operation is repeated twice more, and then it is over. The first stage of the Gaza campaign has ended. The world gives Ariel Sharon a standing ovation.

⁂

At Homesh, the second of two West Bank outposts to be evacuated, the wind hisses and whips the sand in circles as it might have had there never been a settlement here in the first place. Yet one can almost hear the voices of little children in the playground. But then again, one really hears nothing but the sound of an army helicopter landing near the tent that has been set up for the final scrum with the army chief of staff, Dan Halutz, and the police chief, Moshe Karadi. Only a handful of reporters and cameramen have remained behind for the debriefing.

The chief of police opens the session. "A year less a day ago," Karadi says, "the government of Israel gave the overall responsibility for the disengagement of twenty-five settlements to the IDF. The job of evacuating the settlers from their homes fell to the Israeli police. The first of the campaign's four stages is now over."

Halutz continues: "The rules of engagement were set back at the first protests in Kfar Maimon." He goes on to describe the highlights of the past week. As he completes his summary, a senior Israeli journalist raises her hand. "The IDF has shown more discipline than any of us thought possible," she says. "Why can it not do the same in its routine business with the Palestinians?"

Halutz bends forward in mock concentration, as if responding to a trick question. "Isn't the answer obvious, my dear?" he
says. "The Palestinians are our enemy."

From one of the cameramen in the back another question
comes for Halutz. "How do you explain the hundreds if not
thousands of infiltrators from the West Bank that snuck into
Gaza? Why did the IDF let them through the border?"

Halutz's cowboy spirit gets the better of him. "We did it all for
all of you," he quips. "Think about it—had we not let the infiltrators in, what would there have been for the media to report?"

The tent breaks into a buzz. A quick-thinking youngster
calls out, "So, Chief of Staff Halutz, if you love us so much,
how come you don't call more often?"

Karadi picks up the ball, though compared to the arrogant
and nimble Halutz, Karadi stumbles through his explanation.
He is the first Sephardic Jew to have attained the rank of five-star
general in the police force. "Many of the infiltrators entered,
legitimately, before we sealed the border," he says. "They claimed
to be guests at a wedding or a bar mitzvah. And instead of returning home they simply hunkered down. Neither the army nor the
police were prepared to disrupt the lives of the settlers, so we
avoided house-to-house searches. And as far as those infiltrators
are concerned, we decided to let them through and deal with
them wholesale rather than one by one in difficult terrain."

Outside the flapping tent I bump into the senior *Haaretz* correspondent Amos Harel, who had predicted an all-out bloody
civil war.

"It didn't happen," I say to him. "Can you tell me why it
didn't?"

Harel is one of Israel's chief military correspondents. He takes a minute to remember who I am and then says, "To be perfectly frank, I never in my life believed that the IDF was capable of such discipline. Something very profound has changed."

On the way home I call up my friend Anat. "Where is the party tonight? I mean, it is the end of thirty-eight years of occupation, so we must be partying." *no one*

"I don't believe anyone thought to organize one," she answers.

Some weeks after the Main Event, I attend the first public *heshbon nefesh*, or soul-searching session, held not by the old guard, which has forgotten its promise to reflect, but by the badly beaten leaders of the settler movement. The conference takes place at Bar Ilan University, and except for me and a Danish journalist, Hanne Foigel, no other secular Israeli journalist or academic thinks the event important enough to attend. But the religious Zionist leadership is present in full force: members of the Knesset, YESHA leaders, rabbis, army officers who run the religious military academies. In the foyer outside the main hall I overhear an older rabbi saying that "when the rockets start dropping on Sderot and Asquelon and Tel Aviv, we will be vindicated, our powers of prophecy will be rewarded."

The tone is set right off the bat. Nissan Smoliansky, a Knesset member, says that "Sharon's strategy was a rape. He forced us to choose between the three things we love most: Eretz Yisrael (the land of Israel), Am Yisrael (the people of Israel), and Medinat Yisrael (the State of Israel). We could not give up on the people," Smoliansky continues, "but apparently they could very well give up on us. We thought they would support us but we were wrong."

Speaker after speaker touches on similar themes. Some talk only about Sharon's betrayal. Others point a finger at the YESHA leadership, whom the more militant speakers call "fickle and blind and useless." An hour into the talks a clear consensus forms. One of Rabbi Kook's main ideas—that religious Jews ought to respect the seculars—is chucked out the window. No one thinks the religious Zionist community needs to remain true to that old social contract. Instead, they argue, religious Jews need to focus on the national school board. They need to recruit young children into religious schools. Their children must take the top positions in the army. And in a hundred other ways they must win over the hearts and minds, must take over the leadership of the country. The people of Israel must become a unified whole and the only way this unity can come about is under their guidance.

As the evening progresses, I get the message: the civil war was in fact not averted at all but will take the form of a choking embrace. The religious Zionist movement plans to take over the hearts and minds of Israel. They are not interested in negotiating or finding a middle ground between religious and secular Israelis. They want it all, and the plan they come up with in the Bar-Ilan University auditorium arises not a hundred metres from the place where the groundwork for Yitzhak Rabin's assassination was laid.

SEVEN

Losing Rachel

I n early September 2005, my mother and I drove into Tel
Aviv so that I could firm up my return ticket to Toronto.
The disengagement was all but over, and my work in Israel
was done. My mother was quite right to complain that we had
spent hardly an hour together in the six weeks I'd been there,
and I wanted to take this last week to put that right.

My mother was a scary driver, with neither a sense of direction nor the desire to take any advice from me. But with a little
very discreet help, she did get us to the Opera House and then
onto Allenby, where she parked just a few blocks west of the
Carmel market. We got out of the car on the south corner of
the street and walked toward my preferred travel agency. Her
arm was hooked in mine and for a few moments I was leading.
But then she tugged, forcing me to stop in front of a kiosk that
was selling fruit juices of various kinds.

"When I was a little girl," she said wistfully, "there was an ice
cream parlour right here. The owner was a horrible little German
immigrant with bad breath and brown teeth. My friends and
I routinely baited him until he went blue in the face. We called

him *yekke potz*, squarehead, and got him so riled that he had little choice but to chase us out of the store waving his scoop. When we got him far enough from the counter, one of us would lean in and steal maybe half a bucket or more of vanilla ice cream, which we always ate with a thick slice of watermelon."

Indulging in nostalgia was not like my mother, who normally looked forward and not backward. I did not suspect anything from this rare lapse of hers, but only thought that in her manner I detected a hint of regret, a long-repressed sense that this man with bad breath and brown teeth may have had children whose teeth would sparkle and whose breath would be a pleasure if only he could sell enough ice cream. I wondered briefly whether the feisty, devil-may-care attitude that had sustained Rachel for the better part of her life was at long last breaking down.

By the time we got back to her apartment in Ramat HaSharon she was drained, and her face was blotched and pasty. But she avoided the elevator that she had fought so hard to install. Rather than take it up a flight, she pressed her lips together and dragged herself up the stairs. Much later, I realized that she had been out to prove to herself that she was not as weak or as ill as she felt.

"Mrs. Berlin, this is Dr. Goldstein," the message on her answering machine said. "I've checked you into oncology at Ichilov Hospital tomorrow morning at 8 a.m. I've sent all your paperwork ahead. I'm sorry it cannot wait. Please be on time."

"He's an ass, that Goldstein," my mother said. "He damn well knows that nobody in this country works on Friday or on Saturday. Why does he want me to lie around the halls of the hospital? Let him go lie around there himself, if he wants."

I wasn't following. "What's this about oncology? You haven't said a word about being sick."

"Oh well, it's nothing—just a little leukemia that can be removed with some chemotherapy. I would not worry about it and I am not going into the hospital tomorrow."

I was shocked. But there was no use getting angry at my mother for keeping me out of the loop. We had been through all of that before when my father was dying, and I was not going there again. But I did note that it was pretty clear from her tone of voice that she would not resist Dr. Goldstein's referral. Indeed the next morning we checked her into the cancer ward.

"I'm glad you brought her down," the triage nurse said. "Your mother is suffering from acute myeloid leukemia, and the sooner we get to work on her the better."

As we walked to the cancer ward, my mother commented on how eerily empty the hospital halls were, normally a bustle of business. "I told you," she said, but then changed her tune. "Perhaps it is a good thing that I don't have to fight the crowd." Within the hour my mother was hooked into her first dose of that rat poison that doctors call chemotherapy. I left the hospital thinking about the nature of our attachment.

Unlike many psychologists, I think that by the time a person is forty he is responsible for his own face and can no longer blame the patterns and behaviours that insinuated themselves into his system before he was old enough to discriminate. Unfortunately, I finally learned something about the difficult work of detachment much older than forty. For most of my adult life I'd found myself inexplicably depressed at twilight. Tanking like that on such a regular basis was annoying to say the least; for many years, I believed it was caused by my circadian rhythms or blood sugar dips and that there was very little I could do about it. Then one day, not so long ago, I was strolling on the beach in Tel Aviv at twilight and suddenly remembered something that my mother had told me many years earlier. "I don't like the grey stuff," she had said. "I get low each evening when the sun goes down and pick up only when it is gone. I love this country for doing the dirty work of transition so efficiently."

I did not get the significance of this thought right off the top. Rather, I let it bump up against a passage from the Israeli writer Amos Oz's A *Tale of Love and Darkness*, in which Oz described his mother's anger at the Middle Eastern sun, which sank so soon and cared so little about lovers. But once I had truly taken in what she had said, and let it do its cathartic work, I never again experienced that melancholy—her melancholy—at twilight.

But to say this much hardly skims the nature of my attachment to my mother. As is the case with all attachments that unhappily remain past the date of their expiry, this one too is different and unique if only because it wouldn't budge unless I budged it. What would I lose if I lost my mother to her disease? From what was my umbilical cord constructed?

When I was a child, like many children, I thought the world of my mother. I read her my lame poetry and spoke to her endlessly about my hopes and dreams. But the incident at Cedarvale School, when she and my father collaborated (in my eyes) in the denial of my name, began a process of detachment that I achieved with extraordinary inefficiency: rage and remorse and more rage and disappointment and more rage and finally a kind of numbness that left everything important unchanged. All that really happened over time was that I lost my early admiration for her and in fact began to think of her not as the kind of woman she was, but as just one of many Israelis like her—men and women who were perfectly happy living out the communal identity that they'd so strongly developed, both binding and empowering them, in their youth.

The attachment remained in place but its grounds became ever less obvious. As I grew older, for example, I stopped pining for her chicken soup and began actually hating her style of cooking. By the time I married Deborah, I came to believe that my mother was in fact trying to poison me with the powdered garlic, onion and synthetic stuff she called paprika that she applied like rouge to the bloodless flesh of chickens. There were many years when Deborah, the kids and I would return from Friday night dinners at my parents and I would spend the rest of the night vomiting.

What remained of my attachment to my mother had nothing to do with maternal creature comforts or with the unconditional love that some mothers bestow upon their children. I had no doubt that my mother loved me, but I also had no doubt that the only thing that was unconditional about her love was me. In her mind I was entirely a plastic thing, a son without borders and limits, who could be her husband as well as her child. And until she died, and perhaps for a few years after that, I respected the division of labour to which she held so firmly. I copied her relation to me. I was that plasticity. So long as she was the body, I felt disembodied—pure mind in the worst sense of the word.

All of my earliest nightmares had to do with just this division of labour, with being this loose grey matter floating about in space. I used to dream about being called to act in the world, and being unable to do so.

———

I pushed off my departure date, and for the next two weeks I visited my mother daily. When she was discharged, my mother's brother Moti, her sister Talma and I met with a young female oncologist with a lovely bedside manner. "Regretfully, the oncology department at Ichilov Hospital is full," Dr. Dina informed us and suggested that she could get in touch with her colleague at Rambam Hospital in Haifa. "For the particular kind of leukemia that you have," the doctor said, "the treatment at Rambam is great—perhaps even better than here in Tel Aviv."

"But how about the travel?" I asked. "Rambam is more than an hour from her home."

But Moti and Talma thought it would be no problem to ferry her back and forth and so, the following week, we all drove to Haifa to register, meet some of the staff and wait while my mother had a thorough checkup. "The cafeteria serves terrific salads," Moti said and ushered Talma and me down to the lobby. None of us were prepared to express what we all were thinking—that if my mother did not receive a bone marrow transplant, her fate would be sealed. But the doctors at Ramban delivered us some blue-skies news: my mother's red blood cell count had stabilized and the cancer had gone into remission. That night I renewed my plane reservations. I would leave Israel in a week's time, on November 3, a month and a half later than scheduled.

———

Before I left, my mother asked me to drag up some of her old suitcases from the storage room in the basement. Their latches dangling like useless limbs, they were ancient and worn out. I carried up first three large suitcases and then several cardboard boxes that broke open on the way. "These are my life," my mother said. "Would you be interested . . . ? I want to show you . . ."

I was not all that interested and would have much preferred to talk about how she would get along after I went home. I had suggested that she hire live-in help, but she shrugged that notion off as though it were entirely off the wall. I asked her whether she might re-think her decision, maybe do it for me. It would relieve some of my anxiety, I said, and maybe even some of the guilt feelings I had about leaving her alone.

"Why should you feel any guilt?" she replied, making it clear that it was quite all right by her if I felt guilty to the core. I said, "Okay, show me some of your pictures."

My mother poured boiling water over the coffee in her Bodum, not pushing down the press, but scratching her skull beneath the crazy wig she now wore over the baldness that the chemo created. She poured cups for us both and then reached for the dustiest of all the dusty albums, wiped it clean with a wet paper towel and placed it atop a newer album filled with pictures of her grandchildren. Inside it were some letters from dead friends, which she removed, perused, smiled over and then returned to the album. I sipped my coffee and watched. There were many loose pictures with which she did the same: removing them, dusting them off, looking at them and then, with a final smile, returning them to their spots without saying a word. She turned next to a box of souvenirs from a trip to Prague that she and my father took with Talma and her husband, Yair.

Silently, methodically—as if I were not in the room—she reorganized the box and then turned back to the albums.

She cleared off the top of the dish cabinet that stood by the window and went about emptying a shoe-box filled with the trinkets she had gathered during a recent trip to China with the elder of my father's two younger sisters, Aya, and her husband Asher. The trip was to be her debut as an eligible widow, fresh for the plucking. But the cancer put an end to all that.

There was a box filled with her children's old report cards, including one that I don't know how she got her hands on: mine from grade twelve. I remembered that it had been marked "repeat," but here it was, and there was no such word. Had I ever actually seen that report card?

I watched her fussing about and muttering, moving items from one place to another, and it struck me that I could not leave—she had not recovered, she was not in remission at all. She was wrapped in the same kind of bubble that had enveloped my brother's wife, Annie, who died of cancer in her mid-thirties, leaving Daniel to raise two infant boys. My mother looked up at me then, and said, "This coffee is making me feel nauseous. I am going to lie down."

Early the next morning I heard her shuffling about. By the time I got up she was sitting at the kitchen table, which was now piled high with albums. She had the digital thermometer in her mouth. It beeped and she read off the number: "40 Celsius."

I called Moti, who arrived within the hour. Before noon she was back in the hospital in Haifa, where I was told she would remain for the next several days. I called Deborah to say that I would not be home any time soon.

The truth was that I had seen almost all her photos before. On my own that evening, I tried to sort them out and found myself drawn again into the world that had recaptured her. Each photo told a story and many came to mind as I tidied them up.

There was a black-and-white one of Haifa dating from the late 1930s or early 1940s. My mother, who could not have been more than eight or nine years old, stood by an apartment building that was surrounded by tufts of grass that made the lawn seem as though it was balding. By contrast, my mother's pitch-black hair seemed even thicker than usual, and was drawn into a severe bun that made her look older than she was. She was wearing a white dress stiffened by a crinoline. A wide sash wrapped her waist and made her seem like some sort of gift package about to be put under the tree. "In fact, that is exactly what I was," she had once told me. "This was the week my parents shipped me off to visit my father's brother who hunted wild boars in Tiberias. I can't quite remember the trip except that the man was a savage and terribly lewd and maybe even inappropriate. At some point, I remember slapping him as hard as I could and he sent me back to Haifa on the next bus."

I seemed to remember that my maternal grandparents moved from Haifa to Tel Aviv sometime in the early 1940s. In a snapshot I discovered at the bottom of one of the boxes, my mother and her friends are on the Gordon Beach in Tel Aviv. She could not have been more than fifteen. Some of the boys in the picture were wearing Scouts' uniforms and looked as though they hadn't yet shaved for the first time. Rachel stood barefoot. I remembered her telling me how proud she was of the calluses that let her stroll down Keren Kayemet Street to the Mediterranean shore "without feeling a thing."

As a very young boy I remember trying the same. We were on what was perhaps our first trip to Israel since my parents had left in the early 1950s. I was probably eight or nine and I remember coming down from my grandparents' apartment on Philon Street, trying to get to the corncob stand a couple of streets away without my sandals. At the halfway mark my feet felt like they'd caught fire, and I ran home dousing myself with tears.

"Don't you think we were a good-looking bunch?" my mother once asked me proudly as she passed over a series of photos that I now tried to glue back into the oldest album. The album cover was woven from strips of blue and white bamboo and as far as I could remember, it had always sat on the coffee table in Toronto. They were rather good-looking, I thought, just before realizing that this cleaning business could take all year. I quickened my pace.

⸻

Though she soon came out of the hospital again, everyone but my mother realized that the cancer was winning and she would not last for much more than a month. None of her doctors were prepared to break the news to her. Nor did she press any of them to give her more than the most ambiguous predictions. "We're hoping that we can turn this thing around," her oncologist, Dr. Iris, told her. But when I put a direct question to the same doctor, she just shook her head and pointed out the stats, which were brutal. "Her chances of recovery are virtually nil. Very soon the immune system will go and the fevers will surge with ever more regularity. Once a rhythm is established, the organs will no longer be able to hold up for long." I made arrangements for Deborah and our three children to come to Israel, which they did, staying for a couple of weeks.

I would have liked my mother to ask me outright to stay for the duration. But if she had any idea that there was to be a duration, she never let on. Nor did she ask for my company. I simply had to assume that she wished it and I also assumed that I would be useful to her as her condition deteriorated.

But it also occurred to me that under no circumstances could I continue to live in her apartment. I needed a room of my own, which I found rather easily. It was a small but pleasant room, available immediately, inexpensive and most importantly only a five-minute walk from my mother's apartment. The evening before I was to move, I packed my belongings, which included the notes and newspapers I had collected through the disengagement. My mother and I had an early supper, after which she retired almost immediately. I read until midnight and fell asleep on the bed in the extra bedroom, without ever having got undressed.

When I got up the next morning, I noticed that my mother had folded a crisp short-sleeved shirt, a freshly ironed pair of trousers, underwear and a clean pair of socks neatly on the bed table by my head. The scene was unmistakably meant to conjure memories of childhood, and the first day of school. Each year until I was into my early teens, my mother would carefully make just such piles and place them on the bed table. Beside the pile she would put a new lunchbox, a pencil case containing 2HB lead pencils, a sharpener, a plastic ruler and a thermos fit for either hot soup or a cold drink. Some years, as a special treat, she would buy Daniel and me new school bags decorated with one cartoon figure or another. Waking to such a pile of school things was the nearest we got to waking on a Christmas morning. The sight of all these new things filled my brother and me with intense excitement, along with great if false expectations that the world had been reborn. We mostly were forced to acknowledge that it had not been reborn before breakfast, when my father slammed the front door even as my mother was still yelling at him. In better years the spell extended through to the end of breakfast, but it still broke the moment we got to school. All of which is not to deny the enchantment of those moments.

But that was then and this was now and it took no more than five more minutes before I learned what was on my mother's mind.

"You needn't have done this," I said.

"But I really, really wanted to. Could you not perhaps let me play the mother one more time? You could save your money, cancel the rental, stay here, at least for a while?"

My mother's plea was entirely touching. But every instinct I had and many that I didn't have instructed me—as loudly as any instruction I had ever received from myself or from anyone else for that matter—to say no. *Thank her politely, but just say no. Don't try to explain that there is no way to retrieve those times when she was a mother and you were a child. Do not even try to make her see that such a thing is doomed, that it will necessarily lead to disappointment—hers more than yours.* I reminded myself that all it would take would be for me to arrive late for a meal, or miss the last bus home, or be inadvertently or not inadvertently irritated or short-tempered or rude. If anything like that happened, it would trigger her old tantrums or the face-slapping she'd once indulged in so liberally—and our relationship would end with a terrible bang instead of the whimper I was expecting. All of these thoughts crowded my mind and persuaded me that I could not extend my stay in this apartment for even one more day, and that I had to go on with my plan. And then I said, "Fine, I'll stay."

Maybe I felt sorry for her, saw in this plea the final and really not so terribly hard-to-satisfy request of a dying woman, of my dying mother? Probably there was, in this terrible mistake I made, a little of all these things. But there was also something else: a trait that I developed early, largely as a reaction to her, which had to do with thinking of myself as far more able to toe a line than I actually am.

⸺∞⸺

For several weeks, my mother's condition levelled off. Her fevers came only sporadically and there were many days when she seemed almost normal—except that she had lost her appetite entirely and was being sustained by a liquid meal supplement called Ensure. Moti and his wife Efrat and my aunt Talma visited every afternoon. I was with her every morning. Often, I would shop for the guests and sometimes for the meal I planned to cook that evening. Many mornings I would visit the doctor at her behest, fill a prescription, buy a case of Ensure, wash last night's dishes.

In the afternoons I would sometimes conduct interviews that had to do with the aftermath of the disengagement. I did a series of chats with Brigadier General HaCohen, who introduced me to a side of the IDF that I had never known. Some evenings I would stay home, read or write or watch Israeli television, which struck me as droll. Whenever one of my mother's friends came to visit her after supper, I would go out with my own friends.

For a while my mother seemed fine with this. When I got back to the apartment in the late afternoon, she would greet me with a verse whose origins I did not seek out until after she died. "*Shalom adoni haMeleh, eifo hyeeta Umah Useetah*— Hello, Your Majesty the King, where have you been and what have you seen." The verse was part of a children's game that was popular when she was young. The child performing the role of His Majesty was expected to respond with a real or imagined story about his adventures. But I knew nothing of the rhyme and thought she was trying to make me feel guilty for being out and about. That in turn made me irritable to the point where I sometimes did not respond to her at all.

To her credit my mother never allowed herself to express the anger she felt when I did not come home on time or when I was distracted or lost in thought. Though she never said as much, to me it seemed perfectly clear that she had promised herself not to react as she would have in the past—as she undoubtedly still wished to react. Every once in a while I tried to carve out a different kind of relationship with her, something better suited to a relationship between two adults, one of whom was dying. One day I tried to get her to explain why she had been so violent with me when I was a kid. "I didn't know what else to do," she said. "You were out of control. You were doing drugs and you were failing at school and you did not seem to know the difference between good and evil."

"When your mother hit you as a kid, did that help?" I asked her.

"Not for a minute. It only made things worse."

"So?"

"I didn't know what else to do."

"But what did you think I was up to? Wasn't your husband as much out of control as I was? Did it ever occur to you that maybe he was my role model—that I was perhaps acting the way I did as a way of getting closer to him?"

"It never occurred to me," she said. And that was that.

On another occasion, when she asked me how my day had gone, I tried to tell her about a new crop of IDF commanders, whom I found fascinating. "They are thinking about things in entirely different ways," I said, "developing new techniques for dealing with their enemies. In fact they are not thinking about the Arabs as enemies at all but as opponents who could be turned around, sometimes in the midst of a battle." I told her about some new military techniques that I had been studying. I even wondered aloud about the intellectual bubble that helped some younger officers live more easily with their duties. Did she think it was better or worse to think creatively about what amounted to nothing more than killing people, I asked her. But by then she had shut her eyes.

What I realized over time was that she and I had never actually had a conversation that did anything more than chase about its own tail. To attempt to break that circle at this point was hopeless.

One day I came in only to find my aunt Talma sitting on the overstuffed chair across from my mother. Talma was crying, and my mother was violently scratching her skull. Only after my mother died did Talma explain what had transpired.

"When I came in," Talma told me, "my sister did not say a word. I asked her what was wrong, was she feeling okay, but she didn't answer. I made us both a cup of tea and sat down across from her. Quietly at first but working herself into a tizzy, Rachel began berating me for seeing a psychiatrist. 'Why are you spending your hard-earned money,' my sister wanted to know?"

Talma told her she needed help with "separation issues." My mother lost her temper. "You don't need to see some stupid psychiatrist for that. I know everything there is to know about separation. I left my husband for almost seven years, didn't I?"

Talma tried to change the subject, but my mother was relentless. "Finally, I broke down," Talma said. "I told her that the separation issues that I needed help with had nothing to do with my husband but with my older sister. 'I need help separating from you,' I told your mother, who went white and never really spoke to me the same way again."

※

By late November 2005, my mother was refusing visitors and not answering phone calls from her many old girlfriends in Canada. Her days emptied out and the pressure she put on her closest family became almost intolerable. Moti, who had built my grandfather's subsistence-level playing card factory into a successful two-person operation, was chauffeuring her back and forth from Tel Aviv to Haifa on a nearly daily basis. More often than not, Talma took the day off from her law practice and joined them at the hospital. Mostly I would join them by midday, taking the train from Tel Aviv to Haifa. All of this took a serious toll on Talma and Moti's livelihoods and my mother would often acknowledge their effort, excuse herself for being such a handful, a chore, a burden. And she would then offer to relieve us of our duty, though it was never clear how she could do that. Moti and I once spoke about hiring a driver to shuttle her back and forth from the hospital. But we immediately abandoned the idea, for we both knew that she would see it as a betrayal.

Sometimes my mother's natural defiance would make an unexpected appearance. On those occasions she would hold up her childhood like a cross to the devil. "How could you do this to me?" she once muttered, loud enough for me to hear. "I am still that little girl who stole the ice cream and you have no right." Who was she talking to?

One day my mother asked me, "How do they expect me to die? I don't know how they expect me to die. Do you think I should be standing up or should I be sitting or maybe lying in bed like old Ivan Ilyich? I really don't know what they are expecting." I recall thinking how funny a question this was and how charming and how impossible to answer and maybe even realizing that she really was moving backward and that very soon she would no longer be the adult that she maybe never was.

But I needed to talk with her about at least one more adult thing. My money situation was getting bad and I could not figure out how I could possibly stick around for very much longer. I considered applying for a job in Israel and in fact went to an interview for a staff job at one of the newspapers. But since I had no intention of staying in Israel after my mother died, it came to nothing. No institution was interested in an employee who could make no commitment.

Bereft of options, I asked my mother for a loan, which immediately made her face drop to somewhere below her knees. "Okay," she said, as though I had just asked to be paid for services rendered. Then she changed the subject and made it impossible for me to ever ask again. I wondered whether she was not now becoming her father, for whom money had meant everything. The day before he died he wrote Moti, the son with whom he had worked for most of his life, out of his will.

Talma, Moti, my mother and I met with the South African physician who headed the oncology team at Rambam hospital. "Mrs. Berlin," he said, looking stern. "I am very upset with you."

"Why, doctor, what have I done?" my mother said in a voice barely audible.

"It is not what you've done—it is what you haven't done. When we first admitted you, we made a deal, which was that we would do everything to make you better and you would get better. Well, Mrs. Berlin, we have done our part, provided you with the best medical care in the world. But you have not done your part."

I thought this man was insane and had probably only left South Africa because Botha refused to extend apartheid. I considered the idea of rushing him, maybe even helping him out his office window. My mother looked as though the last pint of blood had been siphoned from her. "I am sorry, doctor," she said. "I did my best. And I have to say that I do not feel bad. I do not feel at all ill. So what do you think would happen if I just didn't bother you anymore, stopped the treatment, ignored the disease, and went about my business as if nothing had changed since before we met?"

"I don't think anything," he said. "I know what would happen—in one week you would be dead."

"What are you saying, doctor?" Moti said, with great trepidation.

"Is there something we can do?" Talma asked.

I was still seething, still planning a frontal attack.

"Nothing, really. There is one drug that is still very much at the experimental stage. It is not included in the health care basket. If you wish, I believe I can get it. It is administered in two doses, two pills, which will cost you five thousand dollars US. Should you choose to go this route, you will need to hand me a certified cheque before you leave the hospital today."

"Will it help?" Talma asked.

"I don't know. If I was forced to guess, I would say there is less than a 10 percent chance."

"Do you recommend it?" Moti asked.

"Put it this way. If I or a member of my family was as sick as Rachel is, I would go for it, would not give it a second thought."

"Thank you," Moti said. "We will be back with the money within the hour."

"Is that all?" my mother asked

"Yes, thank you for coming in," the doctor said.

———⁂———

The magic pills did not help stave off the fevers, which had finally established a rhythm. At some point it occurred to me that my mother might have either accepted, or was preparing to accept, her death. I thought she might be prepared to write down her thoughts, perhaps even jot down some things she wished to tell her grandchildren. So I made my way down to the local paper shop, bought the most expensive blank notebook I could find, had the clerk wrap it and quickly went back to the apartment. Then I took my mother for a walk to the parkette at the back of her building. We sat on a bench and she carefully unwrapped my gift.

"There is a chance that you will not be present at your grandchildren's weddings," I said in as gentle a manner as I could manage. "I think it would be wonderful if you wrote down your thoughts and wishes and or whatever else you would like to say to them. If you don't make it, I, or maybe someone else, will read your notes and for a moment you would be there. It would undoubtedly be the most meaningful moment in their lives."

My mother looked down at her shoes and for the life of me I could not tell what she was thinking. A tear rolled down her cheek but she never wrote a word in the album.

Her immune system crashed and the magical pills made no difference. Her fever soared almost daily and by the second week of December, her brother could no longer handle things and hired a driver to be at her beck, to replace him on the road to Rambam hospital. I bought a plane ticket home.

I cannot really speak for Moti, but I have tried to understand my own decision to leave so close to the end. Off the top, I could say that it was no longer possible to stay, that I had come to my wits' end but also to the end of my finances. But this is merely being descriptive, not analytic, and really it is no reason at all. And why did I not summon my family to her bedside again? Together, perhaps by concentrating our feelings, could we not have pulled her back into our world? By leaving or by letting go, we humans think that we give the dying permission to die. What we say is that we the living, whom you the dying love, will be all right—we'll find a way to continue living without you. But what if this thought is profoundly mistaken? Imagine a world in which the next death meant that no one will be all right again. Would we not then find a way of keeping the dying from abandoning us?

What are our real feelings about the dying? Do we not all come to the tug-of-war—in which the body of the dying is the rope—as though the fight is fixed, as though it is written somewhere that we the living will lose, if not now, then some other time? What are the stakes in the relationship between the living and the dying? Is there a moment when the living worry that if they hang around any longer they will be dragged into the abyss with the person who is already halfway there?

I assumed Moti had been so stressed he could no longer take the driving back and forth to the hospital, could no longer worry about my mother's possibly feeling betrayed. She was crazy, he thought, and she was becoming crazier. For my mother, loyalty was everything, but no longer did he think about her need for loyalty. Instead, he told me that the only reason she might become upset that he had hired a driver had to do with the cost. That was maybe the way their father had thought about things; it may also have been the way Moti himself thought about the issue. But it was not the way my mother thought. She thought only about loyalty and she reacted badly. "It is time for me to die," she told me, when we broke the news that I was leaving and Moti had hired a driver; we both were going to betray her. "No one can afford to have me around any longer."

The next morning her fever went through the roof and the cab picked her up and for the first time ever she rode the hour-and-fifteen-minute trip to the hospital on her own. I called the hospital and asked how she was doing. "At the moment your mother is stable," the nurse said.

I had a hundred errands to run but got them done by early evening, at which point I got on the train to Haifa to see her one last time.

My mother was in a private room, IVs in her arm, the snorkels of an oxygen bottle attached to the insides of her nostrils. She asked me to wet her lips and I did so, just as she had done for my father. I told her that I was not comfortable leaving her until she was back at home, that I would cancel my flight and renew it only when she was feeling better. She could hardly speak but managed anyhow. "No," she said. "Go home as you've planned. You don't care about me anyhow and you should leave."

Perhaps I should have expected her to say something like this, but I did not and was mortified. "Why did you say that?" I asked.

"No, no, you don't love me at all," she insisted. "Do you know how many nights I waited up for you? You said you would be home by such and such and I waited and you didn't come."

"But you could have called. I always had my cellphone with me. I would have come home in a minute."

"You should have called me."

"But, Mother, for Christ's sake, you were in bed at 9 p.m. Why would I call you?"

"GO HOME," she said as loudly as she could. "YOU HAVE GOT YOUR REVENGE, NOW GO HOME." And then she passed out.

I knew it would be the last time I would see her. I touched her arm, and then walked out into a cool night in Haifa. Why in the world had she spoken about revenge?

Three days later my brother Daniel took my place at her side. Very soon she was transferred to the hospice near Meir Hospital where my father had died. For the first day all she wanted to know was who was paying for her stay. She said that if they were charging her, she wanted to die right there and then.

One night my brother called me in a tizzy. "Your mother wants to cut you out of her will," he said. "She told Talma that she wants all the documents altered and that none of her money should go to you. She told Talma that you cared for nothing but her money and that she would teach you what that meant."

"What did Talma say?"

"Talma said that if she wanted to change her will, she would have to get herself another lawyer. And then she reminded our mother that your grandfather had done the same thing to his son, Moti. Your mother screamed at her, insisted that this was her money and that this is what she wanted to do with it and that she would teach you what it meant not to love her. But don't worry, if she does get the will changed, I will for sure give you half."

"Daniel, I am not worried. Not for one second. But I am very sad. Very sad."

At four the next morning my mother passed away.

EIGHT

The Dream State

On the morning of Wednesday July 12, 2006, just hours before I arrived in Israel to attend to my parents' estate, Hezbollah's secretary-general, Hassan Nasrallah, launched an attack on two IDF armoured vehicles patrolling the Israeli-Lebanese border. Manning the convoy were seven Israeli reserve soldiers on their final tour of duty. Some had already packed their bags, returned their gear, and crossed the mental border separating military from civilian life. Minutes before the convoy left the base, First Sergeant Ehud Goldwasser, the non-commissioned officer in charge of the outgoing troop, chatted with Nir Laon, the weary lieutenant who had just returned from an earlier patrol. As Goldwasser was brushing his teeth, Laon told him that during the night some twenty Hezbollah fighters had crossed the border from Lebanon into Israel. But for some reason, Goldwasser did not pay attention to Laon's words. Nor did he allow them to spoil his mood. At a quarter to nine, when Goldwasser conducted the routine radio check with his buddies in the patrol, he did not mention Hezbollah's movement, but breezily wished all a good morning, reminded them that this was their final mission, and exhorted everyone to enjoy it. Sixteen minutes later, the two armoured vehicles were ambushed. Ehud Goldwasser and Sergeant Eldad Regev were kidnapped and subsequently killed. Three more soldiers died in the skirmish and eight rescue soldiers were killed in the ensuing chase.

This was not Hezbollah's first offensive. In October of 2000, shortly after Israel's hasty withdrawal from its eighteen-year occupation of Lebanon, a group of Syrian-trained Hezbollah fighters crossed the border into Israel and kidnapped and killed three Israeli soldiers. The Israeli prime minister at the time, Ehud Barak, reacted mildly. He ordered the army to fire a few rounds in the air, put some helicopters into play, and let things go at that. In March of 2002, after Ariel Sharon was elected prime minister, Hezbollah killed another six Israelis. Sharon, whose confidants claimed he could not stomach the idea of re-entering Lebanon, gave strict orders not to escalate the conflict. Over the next four years, Sharon's office routinely played down the threat that Hezbollah's growing missile cache posed to Israel.

"The settlers' claim that Sharon is a traitor and that he was not the father figure we thought he was has been gaining currency, now that we're beginning to understand how much he hid from us," Benzi said as we walked out to the airport's parking lot after he'd met my flight.

"Why do you think he did that?" I asked.

"Hezbollah's rearmament, which he did nothing to stop, made his occupation of Lebanon look like an absolute waste of time," Benzi replied.

"But really," I asked, "are their weapons more than a nuisance? Don't you think Nasrallah's got the Lebanese president, not us, in his sights?"

"Well, Mofaz [the former IDF chief of staff and minister of defence] and Moshe Yaalon [another former IDF chief of staff] don't think so. Besides, Nasrallah is now boasting that he has the capability of destroying Israel any time he wishes," Benzi said.

The truth was that many Israeli military analysts held that Hezbollah's arsenal did not in fact constitute more than a nuisance. Several senior analysts with whom I spoke over the next few days thought Nasrallah's boast was hollow. "Nasrallah knows that Israel's fighter planes could knock out his rocket launchers in no time flat," one analyst told me. "The Sheik authorized this kidnapping raid only because he could not afford to ignore our reluctance to negotiate a prisoner swap. Nasrallah's power depends on the loyalty of his fighters and their loyalty depends on his authority as a protector. Plus there's the disputed Sha'aba farms business. Ordinary Lebanese feel strongly about that issue, and so taking a firm stand about it raises Nasrallah's status in the country, makes him seem not like the chief of some fundamentalist splinter group but a bona fide political leader for all of Lebanon."

However one thought of Nasrallah, General Udi Adam, who was then in command of Israel's north, argued that there was nothing to be gained by military means alone. But Prime Minister Ehud Olmert did not agree, and by nightfall on July 12 the Israeli Air Force was flying round robin sorties over Beirut.

Why did Olmert retaliate with such force? Israeli analysts have offered myriad answers. Some claim that the international consensus encouraging Israel to destroy Hezbollah's internal organization created a mandate that could hardly be turned down. Indeed, rarely had so many Arab leaders, including the Egyptian president Hosni Mubarak, the Saudi foreign minister Saud Al-Faisal, and Jordan's King Abdullah II, given Israel the green light.

Other analysts focused on the IDF's anxiety about Lebanon re-emerging as a second front. Some months earlier Hamas had taken over the reins of power in the Gaza Strip, and only a few weeks before the Hezbollah attack, they'd confused the IDF by kidnapping the Israeli soldier Gilad Shalit. As the Gaza settlers had predicted, Hamas militants were now lobbing missiles into Israeli towns near the border. Some senior IDF staff worried about a Hamas-Hezbollah coalition.

A few Israeli journalists interpreted Olmert's decision in psycho-political terms. They argued that Olmert's decision to hold Lebanon as a whole responsible for Hezbollah's attack had much to do with the prime minister's desire to distance himself from Sharon, his predecessor and his former boss, who had had a visceral aversion to everything that had to do with the Lebanese front. Olmert wanted to show Israel that although he had none of Sharon's military experience he was just as tough and capable a military leader.

By midnight on July 12, the sky above Lebanon was wall-to-wall Israeli jets. "In a matter of thirty-nine minutes, the Israeli Air Force destroyed over sixty long-missile launchers. If there ever had been a threat to Israel, the threat no longer existed," wrote the Israeli journalist Ilan Kfir. "By Friday afternoon, the 14th of

July 2006, Nasrallah was devastated." The Shi'a neighbourhood in South Beirut was in ruins, many senior Hezbollah leaders were dead, and Hassan Nasrallah had barely escaped with his life. "Reports of the extent of damage to his strategic weapons cache reached him and he would have been prepared to accept any terms and conditions which Israel dictated. He was very aware that six years of military build-up was about to vaporize."

But Olmert did not stop there. He continued the Israeli offensive for another month, escalating a campaign that began as a massive but successful retaliation into a full-scale, devastating war. To attempt to understand how and why the Israeli leadership became obsessed with a campaign that should have ended no later than the fourteenth of July is to inquire into something far deeper than the usual assumptions about Israel. It becomes even more of a mystery when one learns just how unprepared for war Israel was at the time. A large number of senior IDF officers had no experience in battle; over the previous six years they had been fighting terrorism in the West Bank and Gaza. A large percentage of the IDF's foot soldiers had never even participated in a military exercise on the scale of the battle that they would now encounter against a disciplined and organized enemy. By 2006 the Israeli army as a whole was becoming a bureaucracy that worried more about budgets and tenure than about military excellence at any cost. The northern Galilee, whose towns, villages and spas constituted the main target of Hezbollah's Katyusha missiles, was impossibly unprepared. The condition of the shelters had been allowed to deteriorate to the point that many were entirely unusable. Magen David Adom, the nation's ambulance service, was on the verge of bankruptcy.

Yet when the news that Hezbollah's long-range missile launchers had been destroyed made its way back to Israel, the Israeli mood went through the roof. Within hours, thousands of automobiles were flying the blue-and-white Israeli flag. At virtually every intersection elated children handed out flags, buttons, T-shirts and bumper stickers. Israeli television ran clips of restless little children confined to the dilapidated shelters in the north. In one clip that I watched, a bunch of giddy six-year-olds reported that they hoped this would all be over soon so that they could resume working on a joint Arab-Israeli school project they had begun before "evil Nasrallah started to shell them." The scene was followed by one in which local reserve officers promised to "tear Nasrallah's every organ out of his still living body." Brigadier-General Ran Shmueli went live to air swearing that he personally would "shatter the head of the snake with a garden shovel."

Meanwhile, in the nation's capital, Noar HaGvaot—a zealous religious youth movement living in the Judean desert—danced the hora hand in hand with Peace Now activists. The pious Chabad Jews drove about the country in their happy synagogues on wheels, piping klezmer songs from loudspeakers into the streets.

Thousands of Israelis offered up spare rooms in their houses to their "brothers in the north." Postings on the internet invited northerners suffering Hezbollah shelling to bring their entire families to the safer environs of Tel Aviv, Beer Sheba and Eilat. Restaurants and hotels advertised special discounts to "our brothers in the Galilee." Private citizens converted vehicles into ambulances. The media, which should have maintained a critical distance, abandoned it. Indeed, the editors of Israel's two largest-circulation newspapers altered their format from tabloid style to double-page broadsheets featuring panoramic shots of the devastation. *Maariv* adopted a new blue logo and headlines that screamed, "We shall win."

On the political front, Israeli leaders were fielding massive numbers of congratulatory notes, many of which encouraged them to finish off the job they had begun. From Washington, Vice President Dick Cheney contacted former Israeli military chief of staff Moshe "Boogie" Ya'alon to discuss the future of the campaign. From the American administration, the Israelis got the message that destroying Hezbollah would strike a blow against the Iranians such as no one had succeeded in doing since the Ayatollah's revolution in 1979. Reacting to all of this, Labor Party stalwarts began contemplating the future of their party. "Come next election we will win, big time," one memo said. "Ever since Yitzhak [which was how the current minister of defence referred to the assassinated Prime Minister Rabin] there has not been a leader like the current defence minister, Amir Peretz: the party has a tradition and a history, and now, given Peretz, a genius leader," another memo records.

The only protest that I noted took place in Rabin Square, where a handful of Israeli Communist Party members rallied against the wanton bombing and the massive collateral damage. But as forty-odd young men and women marched behind the Hammer and Sickle, Israelis of all walks gathered on the sidelines to heckle and boo.

Both the journalist Ilan Kfir, who published the first book on
the war that would be called Lebanon 2, and Ofer Shelah and
Yoav Limor, who put together a 437-page tome on the same
subject, regarded the euphoria that swept Israel in the wake of
the early successes with an understandable degree of cynicism.
"Success inflated the sails," Shelah and Limor wrote. "In the
grip of the euphoria, very few Israelis bothered with finicky
details like the difference between good Lebanese and bad
ones." To most Israelis the Lebanon war was seen as target
practice, and few worried about the consequences the bombing
might have in the post-campaign era.

Indeed, any Israeli old enough to remember the last emotional tidal wave—the euphoria that erupted when news of the
destruction of the Egyptian Air Force hit the streets during the
'67 war—had cause for alarm, because they also could not
forget the dark underside of this celebration. When my mother,
brother and I had visited Israel in July of 1967, I was too young
to understand and all we felt was exhilaration. But when my
uncle Asher, who was a senior officer working for Israel's military industries, took us on a tour of the Golan Heights, I remember being horrified at the site of the ankle shackles the Syrian
military leadership used to keep its soldiers in the bunkers.

It would be another two decades before I understood that
extreme euphoria, which overrides the critical faculties, is itself
a shackle no less binding than the ankle chains the Syrians used.

I learned to appreciate euphoria's serpent-like nature from
reserve General Shlomo Gazit. During the Six Day War, Gazit
had served as a junior officer in an Israeli intelligence agency.
"I was in the war room when news that Israeli fighter planes
had decimated the Egyptian Air Force came over the wire. For

the first while, the mood in the office was tentative and then it became jubilant and triumphal," Gazit told me when I went to see him in his office at Tel Aviv University. "Israelis had lost very little and I was dancing with the rest of them. And then I got hit over the head. One of the few casualties was my sister's son, with whom I was extremely close. The news shocked me and broke the spell. It was at that point that I fired off a memo to the prime minister's office. I argued that no matter how great the victory, we should immediately return the lands that we had conquered. Like David Ben-Gurion and a few others, I argued that there was no way we could rule the Palestinian people. I urged the prime minister to get behind the Palestinian movement, promote their national self-determination. If we did that, I argued, we would be heroes and we would have bought ourselves allies for the future."

"What happened to the memo and to your thinking?" I asked Gazit, who became rather evasive.

"Well, you know, I fired off a dozen memos every day. This was but one of them."

When I insisted, Gazit became wistful.

"Like everyone else, I too was eventually swept up by the euphoria."

Kfir, Shelah and Limor said nothing positive about the intoxication that overtook Israel in the wake of its two greatest military successes. But for all the harm that a euphoric condition can cause, not only in Israel but in any theatre of war, it is still important to understand what the powerful positive aspect of this condition is. Euphoria of this sort is essentially the intimation of unity or wholeness, and whether the unity that we feel when we are under its spell, in the dream state it induces, is a unity that once existed or is simply a profound and sentimental nostalgia for a condition that never was, does not alter the feelings themselves. When the newly installed Israeli minister of defence Amir Peretz shook both his fists at Hassan Nasrallah, saying that "the Sheik shall always remember the name Amir Peretz," all one could do was hope, for his sake, that he would never awake from his dream.

⚙

But Peretz had no choice: he had to awake, and must have considered that possibility as early as Thursday, July 13, 2006, when Haifa was hit by a missile from Lebanon. And if he managed to remain in his waking dream through that event, what followed on July 14 must have seriously disturbed his rest. That evening, as jet squadrons were busy releasing payloads over the Dahiyeh neighbourhood of South Beirut, the first serious alarm must surely have gone off in the minister's offices.

At twenty minutes before nine that evening, a battleship called the *Hanit*, stationed in the waters off the coast of Lebanon, was hit by a land-to-sea missile fired by Hezbollah. What was devastating about this event was not only the death of four of the sailors aboard the vessel but what it revealed about the general state of laxity in the Israeli military.

The blast happened on a Friday night. Fifty-five of the seventy-odd men on board, including most of the senior officers, had retired below deck to celebrate the Sabbath. In their enthusiasm, no one remembered to switch on the *Hanit*'s anti-missile system, which happened to be one of the most expensive and sophisticated systems of its kind. Moreover, the various anti-missile launchers on board were unmanned.

By the time the deck crew observed the lightning-like flash from the Lebanese harbour, it was too late. Seconds later they felt an enormous jolt as the back of the ship was hit and burst into flames, engulfing the helicopter on board. A very damaged ship had to be towed into an Israeli harbour early the next morning.

For the next thirty-some days, Israel escalated the war, but no battle broke decisively in its favour and in many cases the battles were costly. Young men, including the Israeli novelist David Grossman's son, Uri, died in the bungled manoeuvres undertaken in south Lebanon. Inter-IDF communications were a mess, in part because the newspeak that the young generals who had graduated from Shimon Naveh's institute employed as though it were the vernacular was entirely incomprehensible to reserve soldiers.

"We were told to swarm and to *lehishtabel* (ensnail) ourselves," one reserve officer told me.

"How did you respond?" I asked.

"I asked the commanding officer whether he wanted us to swarm and ensnail directly up his ass, or maybe take a detour and then drive up his ass."

Soldiers deployed into combat complained of lack of ammunition.

Time and again, Israeli surges underestimated Hezbollah's resolve.

Throughout the campaign, short-range Katyusha-type rockets rained down on the Galilee, through which I and my Danish journalist friend Hanne Foigel drove many times. "It's demoralizing," Hanne, who has lived in Israel for thirty years, told me. "These rockets remind me of the stones David used against Goliath, except that in this case, we are the giant."

This kind of moral discomfiture affected every Israeli, not least the prime minister, Ehud Olmert, who withdrew from public life for two weeks in the middle of the war. The vacuum that he and his senior ministers left when they disappeared was filled by a cacophony of low-ranking military officers, middle-brow academics and noisy junior politicians who were not authorized to speak for the government. At some point Israelis became so unnerved that they were transfixed by Nasrallah's broadcasts on Al-Manar, Hezbollah's television station.

Israeli parents who worried about their soldier children took it upon themselves to call their sons at the front lines. Or they called the officer in charge in a manner that breached all security restrictions. The cloud of cellular conversations often provided Hezbollah with azimuths that allowed them to pinpoint locations, and cost Israeli soldiers their lives.

Monday, July 31, was a quiet enough day to draw the prime minister out of hiding. He showed up at a gathering of the mayors from the north, and gave what journalists called a "blood, sweat and tears" speech in which he addressed the national tragedy in the south Lebanon village of Bint Jbeil. Olmert spoke into the television cameras of all three of Israel's major networks. He recounted the personal tragedy of one soldier, Roi Klein, who closed his eyes for the final time even as he intoned the martyr's prayer "Shmah Yisrael:" "Hear, oh Israel, our lord is our God, our lord is one." Olmert spoke about Klein's comrade in arms, who had died in a heroic attempt to save an injured soldier. The prime minister looked prime-ministerial. To his viewers he seemed animated and confident, more of an orator than ever before.

Following the speech, Olmert held a press conference to which representatives of both the Israeli and the foreign media were invited. A correspondent from Associated Press International asked him about his post-war plans. Perhaps because he was still under the influence of the euphoric vapours, Olmert responded that "the victory over Hezbollah will pave the road to the ingathering." There was nothing surprising about this statement, which harked back to Olmert's election promise to evacuate a large number of illegal settlements and outposts in the West Bank. Yet the settlers in the West Bank responded as though they had never heard of the "ingathering." Within minutes of his speech, an extraordinary brouhaha broke out. "Who does Olmert think he is?" one YESHA leader cried into a television microphone. "Roi Klein and his friends wore knitted skullcaps. They gave their lives to defend our country, not Olmert's outrageous ingathering." The official statement from YESHA took the form of a question: "Is it possible that soldiers wearing knitted skullcaps should sacrifice their lives so that Olmert will be able to send the army in to destroy their homes?" *Not in this lifetime!* was the resounding response.

Dozens of rabbis and teachers, and hundreds of settlers with children in Lebanon, fired off text messages to their students and children serving on the front lines. "Disobey your commander's orders; abandon the front lines; come home immediately," the messages said. They were declaring mutiny and committing treason. They gave no thought to the possible outcome; no rabbi or settler parent seemed worried about the consequences of such a mutiny for the Israeli soldiers left behind or for the country as a whole.

I was visiting an artillery unit when the messages began coming in. To my surprise, I found myself wishing that Ariel Sharon, and not Olmert, was in power. Had Sharon been in command, he would not have tolerated such behaviour, would have perhaps rounded up the ringleaders and brought them to trial for high treason. Or he would have had the first soldier to abandon his post shot. Olmert did no such thing. In a pitiful attempt to stave off the mutiny, the prime minister called Effie Eitam, one of the leaders of the religious Zionist movement, to apologize for what he referred to as a "gaffe." "For Olmert's ingathering, it was the kiss of death," Ilan Kfir wrote. The blackmail had worked. And then, on August 14, the fighting ended and the funerals began.

On those occasions when grief exceeds the language we have to express it, and does not stop there but becomes bigger still; when it reaches the point where one suspects that no human being could or should or ever will learn how to survive it—then we sometimes get giddy, and funerals become minor celebrations. Thus it was for the many hundreds who came to a moshav called Mazkeret Batya for the military burial of thirty-year-old Captain Yoni Shmoukher. We were noisier and cheerier than anyone should ever be at such an occasion. But it was impossible to cry, not because we had no tears left but because the extent of our despair made crying seem a cliché. Somehow laughter, maybe even coarse, Germanic guffawing seemed more appropriate than tears. We who had come to be with an old friend who had just lost his son, found ourselves too small, too numb for grief. We felt as though it was just a matter of time before our luck would run out too.

Benzi and I arrived late and so we were relegated to the outer reaches of the funeral. Here, at a safe distance from the mourners, smiles and embraces were easier to exchange. As Israel's army rabbi-in-chief began the ceremony I managed to speak with an army buddy I hadn't seen for over thirty years. "This is so much worse than it used to be," Aaron whispered. "Thirty-three years ago when we got together to bury our friends we felt that someone was in charge and that the dead had died for a cause. Now we're in charge, and it is our children we are burying and no one knows why anymore."

The sun's rays damaged a morning that should have been misty and grey but was too bright, over-exposed. Aaron had married a woman named Ye'elah, whose young lover, Gal Avinoam, had been shot through the skull on a similar morning outside of the Jabaliyah refugee camp in Gaza. "I blame the Holocaust for all of this," Aaron said. "Until this nation gets over that trauma we will never be able to act within reason."

I also bumped into Hanan Soreq, who had been our staff officer during the intolerable nine months of our basic training. Soreq still sported Puck's mischievous grin but he had become a religious Hebrew, not only a Jew but the quintessential Israeli, of the sort that must have at some point roamed the Judaean desert freely. He wore a rainbow-coloured knitted skullcap. He was burnt by the desert sun and had he been leaning on a hooked wooden staff, he would have been indistinguishable from any of the ancient prophets. "Are you still living abroad?" he asked me mockingly. "What business have you there?" I asked him whether he knew Yoni. "Yes," he said.

"Yoni was a reserve engineer in a paratrooper unit. He was pursuing a graduate degree in physics. His wife, Shlomit—she is the one hanging on her father's arm over there—is very pregnant."

Bougainvillea draped the back fence. Bouquets and a summer's cornucopia adorned the remains of a young man who had been killed for no better reason than that the war in Lebanon had been fought. Yoni had led a troop into a village in south Lebanon, encountered a cadre of Hezbollah fighters, and requested orders. The troop needed to get out of the line of fire and the officer to whom Yoni was accountable used an aerial photograph to direct him to a villa some hundred metres from where they were crouching. Yoni objected. The villa was far too exposed. If they took shelter there, they would become sitting ducks. But the order was repeated, this time with the kind of stubborn insistence of an officer for whom the need to be obeyed had become more important than the substance of the order. Yoni obeyed and minutes later he was standing at the window of the abandoned villa, watching helplessly as a missile whizzed by and hit a cache of explosives that detonated and took his life.

The IDF's chief rabbi asked Yoni for forgiveness and chanted a prayer that most of the mourners ignored. Then a quivering voice belonging to Ariela Ringel Hoffman, Yoni's mother-in-law, came over the loudspeakers. "No one can understand how life will go on without Yoni," she cried. "No one can understand how the sun will rise without the buoyancy of his spirit, how it will set without his humour." But behind her eulogy storm clouds gathered and would soon burst into the pages of *Yediot Ahronot*, the broadsheet for which Ariela worked as a senior correspondent.

"On August 9, 15 soldiers died in the glorious offensive that got underway even before the decision was properly approved. Their death changed nothing," she wrote. "South Lebanon was not conquered, zero results, and rocket launchers kept firing more than 200 missiles . . . Fifteen families shall stand by gravesites that bring as much pain as they did the day they were dug. Fifteen families and close friends . . . in a desperate search for the boys, the stories of their short lives, and the enigma of their death: How did this happen to us?"

And then there was a shriek such as I had never heard before. Yoni's little sister— she could not have been more than fourteen years old—took the mike. "Abba, Dad," she said, "I know that you are devastated, that you lost Yoni who meant more than life itself to you. I know all that but I don't care. I don't care and I cannot help you and I don't want to help you because I am not your father. You are my father. And all I care about is this black cloud that has descended, that has swallowed me whole. I cannot breathe, I cannot live. You must help me. You must remove this blackness from me . . . now. You are my father and you must do that."

The next morning I had coffee with *Yediot Ahronot* columnist Dr. Ronen Bergman, who had just published *The Point of No Return*. "If I were not Israeli," Ronen told me, "I would pick up the phone to the young Assad in Syria today and let him know in no uncertain terms that the map in the Middle East has changed, that he can no longer count on Israel to act rationally. If there is one incontrovertible lesson we got from this last war it is that Israel is no longer rational, that it has become the madman of the neighbourhood and maybe the madman of the Middle East."

For the most part, tensions between Neturei Karta, the hyper-Orthodox Jewish community living in the Meah She'arim district of Jerusalem, and the State of Israel are negligible. And while it is true that the five-thousand-odd members of this community whose name means "guardians of the city" hold that the State of Israel should be dismantled, they believe the dismantlement should be peaceful. Fewer than a hundred of these Haredim engage in politics; fewer still have gone to the length of consorting with Israel's enemies.

But in late July 2009 all of this changed. The narrow streets of Meah She'arim, normally a bustle of black hats, suddenly became a stream of angry men smashing windows, setting garbage cans on fire, and carrying signs comparing Jewish to Nazi doctors. Over the course of the next few days, eighteen policemen were injured in a rage that one foreign journalist compared to the riots that devastated Watts in 1965.

The incident began when a three-year-old Haredi boy, whose mother belonged to a hyper-Orthodox splinter group associated with Neturei Karta, was admitted to Jerusalem's Hadassah hospital for a condition initially diagnosed as severe malnutrition. Physicians immediately inserted a feeding tube but the boy's condition failed to improve. Suspicious staff installed a surveillance camera that filmed the mother removing the boy's tube. The nurse on duty reported the incident and uniformed officers were dispatched to detain the mother, with whom they caught up with at a welfare office. The arrest sparked angry protests and a ransacking of the office. Police then marched into Meah She'arim and took two more of the mother's six children into the care of social services. Within hours the ultra-Orthodox community exploded into the riots that lasted for four days.

Hadassah doctors diagnosed the mother with a rare condition called Munchausen syndrome by proxy, a subcategory of the equally rare Munchausen syndrome, a psychiatric condition that causes the afflicted to mimic symptoms of diseases to such a degree and with such precision that doctors perform unnecessary operations aimed at relieving the fictitious symptoms. The afflicted are often well aware that they have made up their symptoms but cannot control the obsession, which grows each time doctors are successfully duped. The subcategory called Munchausen syndrome by proxy or MSbP presents in much the same way, except that the body in question is not one's own but another's, commonly a close relative such as a dependent parent or child.

To the great majority of secular Israelis, the Jerusalem riots represented a new low point in the country's relationship with its most extreme religious community. In the daily rounds of conversation, Israelis, whether secular or religious, felt disgusted by the young mother and by an Orthodox community that seemed to them like a medieval if not Neanderthal cult. Photo essays filled the major newspapers. Captions captured the rage, but to most people, the play-by-play seemed to describe a soap opera rather than a national drama of any great import. But popular Jewish economist and columnist Nehemia Shtrasler saw it differently. "The First Temple was destroyed by the Babylonian king Nebuchadnezzer, the second by Titus," Shtrasler wrote in *Haaretz*. "The Third Temple will not be destroyed by any world superpower. We will survive the conflict with the Palestinians and even the nuclear threats from Iran. But the increasing rupture between the secular and the ultra-Orthodox communities in Israel will be the end of us. This is a Greek tragedy with a foregone conclusion. It is a struggle between two contradictory worldviews that cannot exist side by side. The ultra orthodox community makes up some 10 percent of the state's population but the number of their first grade children constitutes 25 percent of all pupils. The larger their number (estimates are that within a decade they will extend well beyond the 50 percent mark), the deeper the economic dependency upon the secular community will become. . . . The secular population will have to support a growing non-working community. So taxes will increase and the young, high-income secular people will buckle. They will leave the country. Entrepreneurs will look elsewhere for high-tech and blue-collar workers who will leave to graze in foreign pastures. The State of Israel as we know it will become a weak, mostly ultra-Orthodox community living off handouts, tithes and donations. There will be no need for a Nebuchadnezzar or a Titus. We are destroying the Third Temple with our own hands."

Needless to say, Shtrasler's opinion is controversial. The Montreal-born professor of finance, Bernard Avishai, for example, believes that Israeli entrepreneurs will not flee the country. On the contrary, as Avishai conceives of the future, it will be the hyper-Orthodox community that will be whittled down by the capitalist class. Which is not to say that the tensions between these two sectors will work themselves out peaceably. On the contrary, if the Canadian professor Yaacov Rabkin, author of *A Threat from Within: A Century of Jewish Opposition to Zionism*, is correct, the trend is toward ever greater violence. But unlike

Shtrasler, who is worried about the State of Israel, Rabkin seems to hope and perhaps even believes that the orthodoxy will prevail and that the Zionist state will indeed fall.

Several days into the riots, Shtrasler published another column that made me think he is far more confused than I had thought. "Secular people are so painfully naïve," Shtrasler wrote this time. "They don't understand that this is a war for home and country. . . . They don't understand that they are facing a well-planned occupation plan, with large, purposeful divisions set on robbing the secular majority of its spiritual and physical home. A halakhic [fundamentalist] state is not a mere slogan. It is an action plan."

"Judaism is not a missionary religion but it is missionary for internal purposes," he continued. "The Lithuanian and Chabad Hasidim want to turn the people into ultra-Orthodox Hasidim like themselves. They want the state to abide by the Torah. They do not accept the halakhic obligation to abide by the law of the land. The revolution they are planning is not like the Iranian revolution, which was carried out with weapons and violence. Here it is a velvet revolution, of money, smiles and kind words. But the goal is still the same—turning Israel into a halakhic state."

By the time I arrived in Jerusalem, Meah She'arim was a complete mess. Women wearing black shawls, their cheeks flushed from the heat, stood in pairs screaming at all and sundry. "They are kidnapping our children," one woman yelled at me. "But she was trying to murder her son," I retorted. "No, she was doing the *akeda* and hoped that God would save the boy," the woman said in a Yiddish that, if I understood correctly, meant that the young mother was sacrificing her son to God with the hope that he would replace the boy with a ram. Others in the streets offered more rational but less probable arguments. "If the mother was truly suffering from a psychiatric condition," one Haredi man told me, "she should have got help, not arrested."

In a nearby clinic, several adolescents with sidelocks tucked behind their ears were being treated for bruises and broken bones. "We do not have tanks," one young man told me. "Our people have no other way to make the secular authorities understand that such an invasion of our neighbourhoods and such lies about our communities cannot be tolerated." Jerusalem mayor Nir Barkat demanded that the rabbinical establishment condemn the violence, and when the rabbis refused, he declared that the city would not clear the garbage. The Neturei Karta would fester in their own stink.

Purposely or not, Shtrasler blurred the distinction between Neturei Karta, who are entirely self-contained and as interested in bringing secular Jews into the fold as the Amish are in converting lapsed Catholics. It is simply mistaken to say that this hyper-Orthodox community wants a Haredi state. The fact is they do not want a Jewish state at all. If they want anything it is for this state to dissolve, which is precisely why they split from the more warlike Agudat Israel in 1938.

By treating the various kinds of Orthodox Jews as if they were of a single stock; by suggesting all sorts of ridiculous strategies, like conscripting young Haredi men into the army (who wants a Haredi soldier by his side?) or cutting them off from state funding, Shtrasler does everything that any good racist does to avoid confrontation. What he does not do is recognize them; he does not see them as they see themselves. Could it not be that somewhere deep inside, Shtrasler is scared to death of this "archetypical Jew"? Could it not be that Shtrasler, like so many secular Jews, treats the hyper-Orthodox Jew as authentic, the real McCoy in the light of which he himself appears wan, inauthentic, perhaps nothing more than "Orthodox lite"? Could it be that Shtrasler wants to have his cake and eat it too: he wants a Jewish state but not for all kinds of Jews and perhaps not for anything that for the past several thousand years has come to represent Judaism?

As I walked away from the Meah She'arim, and for a year afterward as well, I became obsessed with such questions. Was it not the case that the state with which Neturei Karta would have no problem was in fact the state about which superseculars like David Ben-Gurion dreamed? Their dream state, in which the public arena would be purged of all things religious, in which religion would be entirely a private matter, was a state the hyper-Orthodox could easily recognize if only because it was like all the other modern Western states, none of which made any claims to have overridden the Messiah.

Should the secular State of Israel be declared and its principles written into the constitution, would this not unify and please both the Orthodox community and the secular community in a manner that no Jewish state possibly could? And would this kind of state not also satisfy many middle-of-the-road Israelis whose dream amounts to living a normal life, and whose dream state would be nothing other than what is normally referred to as a modern, Western state?

The ancillary advantages of such an effort seemed almost

too good to be true. Consider, for example, the consequence of such a sea change for the Arabs in the neighbourhood. Would not much of the venom that is so liberally directed at the Jewish state vanish if the state in question were in fact not a Jewish state, but only a state rather like New York City—a state in which many Jews live? And if such a state were not to wholly do away with the law of return, but put it on hold to be activated only in times of crisis, would not this new state be acceptable to the Jewish Diaspora from whom the burden of association with the Jewish state would then be lifted?

If such things are true, why aren't the great majority of secular Israelis joining together with the Neturei Karta in an effort to establish a secular state? The answer I gave myself had mostly to do with the absence of a narrative for which this vision served as an end point. It was to the construction of this narrative that I now attended.

—◦◦◦—

As I envisioned the ideal narrative, it would have a Zionist and a secular Jewish component. The Zionist aspect was easy enough to describe. After all, was not Theodore Herzl's "dream state" both secular and cosmopolitan? In fact, Herzl was so committed to a state that would be neither Jewish nor European that his design proposal highlighted not only the idea of secularism and cosmopolitanism but also the notion of a Gemeinschaft or commonwealth that was opposed to the statist concept of a central government. In *Altneuland*, which was the name Herzl gave to his dream state, the vernacular was to be German, not Hebrew, and the government was to be local and voluntary rather than elected. From there it was a small step to the argument that the opposition to Herzl—Ahad HaAm and Buber's cultural Zionism—had done its revival work quite successfully but had now overstayed its welcome.

The second prong of the narrative, which took up the Jewish story now, as opposed to the Zionist one, was far more difficult to construct. For a very short while, I considered the experiment that the so-called Canaanites undertook in the early 1930s. Realizing that to create a new Middle East it was necessary to cut the umbilical cord that attached them to the old and very exclusive Jewish tradition, this group of young Israeli artists attempted to revive pre-Judaic rituals. But mainstream Jews, including Ben-Gurion, would not hear of this practice, in part because the Canaanites revived all sorts of crazy idolatries, but more importantly because their idea erased from memory everything that Judaism had accomplished, including Jewish morality. Clearly this would not and should not be acceptable.

What needed to be rescued from the Canaanite experiment was the idea that neither a new Middle East nor a new Israel could arise so long as the umbilical cord of Jewish exceptionalism remained uncut. Until such time as that cord could be severed, which is to say until such time as secular Judaism could represent itself to itself as a discrete perspective, the concept of monotheism itself would remain no more than a practice whose centre and hold upon the spirit of the practitioner was unknown.

Initially I thought that to cut the cord that bound secular Judaism to the Orthodoxy would be a piece of cake. My idea was to trace this tradition back to its conception in the Enlightenment, and specifically to the works of Moses Mendelssohn, the father of modern secular Judaism. What I needed to find in Mendelsshohn's work was the weakest link to the ancient tradition. Once I found that, it would be, I hoped, just a matter of tugging a little, and I would have it.

The weakest link between Mendelssohn and the old tradition is perhaps best articulated in Mendelssohn's letter to the Swiss writer Johann Kaspar Lavater in which he argues that because no universal morality has been yet expressed, no one who subscribes to any of the major religions has any claim on the truth. In other words, Mendelssohn argued, the only reason we are Jews and not Christians or Muslims has to do with the accident of our birth, nothing else.

To be perfectly honest, I found this argument impossible to refute. The more I thought about it, the more obsessed I became with the idea that birth, which has nothing to do with conscious choice, determines everything. The more obsessed I became, the crazier I found myself becoming. I remained in this heightened state of anxiety until I realized that the thing that was in fact causing the stress was the same thing I was trying to understand—it was the concept of unity, which expresses itself as the idea of biology as a unity we cannot sever, and also as the idea of God, whose inner unity is so transparent as to be entirely opaque.

—⊗⊗⊗—

At some point in the middle of my obsession, I travelled to the West Bank settlement of Psagot in search of a miracle man who claimed he could pull off the unification of the Jewish tradition, which I now thought of as impossible. This miracle man claimed he had pulled off not one but two miracles. The first led to the death of Prime Minister Yitzhak Rabin. The second put Prime Minister Sharon into the coma in which he remains. Although he was born in Mexico of Syrian parents, Rabbi Yosef Dayan calls himself the King of Israel. He traces his lineage back to King David. His website links up to a British scholar named David Hughes, who has not only corroborated Dayan's claim but gone to the trouble of producing a telephone-book-size genealogy complete with thousands of footnotes, all of which serve no other purpose but to prove the lineage and to fix the date of Dayan's coronation.

At the beginning of October 1995, four weeks before the assassination of Prime Minister Yitzhak Rabin, Dayan and nine other rabbis gathered before the prime ministerial home to perform the darkest and most potent curse known to Jews. Called the *pulsa de nura*, or "lashes of fire," this curse is the subject of Rabbi Dayan's book, unsurprisingly titled *Pulsa De Nura: A History of Lashes of Fire*. The account of a conversation with a journalist reads very much like a confession and should have led the state to charge Dayan with either murder or incitement or conspiracy to assassinate a prime minister.

"Are you sure Rabin will die?" the journalist asked Dayan.

"Yes," Dayan said.

"And what if he does not die?"

"He will die."

"Are you so sure?"

"Yes."

"When?"

"Within the month."

"And what if he doesn't die? What then?"

"HE WILL DIE."

On November 4, 1995, when Yigal Amir pulled the trigger that killed Prime Minister Rabin, Dayan made a public statement that the true culprit was not the crazed young man but the curse, which had entered him and transformed him into its operative. Dayan was prepared to take the rap, but when Israeli police arrested him some weeks later, no charges were laid.

Reading about the police interrogation in Dayan's book is an eerie experience. At some point the investigator, Tirzah Deutch, seems anxious, nervous, reluctant to discover more than she absolutely needs to know. Several hours into the questioning, Deutch removes a mirror from her purse, remarks on her ashen complexion, and recommends that Dayan leave the premises at once.

On July 23, 2005, Dayan and his minyan once again gathered, this time at the cemetery in Rosh Pina where ancient Kabbalistic tradition has it that the Messiah will first arise. A young man equipped with a camcorder caught sight of nine men in black and one in white and filmed what he believed to be the entire ritual—but which Dayan told me was only an abbreviated version. He said the full curse on Prime Minister Ariel Sharon, the "traitor king," had been pronounced a day earlier in a yeshiva whose identity Dayan was unwilling to reveal.

The minyan did not demand his death but something worse: "that he live with the weight of every living and deadly curse known to man and to God." When the ritual was posted to YouTube, the nation and the media went absolutely crazy. For a week or so every Israeli I met would take time off from whatever it was we happened to be discussing in order to curse the cursers. Prime Minister Sharon was less perturbed. "How long before the curse takes effect?" Arik asked his aides, who claimed

that it could take decades. "Then I don't give a damn," he shot
back and that was the last Israelis heard about it. Except that no
one had ever requested that Dayan lift the curse, which a great
majority of religious settlers believed was the reason that
Sharon remains frozen in time. That, plus the possibility of
learning something about unity, was good enough reason for
me to pay a visit to the good rabbi.

I called a professor who I believed knew Dayan, and asked
him whether he could set up the appointment. A day later my
acquaintance called back to say that Dayan would not see me.
But I was determined to see him anyhow. My big idea was to
threaten to bring him to court on a murder charge. To add a
little weight to the idea, I called up a judge in the Israeli court
system and asked whether the *pulsa de nura* could be interpreted in court as a lethal weapon. The answer the judge gave
was perfectly clear: "No way." But he added as an afterthought
that a religious court might have a different opinion.

I got this message to Dayan: "If you will not see me and if
Arik Sharon dies, I personally will bring you to a religious court
on the charge of murder." Dayan did not budge, but after he
received a call from Ahikam, a young photojournalist I knew to
whom he had taken a shine, he finally agreed to see me anyhow.

On the evening before I set out for his home in Psagot, I got
a taste of the kind of anxiety Kabbalistic sorcery strikes in the
heart of secular Israelis. "Do you own a copy of the Psalms?"
my friend Nemet inquired on the phone. "You should perhaps
pick one up, have it with you, in your pocket when you meet
Dayan. I mean it may not help but it certainly can't hurt."

I received half a dozen such calls from friends and acquaint-
ances, none of whom seemed the least bit embarrassed by their

own superstitions. "If Dayan gets Arik out of his coma, then I will definitely, for sure, believe in God," my very secular friend Naomi Omessi admitted almost too happily.

I arranged for Ahikam to pick me up at the Jerusalem bus station. From there we planned to drive the thirty kilometres to Psagot, a settlement of approximately 250 families overlooking Ramallah, the capital city of the Palestinian Authority. Ahikam is a wonderfully bright and warm young man who was born in the Jerusalem area. He claimed to know the road to Psagot like the back of his hand, except that on this particular morning he became so agitated that he drove around in circles until I asked him to stop for coffee. "Are you nervous?" I asked Ahikam, who had met Dayan on several occasions.

"Not for a minute," Ahikam said, his voice hitting a register that surprised even him.

We were scheduled to meet Dayan at 10 a.m. and at fifteen minutes past the hour we were still taking wrong turns out of Jerusalem. But we did eventually get there and as we turned onto the road where Dayan lives, the rabbi, a nondescript-looking man of medium weight, with a stringy speckled grey beard and a flat Aztec nose, waved us down.

Dayan shook my hand and embraced Ahikam. He walked up to the lookout next to his home.

"Look out, what is it that you see?" Dayan said.

"Ramallah," I replied.

"Look again," Dayan said, stroking his beard.

"Just Ramallah."

"Take in the aerial view," Dayan said, waving his arm across the horizon. "What you see before you is not this lousy Arab city but the entire history of the Jews. Over there . . . Abraham walked with his son. Down there Moses overlooked the Promised Land."

Dayan's voice was drowned out by the muezzin's call to prayer. Below us, an Arab man stepped out and began making his way toward the mosque.

"It is not altogether their fault that they are crazy. Five times a day they are confronted with the nasal sounds of this muezzin. It is enough to make anyone crazy."

"But, Rabbi," I said, "from where you live you too hear the muezzin just as many times as they do. How come you manage to preserve your sanity?"

Clearly Dayan did not appreciate my quip. "I am simply not prepared to consider that the Arab man down there and I are made of the same stock," he said. "We, not they, are the chosen people."

Around eleven that morning, Dayan ushered us into his whitewashed bungalow. The living room was decorated in early Salvation Army; an understuffed couch in gaudy floral pattern by the wall faced two extraordinarily mismatched plastic chairs. Between them was a pressed-wood coffee table with a Mactac top upon which Dayan placed the largest bottle of McCormick vodka in the world. "Americans still make vodka much better than the Russians," he said. "Vodka with Coke goes well." Dayan poured himself a tall glass of vodka, with a splash of Coke for colour. Ahikam began snapping pictures.

"I take it that you claim to be a direct descendant of King David?" I began.

"No," Dayan said. The room went silent for what seemed like a full half hour but probably was no more than twenty-eight minutes. I struggled desperately for my next words. They finally hit me.

"You are a direct descendant of King David," I said, and Dayan nodded. The interview was on again. Dayan left the room and returned moments later hauling a monster book of genealogy that showed his lineage.

"Democracy is totally bunk," he said. "It has nothing at all to do with Judaism. Everyone knows that. In fact there are only two forms of governance that have anything at all to do with our tradition—anarchy, which we will get the day after the Messiah invests us all with the power of revelation, and monarchy, which is what we need to keep us going until then."

"Rabbi, I came to talk to you about the *pulsa de nura* . . . I understand that back in July of 2005 . . ."

"Yes, yes. We put a curse on Arik. I will tell you about it."

Dayan had an agenda, and he would get to my questions in his own time.

"What does it mean to be a rabbi in Israel today?" Dayan asked. "Nothing. It means nothing except that you work for the government, get paid by the government. And any Jew who is prepared to put up the money can become a rabbi.

"Most rabbis are prepared to run a cleaver through their own breast and through the chests of their students if there is a shekel in it for them," he continued. "They are scared of their own shadows. That is what happened in Gaza. At the beginning I went to meetings. I argued that we should not allow the state to push us around. We should not let anyone collect our weapons. I argued that any soldier coming to force us out of our homes is by definition not a Jewish soldier, is a *shegitz* that needs to be stopped."

"By stopped do you mean shot?" I asked. Dayan simply repeated that any soldier coming to force Jews from their homes was by definition not a Jewish soldier.

"And the pulsa? What about the pulsa?"

Dayan poured himself another drink. This time he left out the Coke.

"No responsible rabbi would perform a pulsa in public lest he give away its deadly secrets. Just so you understand how deadly the curse is . . . in 1991 a number of rabbis brought the curse upon Saddam Hussein. Apparently someone on high did not think that Hussein should die. So the pulsa boomeranged and the morning after the ritual, one of our brightest young students died in midsentence. But except for the judgment of heaven, the pulsa operates under no constraints. Rabbis were very successful in 1939 when they laid the curse upon Leon Trotsky. We have to be very careful not to expose too much. This is what we have learned from the terrible case of Elijah the Prophet who is the only righteous man blessed with immortality but also cursed. I shall tell you how that happened.

"It was on the holy days of the month and Elijah arrived late for prayers. Why have you tarried? the rabbis asked him. Because it is Rosh Hodesh, the holy first day of the month, Elijah said. *Al akhat kama vekama*, it is on just such days that we expect you on time. No, Elijah said. On the first days of the month I go to the Tomb of the Patriarchs. There I take Abraham, our first father, out of his crypt. I wash him, I pray with him, and I return him to his grave. Then I do the same with Isaac and I repeat the same with Jakob. But Rabbi Elijah, the rabbis say, Why would you not remove all three patriarchs, wash, dress and pray with them all at the same time? That way you could still be on time for the service? I could not do that, Elijah responds. For if these three patriarchs are permitted to pray together it will bring about redemption and the world is not yet ready for redemption. Are there perhaps other men alive today who, if they prayed together, would force the coming of the Messiah? the rabbis ask Elijah. And Elijah, always generous Elijah, wanting to please the rabbis, responded in the affirmative. Yes, indeed. If Rabbi Nathan and his two sons were to pray together, that would force the Messiah. Immediately, the skies opened and Elijah the prophet received forty lashes of fire for exposing the secrets of redemption.

"Do you understand my story?" Dayan asked. "We cannot, must not, expose the secrets of the lashes of fire, which is why I shall tell you everything but must leave out one thing. Most rabbis make a distinction between a blessing and a curse, but there is no distinction. In both cases we ask for divine intervention for the sake of the people. In both cases God knows whether we are within our rights to ask. And if the intervention is necessary it happens and if it is uncalled for then nothing happens."

Then Dayan said something that threw me off guard. "I am not so sure that Arik is in a coma because of the curse. After all he was an old fat man. It could very well be that the cause of his coma was his fat, that the pulsa had not yet reached him."

My plan had been to demand that Dayan remove the curse and get Arik back again. I wanted to see him do that not only because I thought it would be fun, but because I thought it would unify the country in ways that perhaps nothing else could. But now the carpet was pulled out from under me.

I felt as though I would find the right thing to say but it wouldn't be inside this house. I had no idea what this something would be, but I had an intense need to get out of the house and to take this man with me. Ahikam felt my jitters and began to pack up his gear.

"Can you point me to the washroom," I asked, and Dayan did so. On the wall behind the toilet there was a poster that read *Din manhieegei Israel kedim Rabin*, Rabin's fate is the fate of all Israel's leaders.

Returning from the john, I asked Dayan whether we might take a walk and he agreed. And then we were again looking out upon the city of Ramallah, or perhaps out upon the entire realm of Jewish history, which was looking back at us.

"I have been listening to you for the past two hours," I said to Dayan. "Now I would like you to hear me out. You told me that you are not so sure that Sharon is in a coma because of your curse. But I am absolutely sure. And I am also sure that you need to lift the curse. This would be a noble act and would go a great distance toward your coronation. If Arik were to rise from near death, it would be a miracle and that would strengthen the faith of the nation. And that too would be a good thing. Zion is very much in need of a miracle. Now, if you do not mind, Ahikam and I must go."

Rabbi Dayan stood there for a long moment, as astonished by what I said as I was myself. Perhaps he was wondering where exactly I got my chutzpah. In any case he soon enough turned around and walked away without saying another word.

Ahikam looked at me and broke into a rip-roaring laugh. "You are out of your mind," he said. "What on earth possessed you to talk to him like that and in his own language?"

"I have no clue," I said, then laughed too. "Maybe I just wanted to test something that I thought I learned from him."

"What is that?" Ahikam asked.

"How not to blink," I said, and blinked.

I can think of no better way to describe the past decade of Israeli history than Gibbon's description of human history as a whole. "History," the eighteenth-century British curmudgeon claimed, "is nothing more than a series of crimes, follies and misfortunes." But for the individual who is implicated in history and who must, in any event, come to terms with it one way or another, it sometimes pays to step back from the flux, return to basics, and ask what drives the business of history. And how human beings can put themselves back in the driver's seat rather than be driven crazy or into oblivion.

To step back and ask oneself some of the basic questions is not to do more history but to engage our moral underpinnings, which I think of as the engine of history. This is what I've tried to do. I asked myself not only about the extent to which we Israelis are responsible for the predicament in which we find ourselves, not only how the state spiralled out of control, but also how we might work ourselves out of this bottleneck. What

I never asked myself and never will ask myself is whether Israel has a right to exist. As far as I am concerned, that is not in question.

The questions I did ask broke into a thousand other questions and these sent me down dozens of trails and required a huge number of thought experiments. The result of all these efforts is the substance of this book, but also made a substantial change in its author. What happened to me is perhaps best described as an existential reorientation. In small and often imperceptible increments I was transformed from a secular Jewish Israeli into a Jewish secular Israeli. The former is a kind of Jew. The latter is a kind of secular being existing at a point in time in which the idea of secularism appears as a positive morality or faith that has yet to be fleshed out in detail.

I have my parents, Asher and Rachel, who died while I was working on this book, to thank not only for the usual things but also for letting me experience what it means to be Israeli from up close. To my wife, Deborah, who is the love of my life and my muse and for whom I would do nothing but sing her praises except that she would probably tell me that I was singing out of tune and send me off to the cleaners—to her I will always be impossibly indebted. To my sister-in-law Joan Moss and her partner Earl Berger and to my cousins Aaron Peleg and Ariel Meriav, who set me straight on so many occasions, and to friends including Joseph Omessie and Benzi Netzer, Alex and Anat Biletski, Naomi Segal, Bernard Schiff, Sholom Glouberman and Sydney Nestel, all of whom suffered through the many rethinkings and revisions that went into the final narrative—and to Angelika Glover and Eyal Pundik-Sagie, who contributed from their immense skills as editors—and to dozens more who I do not mention here but do mention in the book: to all of these I extend a great thanks.

My children, Natalia, Mira and Mischa, who stood in as the first citizens of the dream state and the first inhabitants of the world I should like to leave behind—to them, whom I love more than anything and from whose wellspring I am constantly drawing energy, I owe not only my capacity to fantasize but my far more profound need to keep on dreaming.

Over the course of sixty years I have had many teachers and mentors but none so great and so important to me as Professor Alan Blum and the late Professor Peter McHugh. These two thinkers not only taught me how important it is to think for oneself but also brought the action of thinking, which always occurs in the privacy of a mind and mostly in a manner that is outside of experience, out into the open. Through their collaboration and friendship, which they played out for the benefit of their students, I got to see how a model begins to take shape and just how much work it takes to play the oft-times thankless role of midwife.

To Anne Collins, who challenged me to write the final word on a subject about which hardly a word had been written and who believed in me more than I believed in myself and who stood by her convictions when anyone in their right mind would have declared the entire idea of conviction entirely bankrupt, I do not have enough words to thank. To Daniel Baird who is more capable than anyone of being transported by a good idea and who is equally capable of being impaled by a bad one, I should also like also to extend my love and gratitude.

The moral history I have made, or that has made me into something I was not when I began, is only a baby step, a reconnaissance trip in the direction of a morality that remains to be envisioned. That history should be oriented to the concept of secularism, not as a form of humanism or an abstract and chaotic intermingling with the faith traditions, but as a positive faith in Life written in the upper case. Secularism is a move beyond the monotheistic traditions, which it nonetheless does not wholly leave behind. Secularism embraces the three streams of monotheism, places them in a creative tension with each other. A secularist as I imagine her may prefer not to use the word God if only because of the awe or ridicule which that term tends to inspire. But she could not and would never deny the existence of spirit. As I imagine the secularist of the future, she is one who has entirely internalized the spirit and put it in the service of life from which it first arose. To her this spirit works as prism and as the guiding hand that grants the unity of perception without which no real encounter with life is possible.

The Unity of Perception

DAVID BERLIN is an Israeli-born journalist and editor who grew up in Canada but returned for a time to live in Israel. He served his military duty in Ariel Sharon's reconnaissance unit, Sayeret Shaked, and took part in Sharon's Suez campaign. After attending medical school at Tel-Aviv University, he graduated from the University of Chicago's program on social and political thought, and taught at several universities. His work has appeared in *Saturday Night*, the *Literary Review of Canada* (where he was the editor-in-chief from 1998-2001), the *Globe and Mail*, the *National Post* and *Haaretz Newspaper*, among others. He is a founding editor of the *Walrus*. He lives in Toronto with his wife, Deborah, a violinist, and their three children.

A NOTE ABOUT THE TYPE

The Moral Lives of Israelis is set in Electra, designed in 1935 by William Addison Dwiggins. A popular face for book-length work since its release, Electra is noted for its evenness and high legibility in both text sizes and display settings.